IMAGES
of America

THE GREAT OHIO RIVER FLOOD OF 1937

ON THE COVER: On a flooded Ninth Street in the heart of downtown Huntington, West Virginia, a group of volunteers can be seen with a boatload of bread and other emergency food supplies for victims of 1937's flooding. (Courtesy author's collection.)

IMAGES
of America

THE GREAT OHIO RIVER FLOOD OF 1937

James E. Casto

ARCADIA
PUBLISHING

ISBN 978-0-7385-6858-4

Published by Arcadia Publishing
Charleston, South Carolina

Printed in the United States of America

Library of Congress Catalog Card Number: 2008936275

For all general information contact Arcadia Publishing at:
Telephone 843-853-2070
Fax 843-853-0044
E-mail sales@arcadiapublishing.com
For customer service and orders:
Toll-Free 1-888-313-2665

Visit us on the Internet at www.arcadiapublishing.com

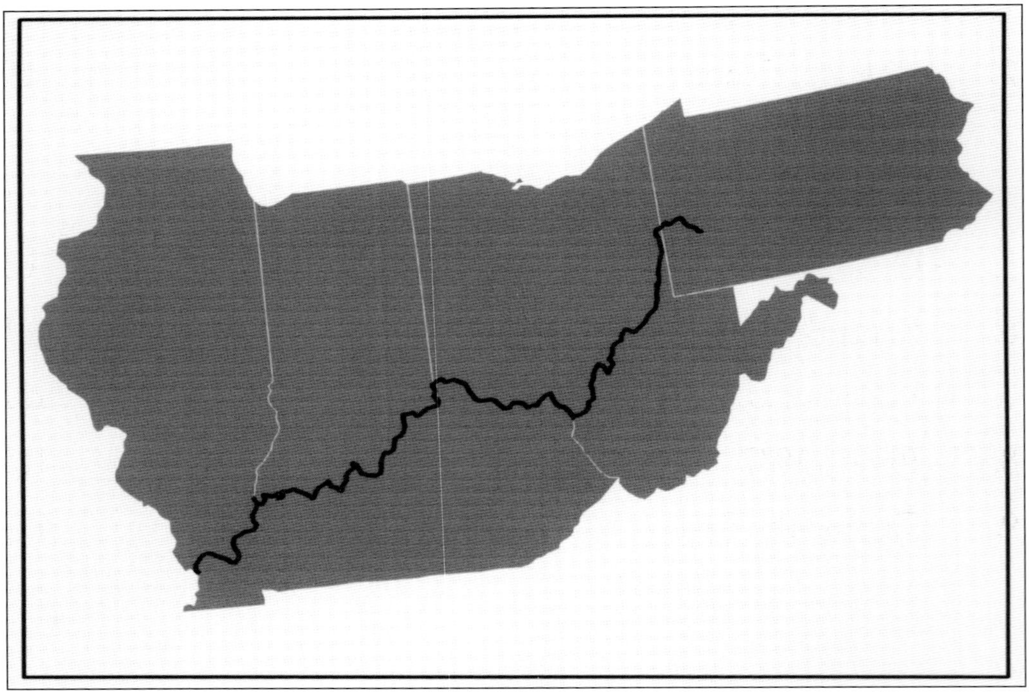

Born at Pittsburgh, Pennsylvania, where the Allegheny and Monongahela Rivers join, the Ohio River follows a mostly southwestern course for 981 miles until it reaches Cairo, Illinois, where it meets the Mississippi River. To the south of the river are the states of West Virginia and Kentucky. To the north are Ohio, Indiana, and Illinois. From the time the first settlers arrived in the valley, floods have been a familiar part of life for those who live along the Ohio River. (Courtesy MotionMasters, Charleston, West Virginia.)

Contents

ACKNOWLEDGMENTS

This is a book I have wanted to do for at least 20 years, and I have been researching information and gathering vintage photographs and postcards for that long and maybe longer. Thus, many of the images collected in these pages are drawn from my own collection. But as I began work on the book, it was quickly clear I would need help filling in a great many parts of the 1937 flood story. So I sought help and am happy to report that, without exception, my pleas were answered.

Pres. Diana Sole and designer Amy Drake of MotionMasters in Charleston, West Virginia, provided a useful introductory map showing the course of the Ohio River. Paul Borelli of Artcraft Studio in Parkersburg, West Virginia, has a carefully tended treasure trove of thousands of old Parkersburg-area photographs and was more than willing to share a few with me. When I needed flood photographs from Point Pleasant, West Virginia, director Jack Fowler of the Point Pleasant River Museum came through with exactly what I hoped for. Thomas W. Dixon Jr., chairman and president emeritus of the Chesapeake and Ohio Historical Society, Inc. (C&OHS), provided me with photographs from the C&OHS collection. Charles R. Nichols of Russell, Kentucky, loaned me some of his Ashland flood photographs. And Kent Keyser, longtime aide to U.S. representative Nick J. Rahall (D–West Virginia), was quick to help when I needed prints of historic photographs in the U.S. Library of Congress collection. Unless otherwise noted, all images are from the author's collection.

I thank all those who helped—and offer a special salute to the many photographers, most of them unidentified, who chronicled this dark chapter in Ohio Valley history.

INTRODUCTION

As a boy, I grew up listening to my mother, stepfather, and other adults talk about the great Ohio River flood of 1937. They recalled the flood in much the same way other Americans would later remember where they were when U.S. president John F. Kennedy was killed or when the terrorists struck on September 11, 2001. Looking back, I suspect listening to their flood stories may have planted the seed that has grown into this book.

My hometown of Huntington, West Virginia, was one of the Ohio River communities devastated by the 1937 flood. I was born in 1941, and when I was five or six years old, we moved into one side of a frame duplex that stood on Huntington's Fourth Avenue, just around the corner from the flooded houses on Fifteenth Street shown in a photograph on page 61. When the talk turned to the 1937 flood, I would look at our little house and try to imagine what it must have been like with the floodwaters lapping at the roofline of our front porch.

"Hell and High Water" was the way *Time* magazine of February 1, 1937, described the flood, and the description could not have been more accurate. The raging floodwaters inundated thousands of houses and businesses, factories and farms in a half dozen states, drove a million people from their homes, claimed nearly 400 lives, and recorded $500 million in damages. Taking inflation into account, that figure would translate into more than $7 billion today. Adding to the misery was the fact that the disaster came during the depths of the Great Depression, when so many American families already were struggling simply to put food on their tables.

There had been Ohio River floods before, of course. When the first settlers made their way into the Ohio Valley in the early and mid-1700s, they found the river was subject to dramatic changes. When the weather was dry for weeks at a time, it could be so shallow that one early settler described it as "a mile across and a foot deep." At some points you could walk across it and hardly get your feet wet. Yet, in periods of heavy rainfall or when a sudden thaw quickly melted the accumulated winter snow from the nearby hillsides, the Ohio River could become a raging torrent.

Major Ohio River floods were recorded in 1862, 1883, and 1884, when the river washed away an estimated 2,000 homes along its length. Although it hardly seems a laughing matter, people familiar with the Ohio and its history joke about the firehouse in Marietta, Ohio, that was swept away, fire engine and all, by the flood and, six days and many miles later, "turned up as part of the Louisville Fire Department."

The Ohio flooded again in 1901, 1907, and 1913. The high water of 1913 brought with it a flood of public protest. Former U.S. president Theodore Roosevelt complained that millions of dollars were going to aid the flood victims but not one penny had been spent on flood prevention. U.S. president Woodrow Wilson also was concerned and convened a special commission to study what could be done to tame the river. The commission examined several options, including the erection of levees and the construction of flood-reducing reservoirs. But the outbreak of World War I shelved such plans. And their revival after the war again was sidetracked by the "Black October" crash of 1929 and the ensuing Depression.

In 1933, the Ohio River flooded yet again, but in the upper end of the Ohio Valley that was just a curtain raiser to the history-making flood of 1936. On St. Patrick's Day that year, Pittsburgh, Pennsylvania,—where the Allegheny and Monongahela Rivers come together to form the Ohio River—saw its worst flood ever. Fed by extraordinary snowmelt and rain, the three ice-filled rivers quickly left their banks, and soon the city's downtown was under as much as 15 feet of water. It should come as no surprise that when people in Pittsburgh and other towns along the upper Ohio talk about flooding, they generally offer remembrances of what happened in 1936, not 1937.

Chapter one of this book offers a number of images of early Ohio River floods, and chapter two chronicles the 1936 flood. What then follows is a state-by-state look at the devastation wrought by the 1937 flood.

Pittsburgh and other Pennsylvania towns again were flooded but escaped a repeat of the record-setting crests of the year before. Huntington and other West Virginia communities bore the flood's brunt in the mid-Ohio Valley. In Ohio, the river that gives the state its name broke all previous flood records. Portsmouth was protected by a floodwall, but fears that the river would come crashing over the wall prompted officials to open the sewers and let the floodwaters slowly creep in. Cincinnati was confronted by the twin menaces of flood and fire.

In Kentucky, Louisville was perhaps hit harder than any other city along the river. The flood turned Paducah into a ghost town with more than 27,000 of its 33,000 residents carried to safety by a makeshift flotilla of rescue boats. River towns in Indiana were devastated. And at Cairo, Illinois, where the Ohio River joins the Mississippi River, army engineers had to use force to disband armed farmers determined to prevent them from blasting out a "fuse plug" to route the floodwaters away from the town.

The widespread death and devastation inflicted by the 1937 flood proved flood control was no longer something that could be ignored, and the federal government finally began to take meaningful action.

Again, as had happened earlier in the century, the outbreak of war halted most flood-control efforts. But this time, the defeat of Nazi Germany and Japan, and the arrival of peace saw not only the erection of more earth levees and concrete floodwalls along the Ohio River, but also the construction of a major network of flood-control dams and reservoirs on its tributaries. As detailed in chapter nine, these reservoirs, many constructed on tributaries at great distances from the Ohio River itself, are designed to hold water back when flooding threatens and then release it as the rivers begin to fall to a safe level.

Time and time again, the region's floodwalls and flood-control reservoirs have proven they are more than worth every tax dollar that has been invested in them, preventing untold devastation to communities along the Ohio River and its tributaries.

One

ANGRY WATERS

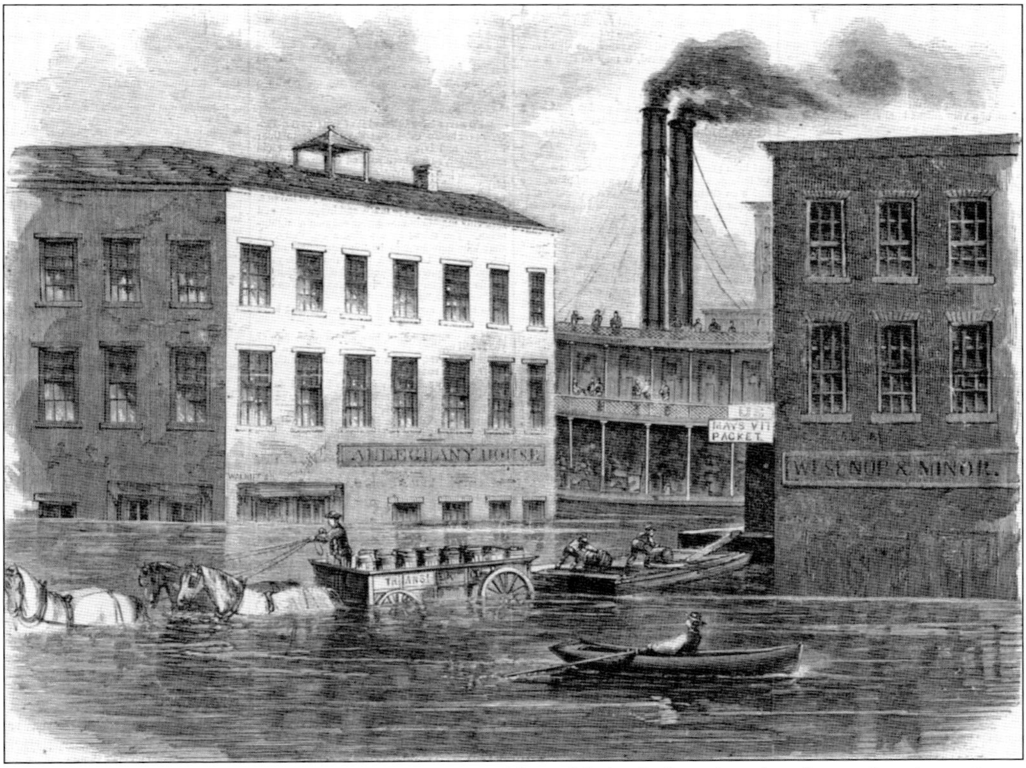

The February 22, 1862, issue of *Harper's Weekly* published this sketch of a packet boat from Maysville, Kentucky, landing at the wharf at Cincinnati, Ohio, during a flood a few weeks earlier, on January 25. In submitting his sketch, artist George M. Finch wrote that such floods "only occur about once in 15 years." It seems Finch was better at sketching than he was at river forecasting. In fact, major floods often swept down the Ohio in back-to-back years.

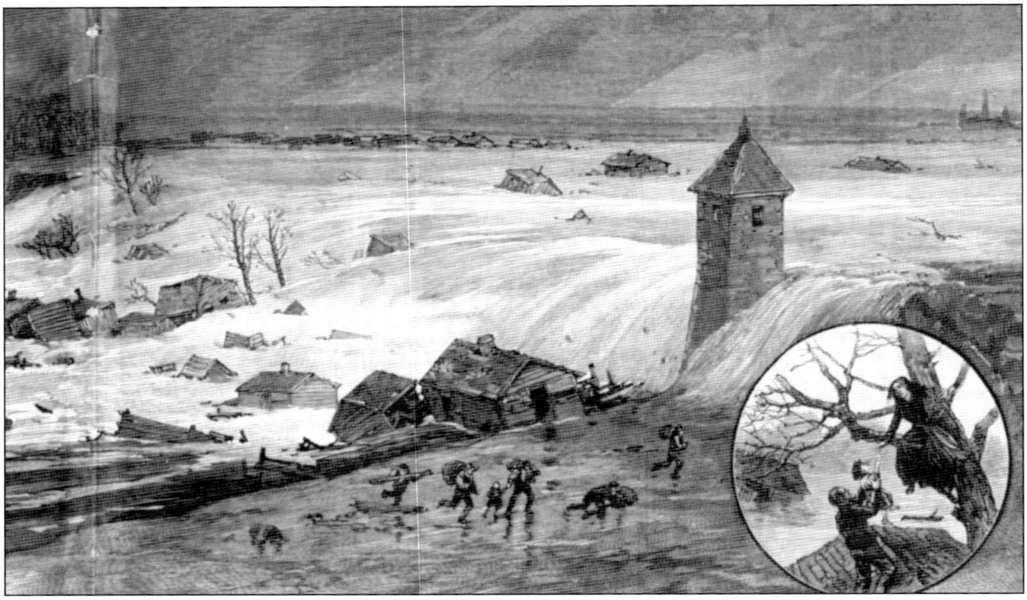

This detail is from a larger sketch published in *Harper's Weekly* of March 3, 1883, titled "The Breaking of the Embankment at Louisville, Kentucky." Houses caught by the rushing floodwaters float down the river while hapless residents flee for their lives. Note the drawing inset at lower right showing a family seeking refuge in a tree.

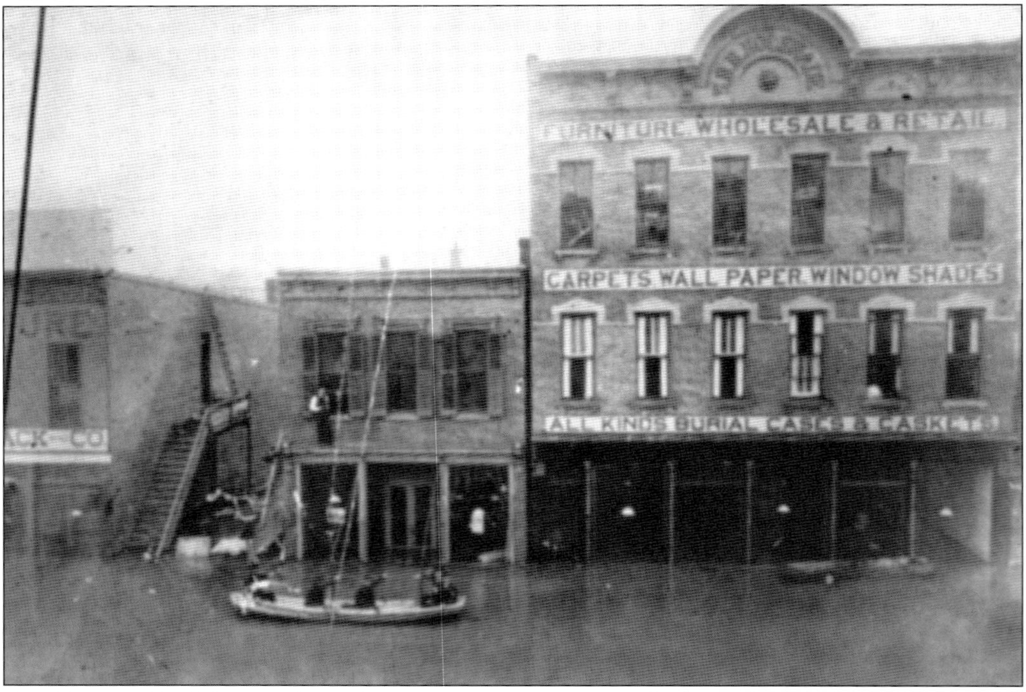

On February 12, 1884, people in Huntington, West Virginia, had to helplessly watch as the Ohio River flooded their young town, then an unlucky 13 years old. The large three-story building in this photograph was home to W. H. H. Holswade's furniture store, located on the south side of Third Avenue between Ninth and Tenth Streets. As was the custom at the time, Holswade sold not only rocking chairs and kitchen tables, but also caskets and other funeral goods.

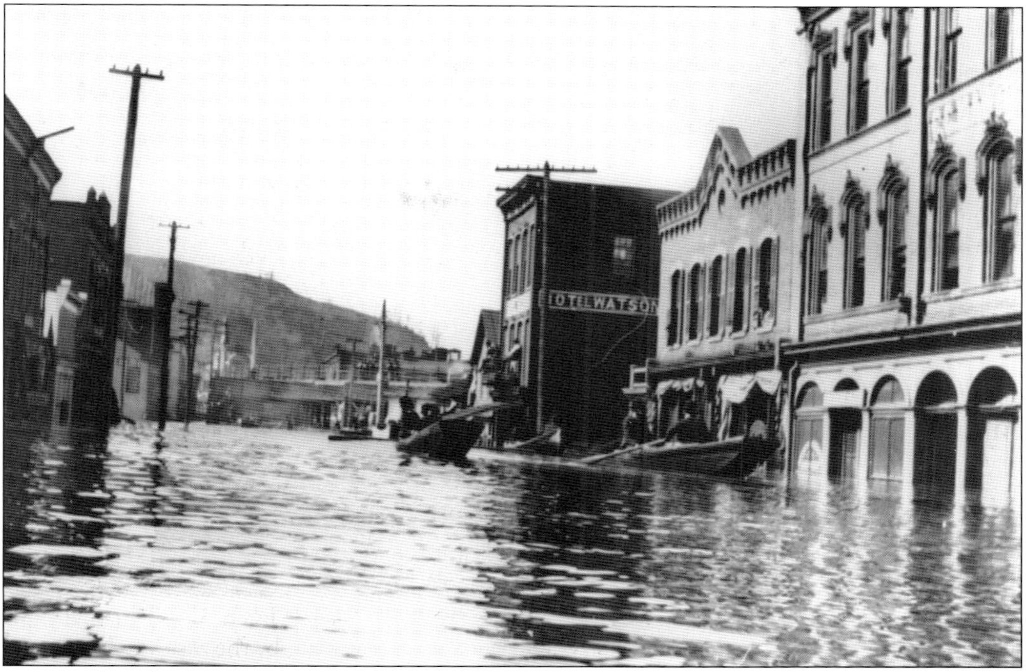

In 1889, the Ohio again flooded a number of towns up and down the valley, including Parkersburg, West Virginia, shown here in a vintage photograph taken at Second and Ann Streets. In the background can be seen Fort Boreman hill and a railroad trestle. The only business that can be identified is the Hotel Watson. When the Ohio flooded in 1913, several buildings in this section burned down to the water line.

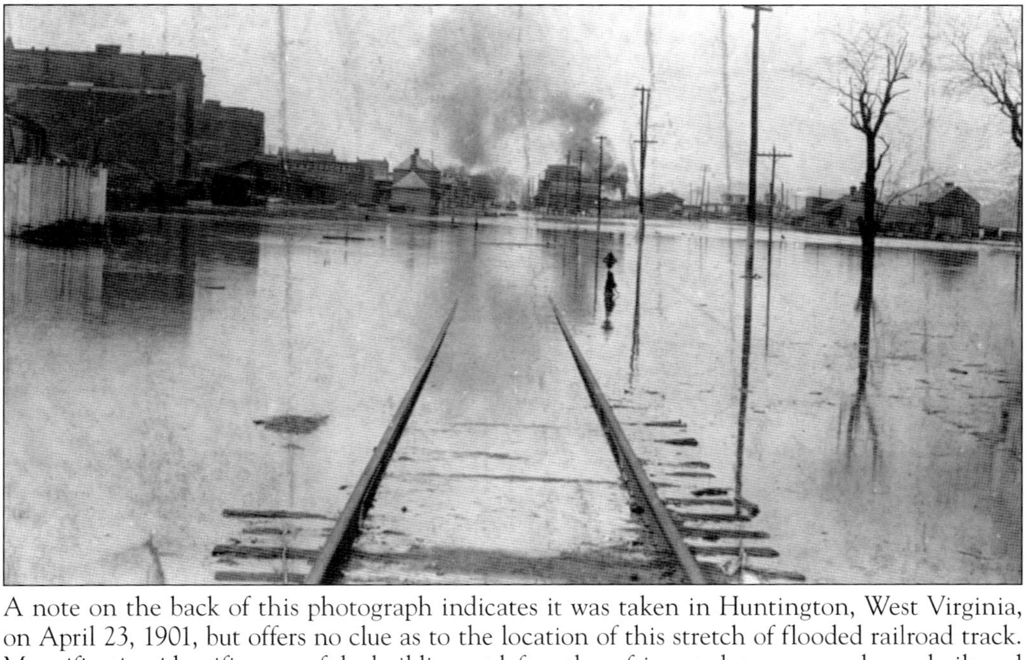

A note on the back of this photograph indicates it was taken in Huntington, West Virginia, on April 23, 1901, but offers no clue as to the location of this stretch of flooded railroad track. Magnification identifies one of the buildings at left as the refrigerated storage warehouse built and operated by J. M. McCoach and Company, which means this is the main line of the Chesapeake and Ohio Railway, looking east from a point just past the city's downtown.

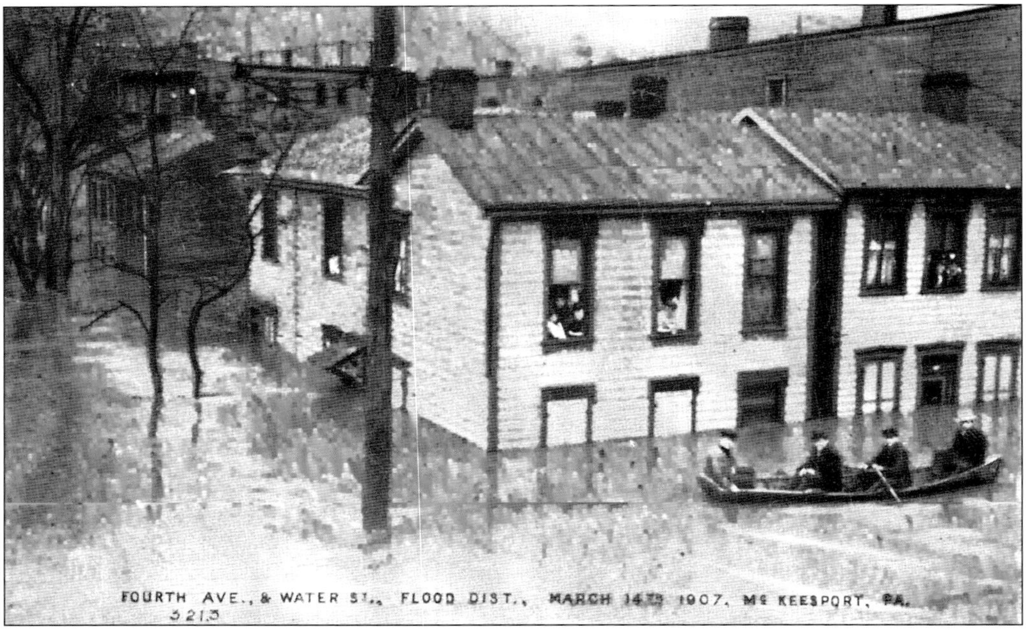

This postcard from McKeesport, Pennsylvania, shows the flooded intersection of Fourth Avenue and Water Street on March 14, 1907. McKeesport is located about 12 miles up the Monongahela River from Pittsburgh, Pennsylvania, where the Monongahela and Allegheny Rivers join to form the Ohio River. Thus, strictly speaking, this is not an Ohio River flood scene. Nonetheless, it is a good example of how swollen tributaries add to the Ohio's floodwaters.

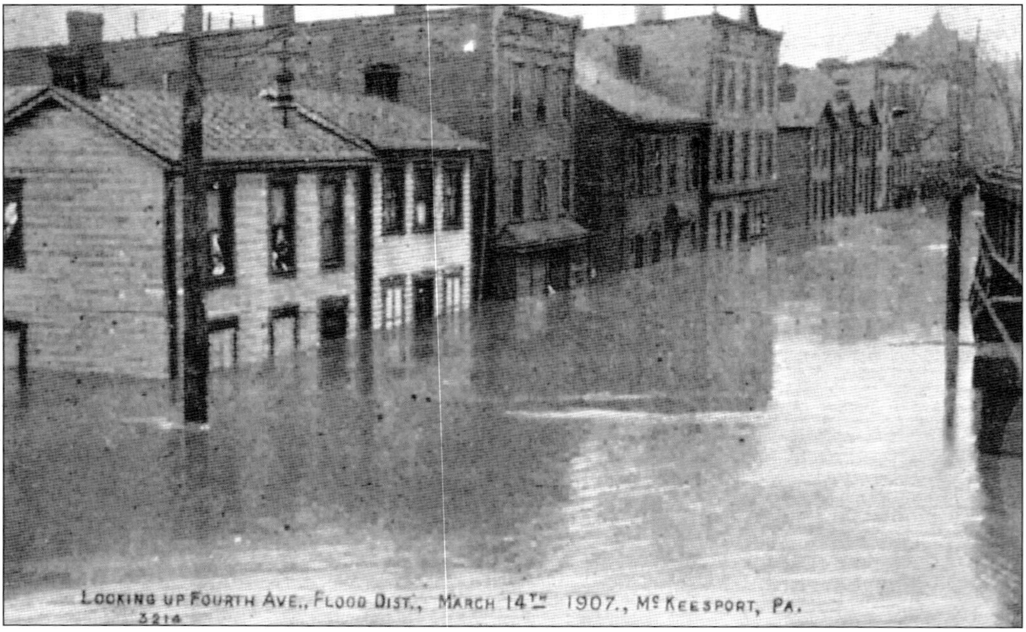

This second view from the 1907 flood in McKeesport shows the same two houses as the earlier card but looks along Fourth Avenue, showing some of the street's other flooded houses and buildings. Settled in 1795 and named in honor of John McKee, its founder, McKeesport in the 1930s was home to more than 50,000 people. Today its population is less than half that, a decrease attributable to the decline of the region's steel industry.

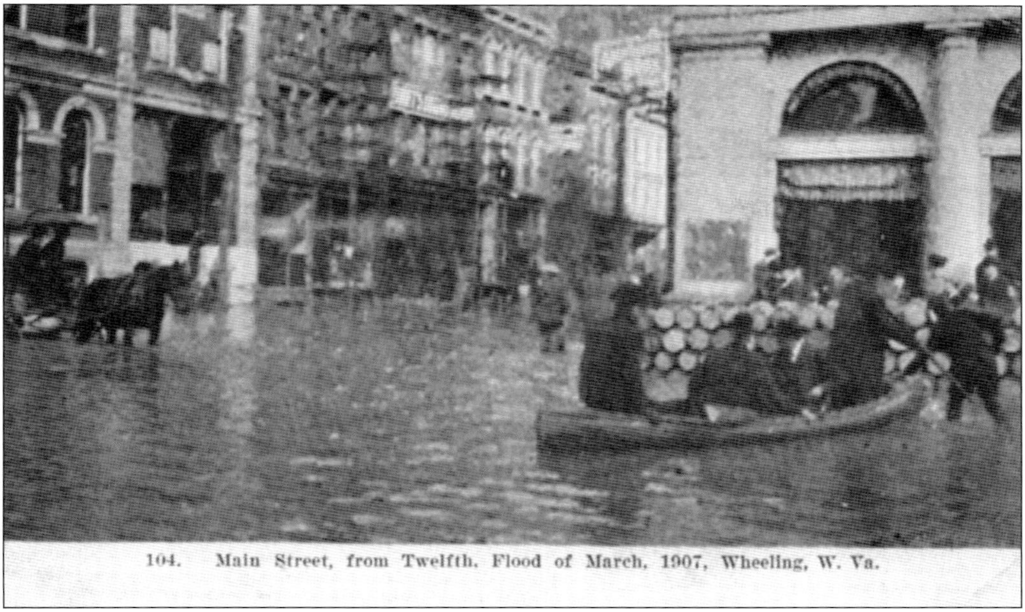

The Ohio River flood of March 1907, one of Wheeling, West Virginia's worst ever, was well documented by enterprising photographers who turned their work into souvenir postcards, such as this one showing the flooded intersection of Main and Twelfth Streets. Within days of the flood, Nicoll's Art Store ran a newspaper advertisement for its postcards, boasting, "Our Camera Experts were active and caught everything worth seeing."

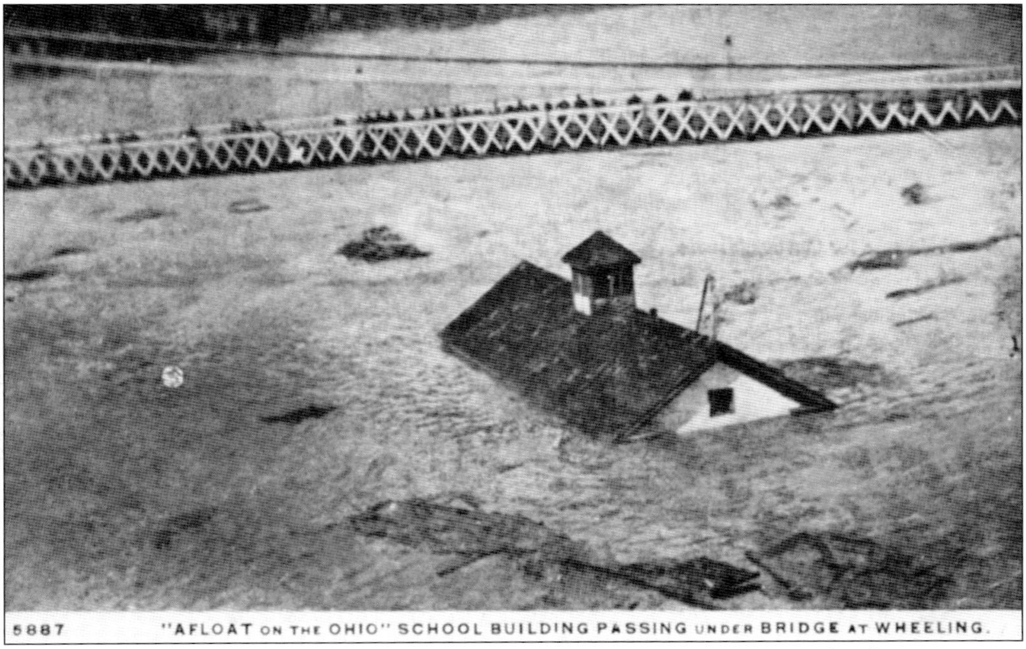

A widely reprinted postcard from the 1907 flood in Wheeling shows this schoolhouse passing under the city's suspension bridge. The school building was reported to have floated down the river from Warrenton, Ohio, to Sistersville, West Virginia, a distance of more than 100 miles. If you listen, you can almost hear the school bell clanging as the river tosses the little building about and sweeps it downstream.

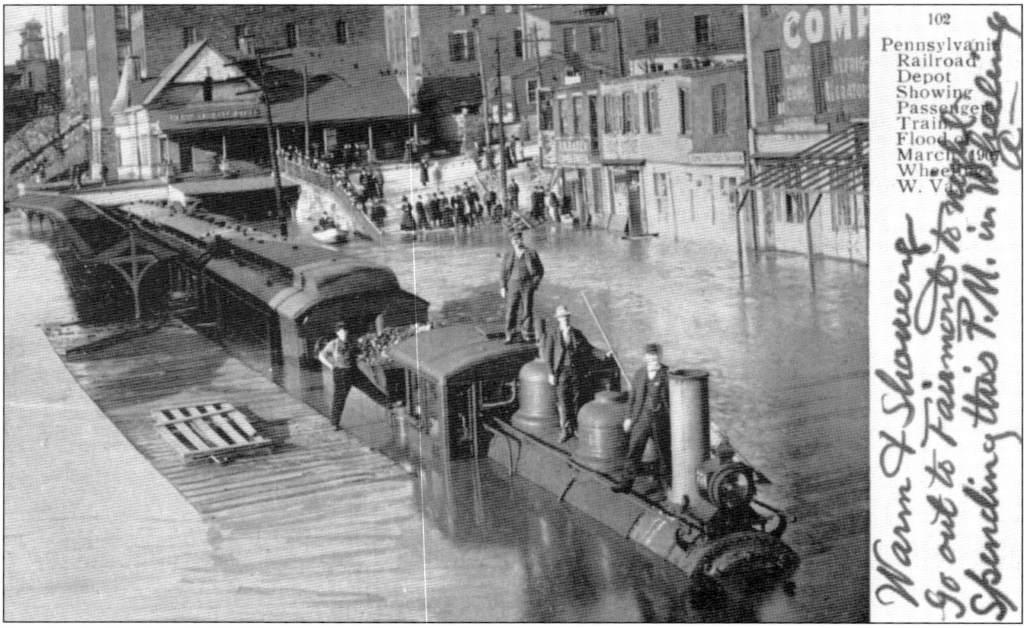

The 1907 flood in Wheeling rose so rapidly that it trapped this Pennsylvania Railroad train at the rail depot at Eleventh and Water Streets. Stranded passengers had to be put up in local hotels until the water went down and the railroad could bring in a new train. The flood crested at 50.1 feet. That is 14.1 feet over the official flood stage at Wheeling.

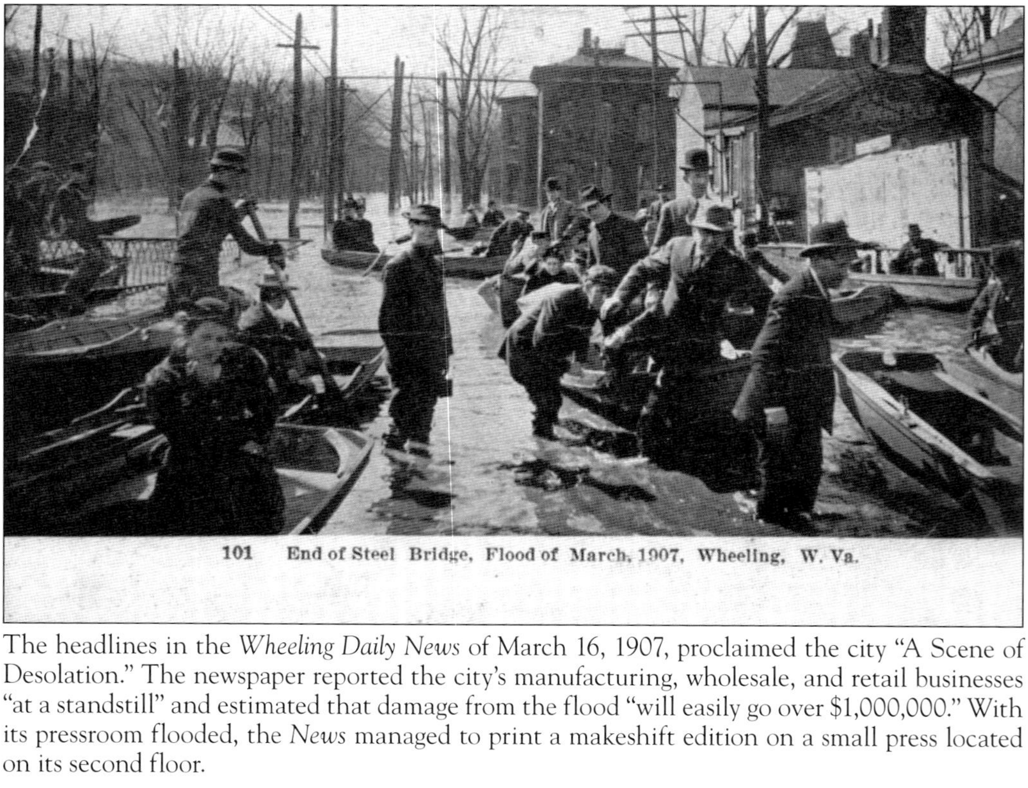

The headlines in the *Wheeling Daily News* of March 16, 1907, proclaimed the city "A Scene of Desolation." The newspaper reported the city's manufacturing, wholesale, and retail businesses "at a standstill" and estimated that damage from the flood "will easily go over $1,000,000." With its pressroom flooded, the *News* managed to print a makeshift edition on a small press located on its second floor.

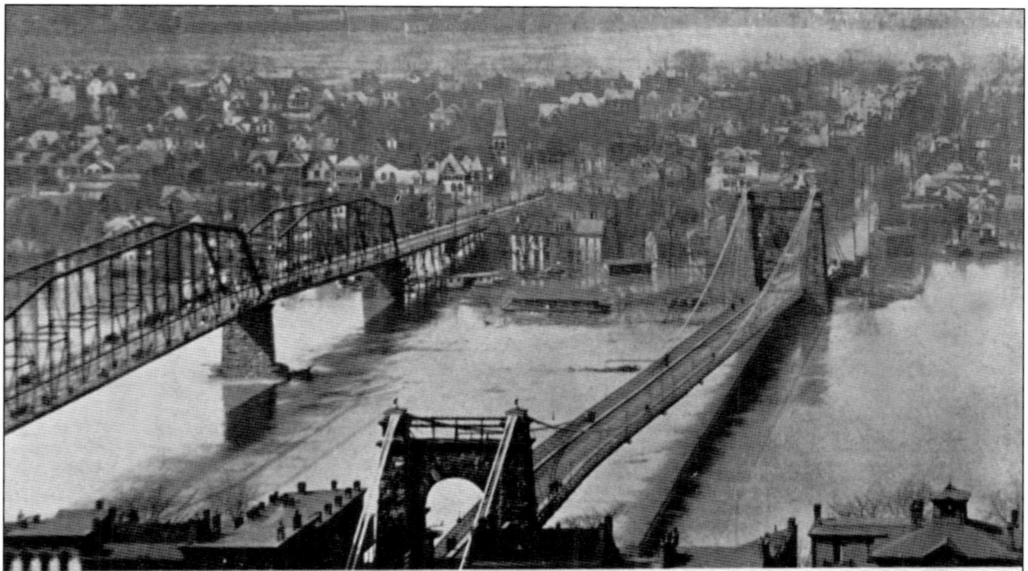

115. Wheeling Island Under 14 Feet of Water, Flood of March 15, 1907, Wheeling, W. Va.

Legend has it Ebenezer Zane bought Wheeling Island from the Native Americans for a keg of whiskey. Construction of the city's famed suspension bridge in 1849 transformed the once-uninhabited island into a popular place for residents and visitors to the racetrack that was built there. But flooding would be a constant threat. The 1907 flood, shown here, covered the island with 14 feet of water. (For a sketch of the island in the 1936 flood, see page 36.)

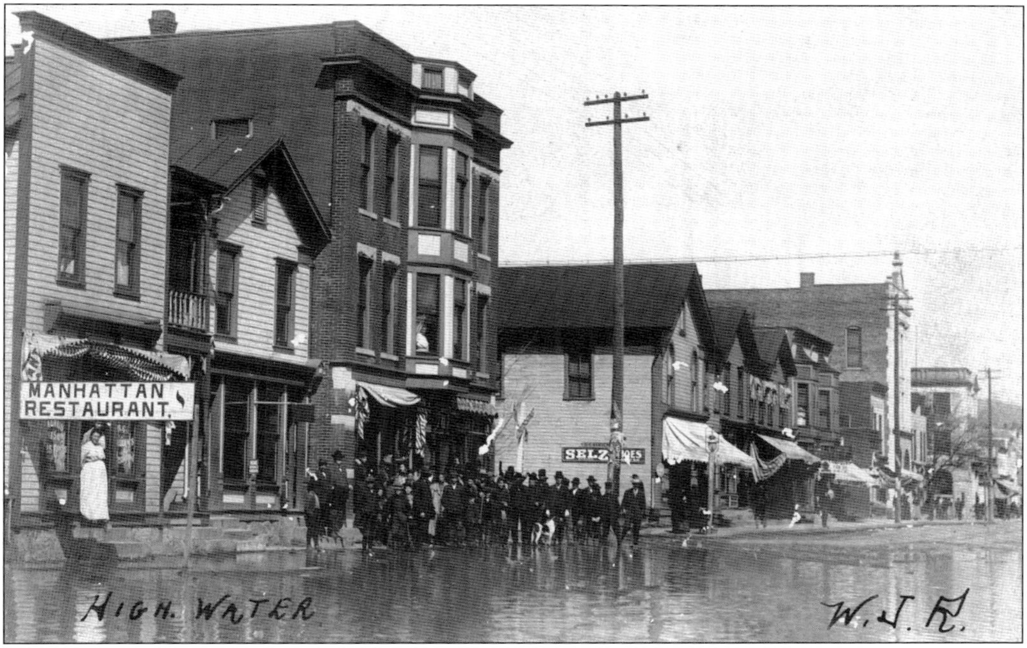

Founder Alexander H. Creel named St. Mary's, the county seat of Pleasants County, West Virginia, in honor of the Virgin Mary. Creel said Mary appeared to him in a vision one night as the steamboat on which he was traveling passed the point where he afterward established the town. Here a curious crowd checks out the high water during the 1907 flood. Note the women in white standing in the doorway of the Manhattan Restaurant.

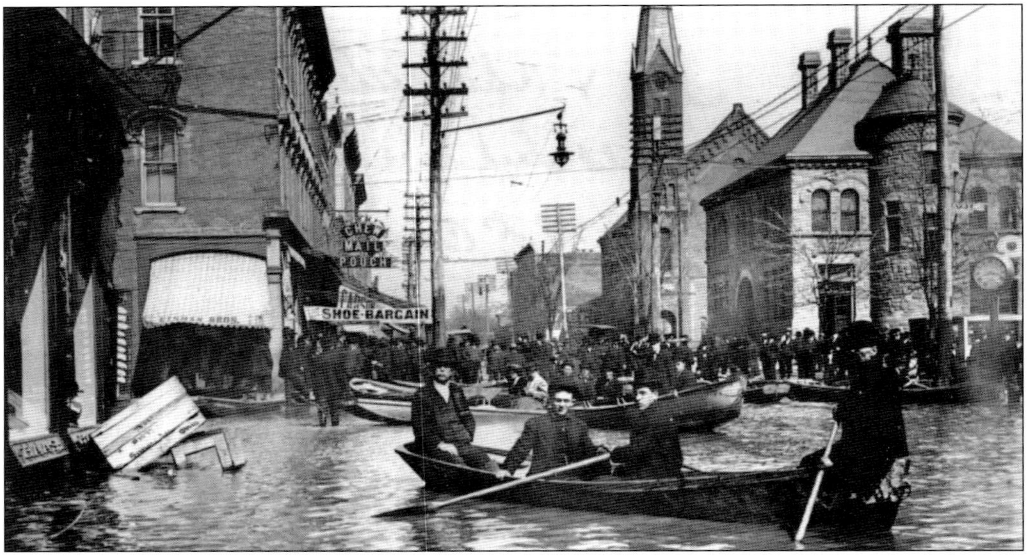

Portsmouth, Ohio, was inundated by the 1907 flood, but on Sunday, March 17, the cold weather broke, and the temperature reached a balmy 70 degrees. According to a contemporary newspaper account, "thousands took advantage of the fine weather to row about the city's streets." The camera captured these Sunday boaters at Fifth and Chillicothe Streets.

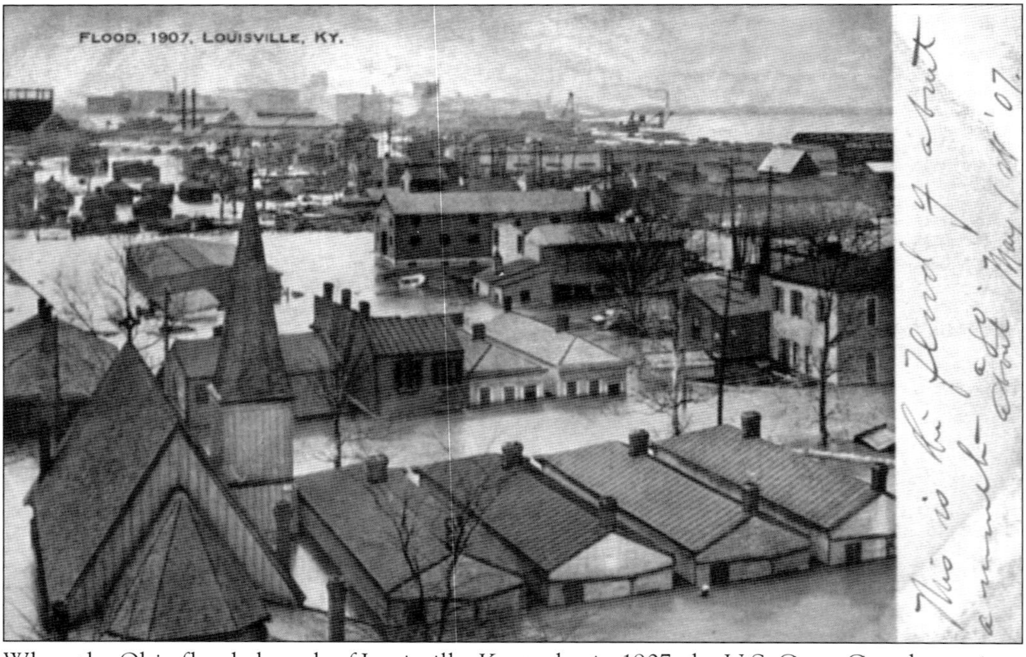

When the Ohio flooded much of Louisville, Kentucky, in 1907, the U.S. Coast Guard went into action and evacuated more than 400 people to safety. The coast guard also distributed food and fuel to hundreds more, transported physicians, performed ambulance duty, and even helped the mail get through by transporting the city's letter carriers.

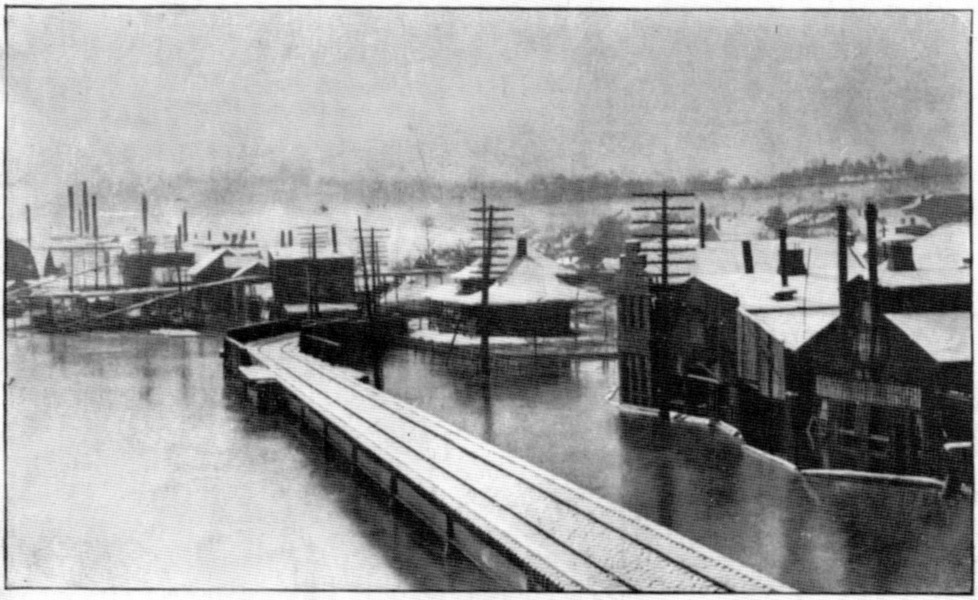

OHIO RIVER FRONT, WEST, FLOOD OF 1907, NEW ALBANY, IND.

Founded in 1813, New Albany was briefly—in the 1840s and 1850s—Indiana's largest city, but by 1907, it had long since lost that distinction. Even so, it remained an important rail hub and manufacturing center. This view from the 1907 flood shows the city's riverfront looking to the west. Note the snow covering the elevated train tracks and the rooftops of the flooded buildings.

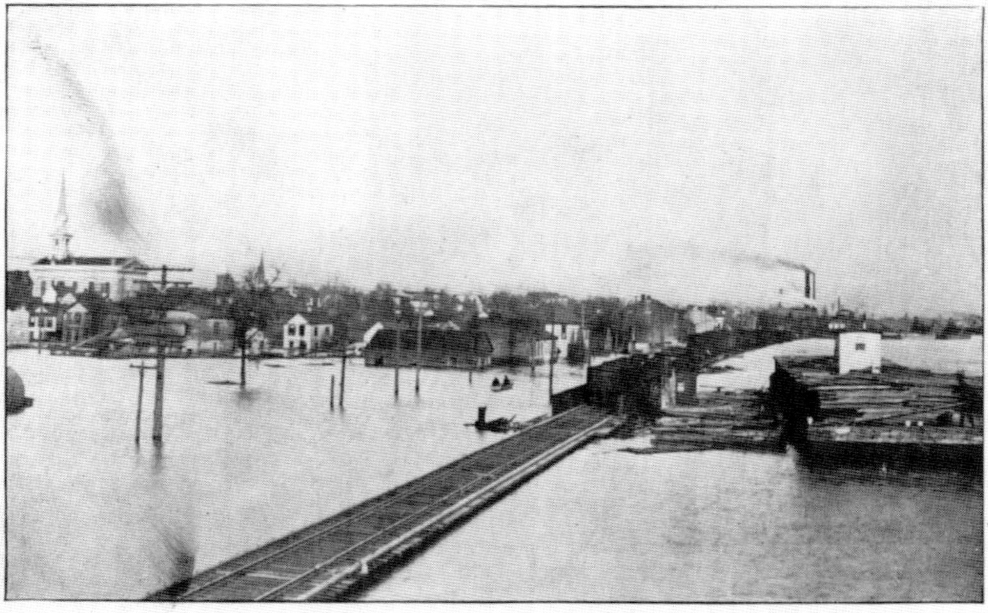

OHIO RIVER FRONT, EAST, FLOOD OF 1907, NEW ALBANY, IND.

This 1907 photograph of the New Albany riverfront shows the view looking to the east. There is no trace of snow, suggesting that it may have been taken a day or two after the earlier photograph when the constant rain had melted the show. However, it is clear the river is still high. When this photograph was taken, New Albany industries included boatbuilding, glassmaking, ironworks, woolen and cotton mills, and woodworking.

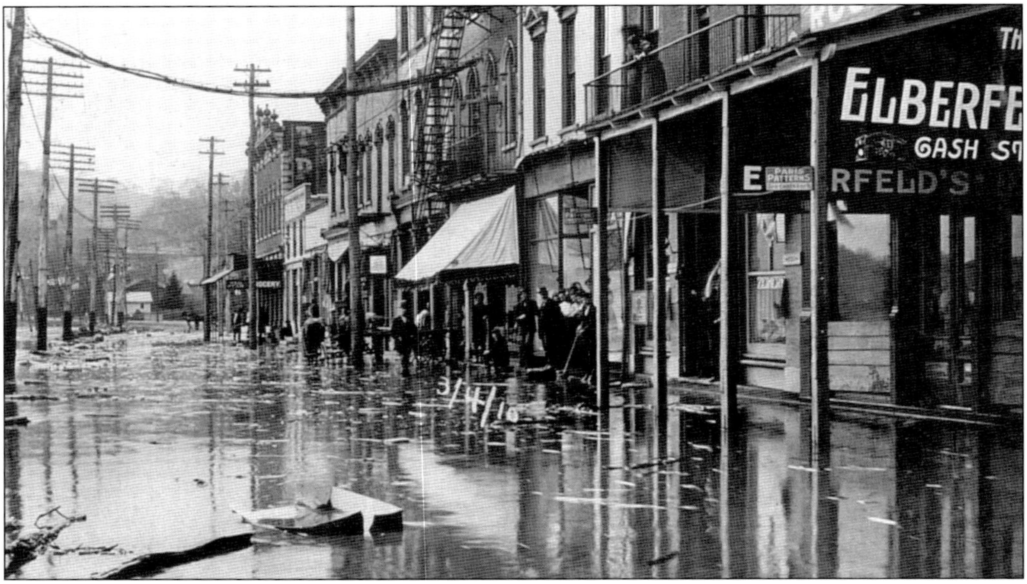

During the latter part of the 19th century and earliest years of the 20th century, Pomeroy, a small Ohio River town in Meigs County, Ohio, was an important shipper of coal and salt. It is said the first coal barges to travel the Ohio River were loaded there. Like other river towns, Pomeroy was regularly visited by Old Man River. Here is the aftermath from one such visit in March 1910.

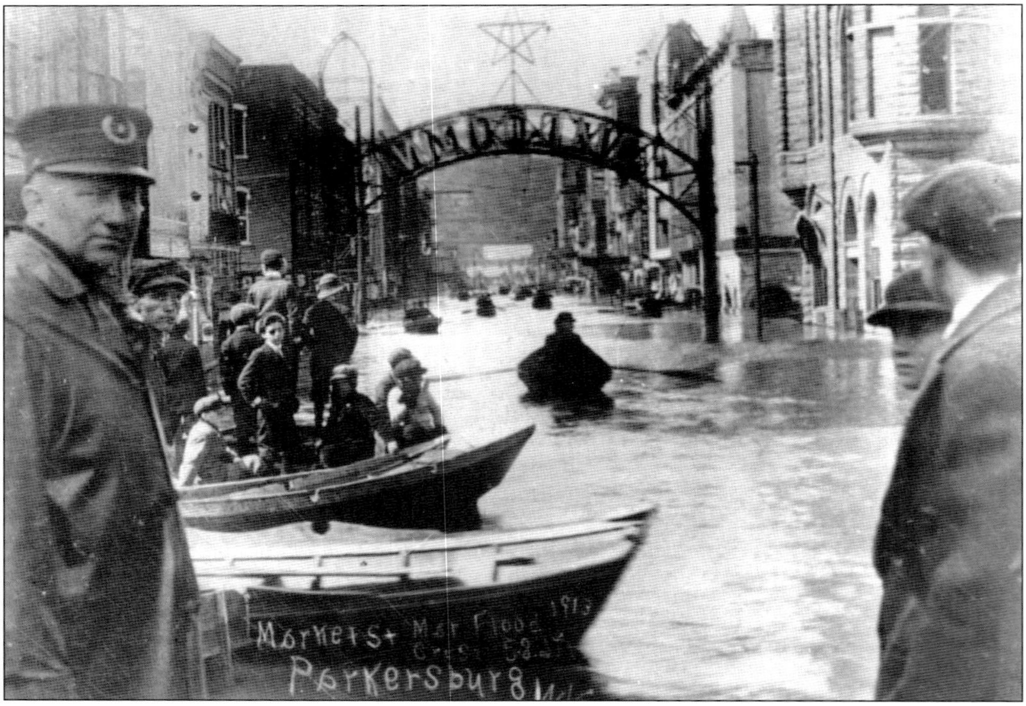

In March 1913, it rained steadily for five days over much of the Ohio Valley, and the Ohio River and its tributaries begin rising rapidly. In Parkersburg, West Virginia, the Ohio crested at 56 feet, covering nearly half the downtown and reaching as far as Market and Fifth Streets (shown here). With no railroad, telephone, or telegraph service, the city was cut off from the outside world. The flood would prove to be the city's worst ever. (Photograph by Artcraft Studio.)

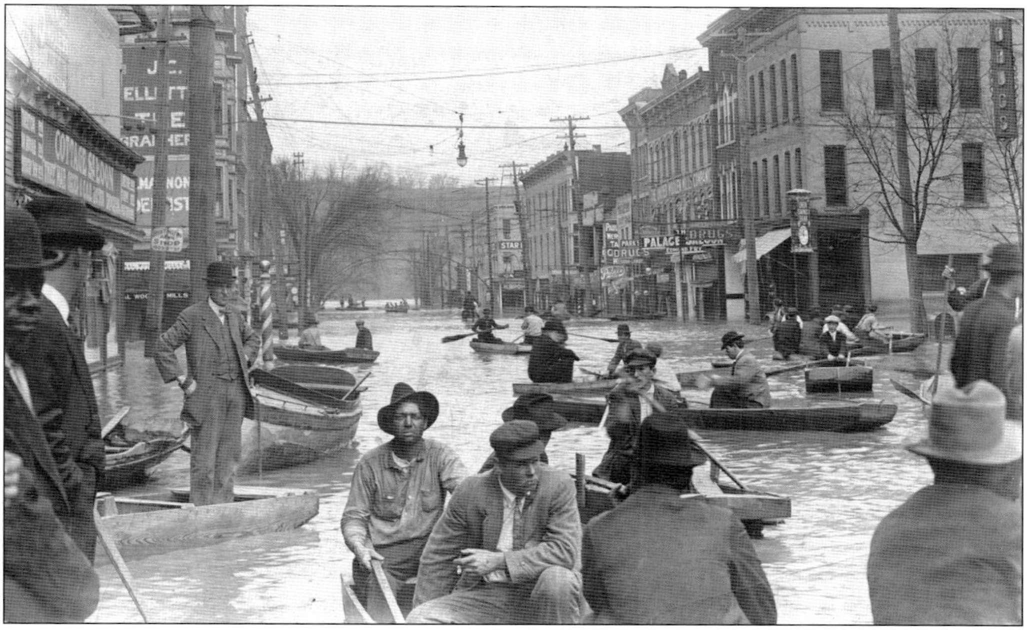

The 1913 flood hit Huntington, West Virginia, hard. "Never since the flood of 1884 has the city of Huntington been in worse condition," warned the March 30 edition of the *Herald-Dispatch*. Churches, schools, and other public buildings soon were crowded with an estimated 2,000 men, women, and children who had been driven from their homes. Shown here in this postcard view is the flooded intersection of Fourth Avenue and Ninth Street.

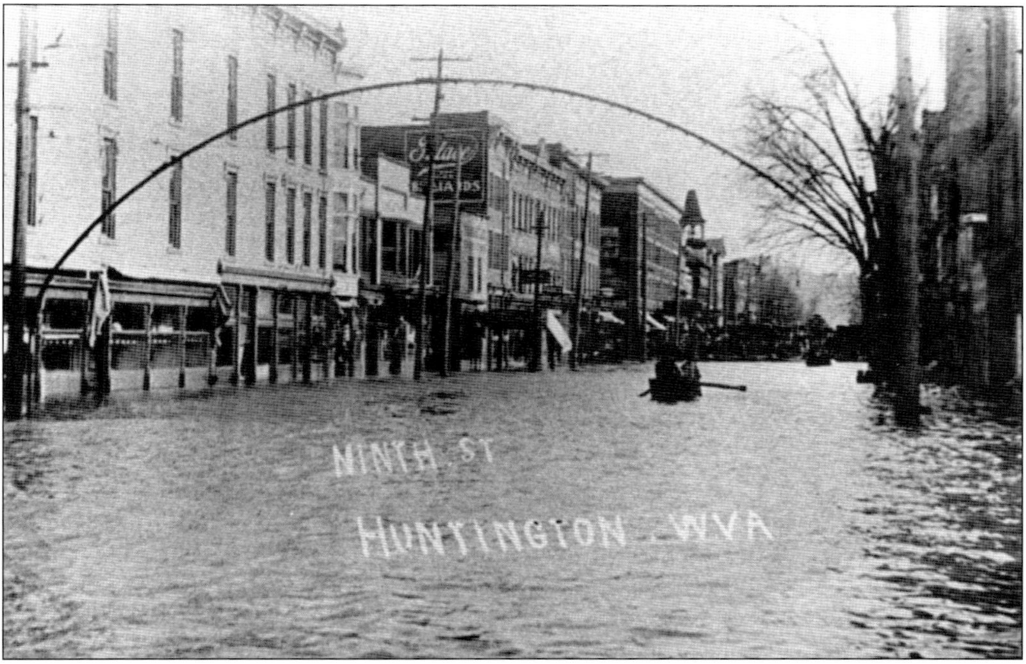

This view of Huntington's flooded Ninth Street in 1913 looks south from Third Avenue. The bell tower just right of center in the photograph is Huntington's first city hall, which also housed the fire department and city jail. The arch extending over the flooded street was part of an early system of electric lights used to illuminate the streets at night.

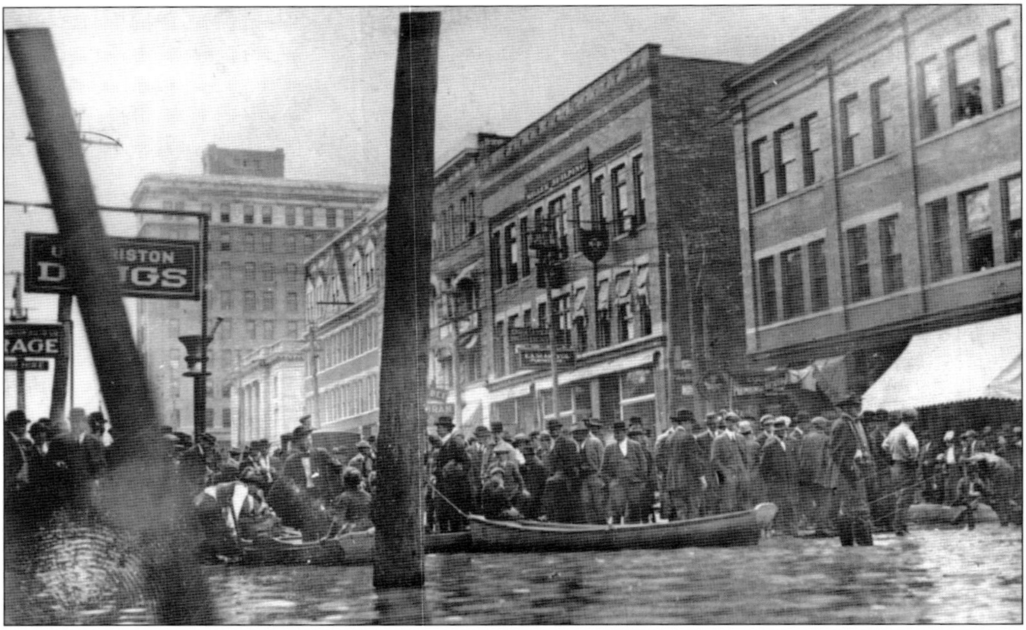

Here is another view of Huntington's flooded Ninth Street in 1913, this one showing the block between Fourth and Fifth Avenues. The tall structure at the rear of the photograph is the Robson-Prichard building. The U.S. Post Office stands beside it. The men gathered in the street do not seem suitably dressed for wading in the floodwaters. With their coats and ties, they might as well be on their way to church.

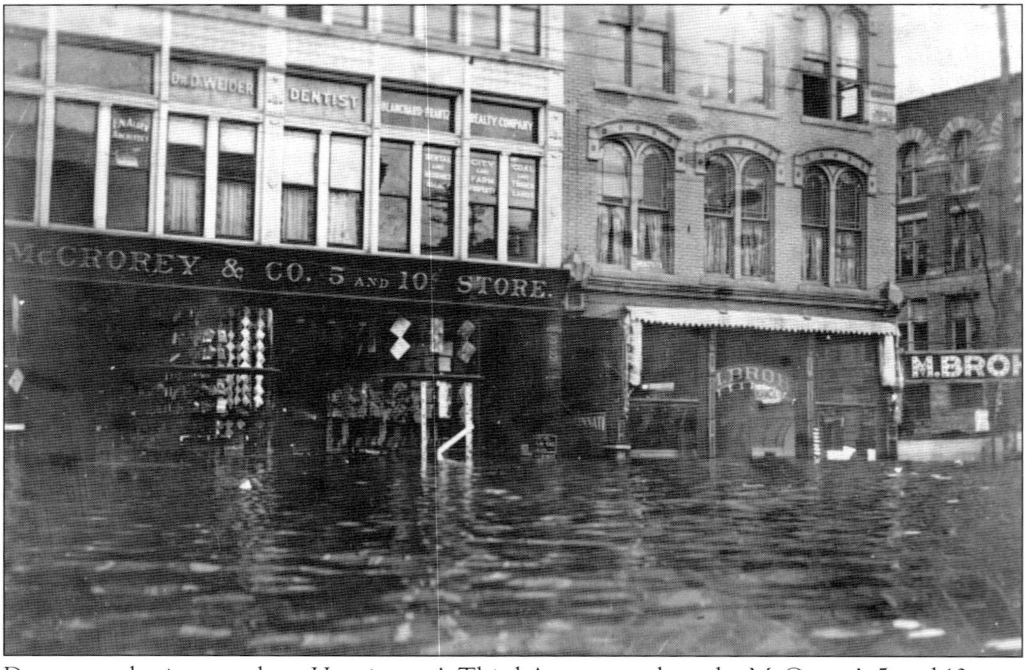

Downtown businesses along Huntington's Third Avenue, such as the McCrorey's 5-and-10-cent store and the M. Broh clothing store, located on the southeast corner of Third Avenue and Ninth Street, were badly damaged by the 1913 flood. Other businesses simply adapted to the emergency. When the saloons were closed by city edict, bootleggers did a busy trade by boat.

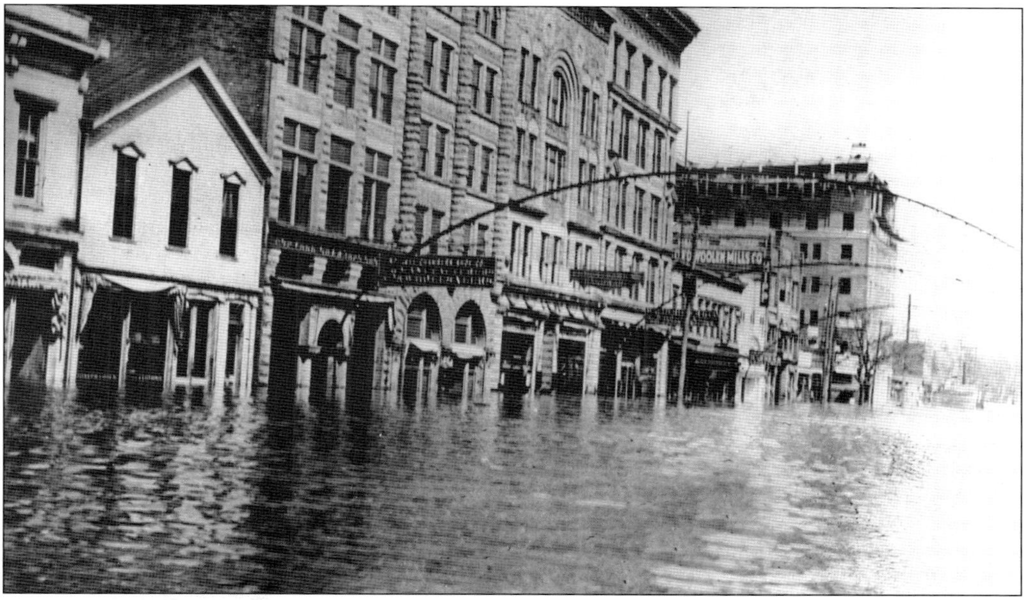

Many of the Third Avenue buildings shown in this 1913 Huntington flood view housed the busy wholesale houses that once played such an important role in the city's economy. The buildings shown line the north side of the avenue in the 1000 block. In the background, at Eleventh Street, can be seen the city's Masonic Temple, then still under construction.

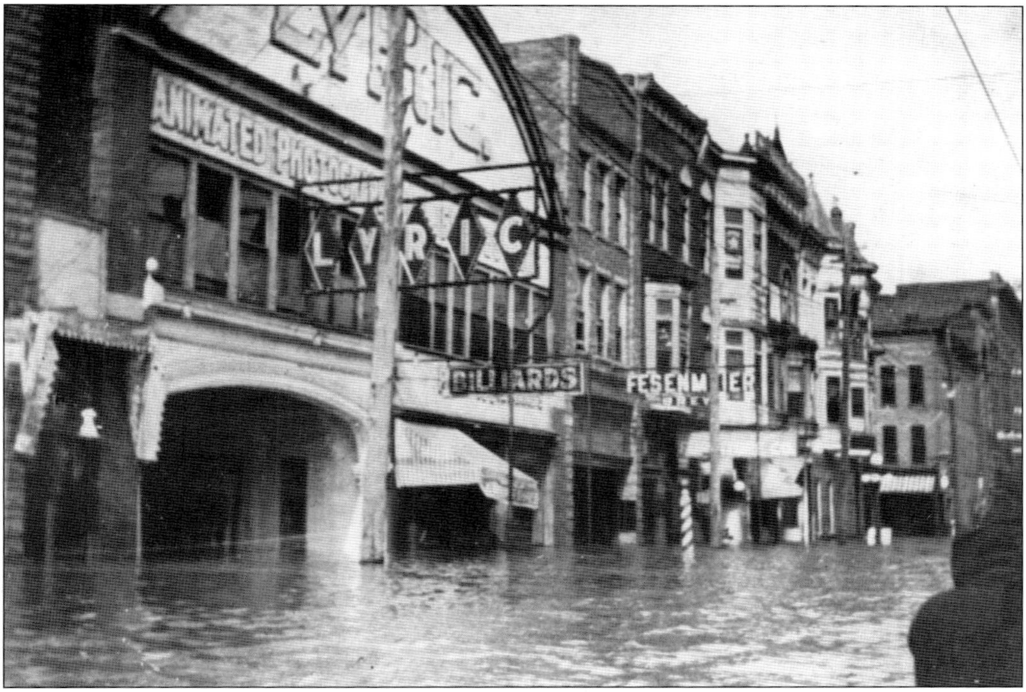

Huntington's first motion-picture theater opened in 1905, and within five years, the downtown was home to a half dozen of the popular attractions. In 1905, Floyd S. Chapman took over an old skating rink on Fourth Avenue between Eighth and Ninth Streets, and turned it into the Lyric movie house. Chapman was elected Huntington mayor in 1912—just in time to preside over a flooded town in 1913.

Type Set by Hand as Office Machines Are Under Water

HUNTINGTON HERALD-DISPATCH

One Page Today

PRICE THREE CENTS — HUNTINGTON, W. VA., SUNDAY MORNING, MARCH 30, 1913 — FOUTH YEAR

REPORT CREST OF FLOOD HERE TODAY; STAGE OF 66 FEET IS NOW PREDICTED

RIVER IS HIGHER THAN IN YEAR 1884

Refugees In Pitiful Condition Are Housed and Fed In Schools and Chnrches.

THOUSANDS HOMELESS

Many Marooned In Second Stories of Homes Are Unable to Get Food.

BULLETIN

Cincinnati, O., March 29.—Unofficial reports state that Parkersburg is fifty eight tonight, this is four feet above eighty four flood. River at Huntington will continue to rise reaching crest stage of about 66 or 67 feet Sunday.

DEVEREAUX

At 8 o'clock last night the flood mark of 1884 was passed in Huntington. It was believed later in the night a stage of at least 66 feet of water would be reached before tonight.

Never since the flood of 1884 has the city of Huntington been in worse condition than it was Saturday night with the river at a stage of 64.8 feet at 8 o'clock and climbing upward at the rate of slightly more than an inch an hour.

The churches, public school buildings, city hall, city jail, court house and every vacant building in Huntington is occupied with a crowd of flood refugees, numbering at least 2,000.

At Guyandotte 500 unfortunates were forced to the hills for safety marooned without anything to eat, without shelter or any way in which to cook. The city sent a boat of sandwiches to them.

In every ward in the city the commissioners, police, special men, sanitary officer and others were working like slaves to relieve situation.

On the orders of the mayor the officers were given the authority to take charge of any boat needed and many times during the day were forces to do so to rescue some flood bound family.

There was pitiful sights to be seen on every side where the pathetic looking refugees gathered in church or school or city building.

In the city hall the upstairs was crowded with the most pitiful looking woe-begone specimens of men, women and children on earth. They were gathered in from all sections where the merciless waters had crept into their homes and driven them out. Unkempt, uncombed and un-everything save fed, they clustered in hopeless looking crowds staring with unseeing eyes from the windows or looking away into space. Over all, the reek of foul odors hung like a stifling wave and yet it was but one scene of many in every school building throughout the city; in many churches and in the city hall where the unfortunate poor had gathered.

Four alarms of fire were turned in during the day, and a great deal of excitement was caused.

The first prooved to be a false alarm at the corner of sixth avenue and Eleventh Street.

The second was extinguished by buckets of water at the store of A. G. Blake & company on Third avenue Twentieth street. The third was a false alarm at West Huntington, and the fourth originated in the home of Ferguson Thompson at 1018 Fifth avenue. This was extinguished. A large flambeau at Seventh avenue and Fifth street caused a number of persons to believe that a big blaze was raging in that section, and considerable excitecent was caused

Crest Is At Wheeling

Pittsburg, March 29, 9 p. m.—The crest of the Ohio river flood is at Wheeling, W. Va. The flood waters are coming rapidly to points below and the volume of the water is large. Southern West Virginia points it is believed will be battling with the highest water in their history by Sunday morning.

Flee To Hills

Cincinnati, O., March 29.—The telephone operator at Aurora, Indiana notified the Cincinnati authorities late today that the rising waters of the Ohio river had broken over the levee at Lawrenceburg, Indiana, and that the people were fleeing to the highlands.

Doubt Parkersburg Report

Washington, March 29.—Weather bureau flood experts today were inclined to doubt the accuracy of the report of a stage of 64 feet in the Ohio river at Parkersburg, W. Va. The crest of the flood they estimated was about due at Parkersburg, but the highest was much greater than at Pittsburg, where the water was reported this morning as falling.

Kanawha Falling Rapidly

Charleston, W. Va. March 29.—The Kanawha began falling here Friday night after reaching a stage of 34.8 feet and at 6 o'clock tonight was down to 28 feet. Everything is moving fine with general conditions good. No loss of life and a property loss not near so large as at most points.

Point Pleasant Helpless

Pt. Pleasant, W. Va. Mar. 29.—The city is in desperate straits and has sent out a call for help. There is great danger here with 60 feet of water covering the country and town. There is no food to be had and a state of famine exists. Charleston has responded with word that two government boats would leave there at the earliest possible moment loaded with food supplies.

Send Supplies By Boat

Charleston, W. Va. Mar. 29.—8:19 p. m.—Two boats loaded to the guards with provisions for flood and famine stricken Pt. Pleasant left here tonight at 6:30 o'clock.

Parkersburg Submerged

Parkersburg, W. Va., March 29.—The whole city practically is under water, the flood having climbed to the Chancellor hotel the highest point in the business district. The entire down town sections is almost hidden from sight and the loss will run into many thousands of dollars. All Riverside has been driven to the high ground and the 400 families residing in the bottoms above the city near the steel plant have been forced to leave their homes tho the waters.

Sixty Feet at Gallipolis

Gallipolis, O., March 29.—The river here has gone so far that it is almost impossible to tell what the exact stage is and the rate of rise seems to have increased since 5 o'clock. It is known that it is close to 60 feet.

Lexington Ky. Mch. 29— Fully one thousand head of stock in Kentucky valley are reported drowned and great quantities of logs have been swept from the hills in the rapidly rising Kentucky river.

COURTEOUS TREATMENT

Through the courtesy of the Chesapeake and Potomac Telephone company The Herald - Dispatch staff was permitted to occupy their offices last night. Free use of the telephone and office equipment was allowed. This paper is printed through the courtesy of the Blagg Printing Company.

The Herald- Dispatch office is flooded.

RISING AT PARKERSBURG

Pittsburg Mch. 29

For a few minutes this afternoon the Associated Press succeeded in gaining telephone communication with Parkersburg W. Va.

The correspondent there reported that the river stage had risen higher than ever was known and still rising.

Offers Help

Charleston, W. Va. Mar. 29., 8:30 p. m.—Mayor Bedell desires to inform the people of Huntington through its mayor and the press of that city that if in any way whatever he and the city of Charleston can aid the flood sufferers in Huntington every service possible will be rendered with pleasure. If provisions are needed they will be forwarded at once.

Send Supplies

Charleston, W. Va., Mar. 29., 8:30 p. m.—The packet Evergreen left here tonight at 8 o'clock with $3,500 worth of provisions on board for Pt. Pleasant. Two government launches will reach that town about 8 o'clock Sunday morning, laden with provisions. After the town has been taken care of the boats will visit the surrounding West Virginia towns to provide food for the homeless. The Chamber of Commerce has been working hard since noon to load the boats with food and get them started on the way.

Marietta Deluged

Marietta, O., March, 29— Via Whipple, to Cambridge, O. Via telephone to Pittsburg. Flood conditions in Marietta this morning are beyond description. The river rose rapidly until the stage at eight o'clock was six tenths and rising.

FLOOD SUFFERER TRIES SUICIDE

Despondent because of terrible suffering he had endured since he was driven from his home by the flood, Will Sullivan, a refugee, attempted suicide by drinking carbolic acid in the city hall building at one o'clock Saturday afternoon. Two trained nurses who chanced to be in the building administered first aid remedies, and it was believed saved his life. No physician was available until four hours later.

Sullivan, who is a militiaman, with his young wife had been driven from their home near Seventh street and Third avenue Friday and had spent the night in the city building. He was thirty-five years old, and had just arrived in Huntington from the Paint Creek strike zone where he had been on duty for many weeks. He was a member of Company "H" of Huntington.

His aged mother, Mrs. S. J. Sullivan, also a refugee, said that Will was the second of her children to attempt suicide. Two years ago her daughter killed herself with carbolic acid.

BULLETIN.

PARKERSBURG, W. VA. MARCH 30.—ONE O'CLOCK.—THE WATER IS STATIONARY HERE AT MIDNIGHT.

Declares Holiday to Protect Banks

Charleston, W. Va., March 29.—Governor Hatfield today declared March 28th, 29th and 31st legal holidays to protect the banks in the flood district of the state. The action was taken at the request of business men.

Twelve Thousand Homeless

Cincinnati, March 29.—In the six towns across the Ohio river from here it is estimated there are 12,000 homeless and that more than three thousand five hundred houses are flood.

No Services In Church Today

"I think this the time to practice Christianity, rather than preach it" declared Rev. U. V. W. Darlington, yesterday announcing that there would be no services in the Johnson Memorial church today. He stated that the basement of the basement of the building at Tenth street and Fifth avenue would be open all day today, and those who wished cooked food could secure it. A force of the church women will be busy all day preparing food for the homeless. Dr. Darlington is heading a force of churchmen in rescue work.

Huntington was cut off from the world last night with the one exception of The Herald-Dispatch leased 'phone wire to Pittsburg. By this route authentic Associated Press reports were received and appear in the regular edition today.

Huntington's newspapers continued publishing during the 1913 flood, but accomplishing that feat was not easy. The Fourth Avenue plant of the *Herald-Dispatch* was underwater, so the type for the March 30 edition was set by hand in the offices of the Chesapeake and Potomac Telephone Company and then rushed to a commercial print shop.

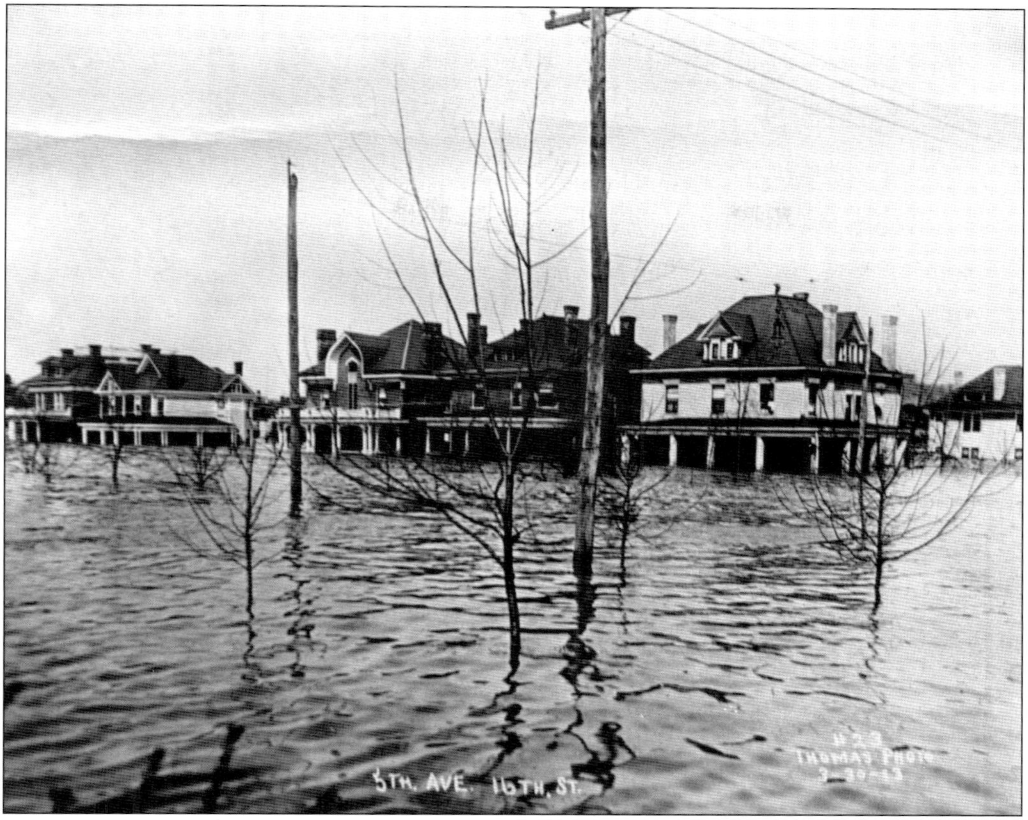

The 1913 flood inundated a number of Huntington residential neighborhoods, including this one at Fifth Avenue and Sixteenth Street (now Hal Greer Boulevard). The *Herald-Dispatch* reported that during the flood, three babies were born at the refugee center at Oley School, only three blocks from where this photograph was taken.

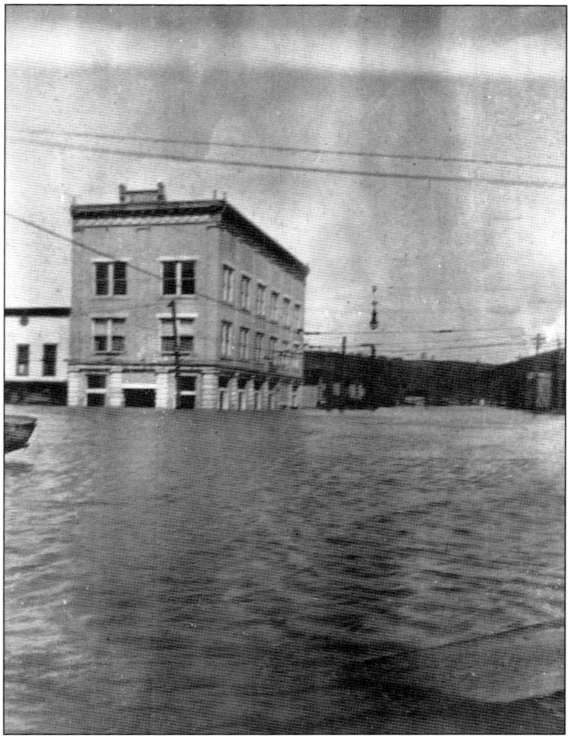

Founded in 1905, the Twentieth Street Bank was long the centerpiece of the busy East Huntington business community. Here the bank's sturdy stone building at the corner of Third Avenue and Twentieth Street is surrounded by the 1913 floodwaters. With the riverbank only blocks away, the neighborhood's homes, businesses, and factories were quickly inundated. (For a view showing the Twentieth Street Bank in 1937, see page 62.)

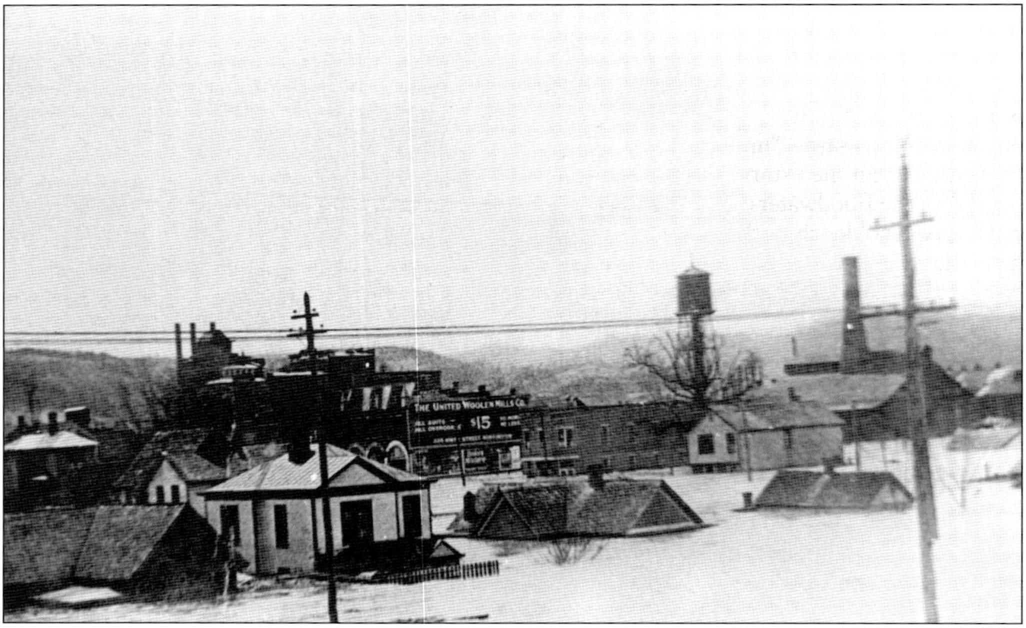

Incorporated in 1893, Central City was originally an independent community just west of Huntington, but in 1909, the little town's voters agreed to be annexed into Huntington. Here the 1913 flood can be seen all but covering a number of one-story houses along Jefferson Avenue in Central City. At the center can be seen a large painted sign advertising United Woolen Mills ("All Suits $15"). At right are the water tower and smokestack of the Huntington Tumbler Company.

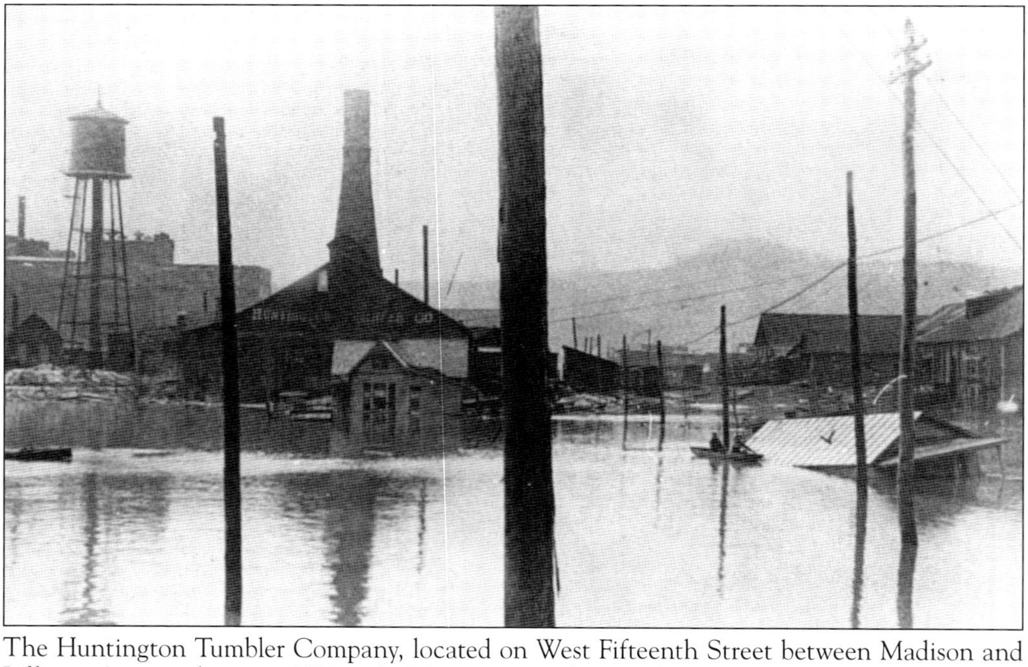

The Huntington Tumbler Company, located on West Fifteenth Street between Madison and Jefferson Avenues, began in 1891 as the West Virginia Flint Bottle Company. In 1900, German-born Anton Zihlman purchased the plant (shown here surrounded by the 1913 floodwaters), changed its name, and switched production from glass bottles and jars to barware and fine glassware for the home. At one time, the plant employed as many as 150 workers.

In the early 1900s, the Chinese community in Ashland, Kentucky, was small but industrious. Pictured on this postcard from the 1913 flood is a Chinese store selling—the lettering on the windows says—"imported teas" and "novelties." Four men stand in the doorway surveying the floodwaters. The man at the right appears older than the others. Perhaps he is the shop's owner. A handwritten caption on the card identifies it as being on "Lower Broadway." (Courtesy Charles R. Nichols.)

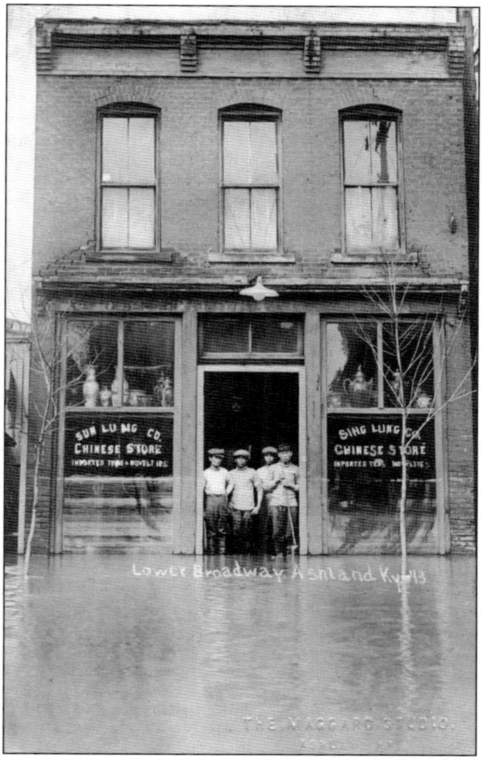

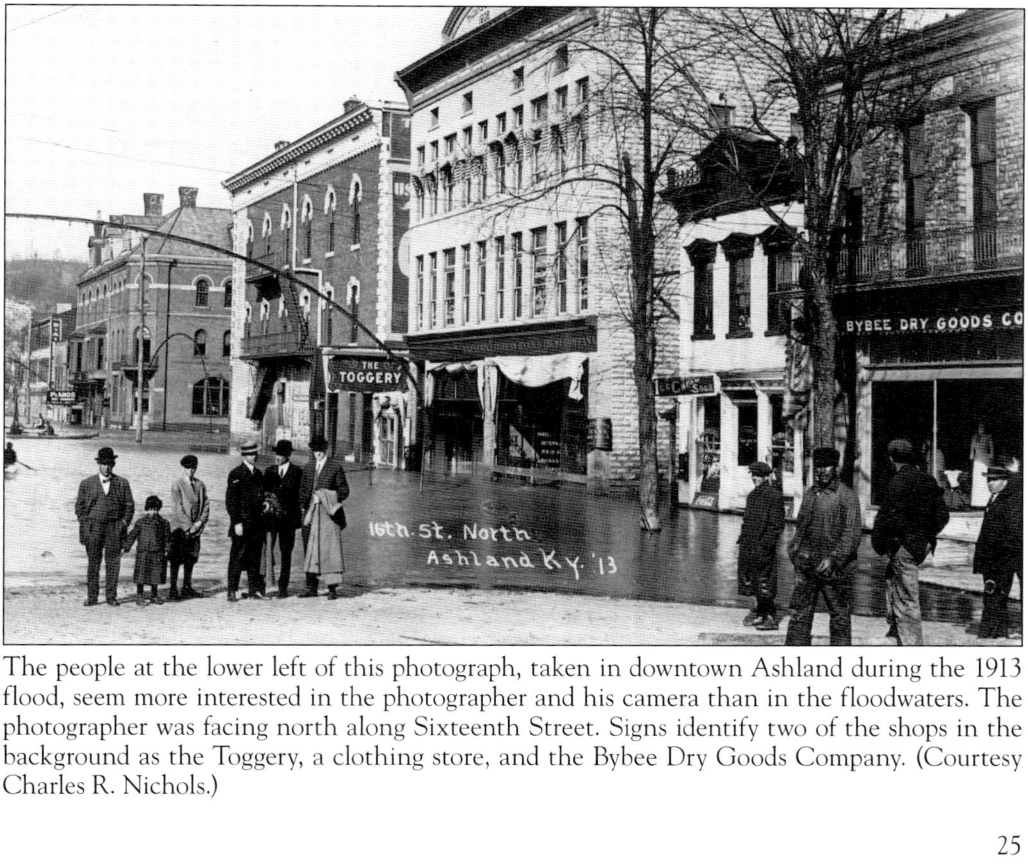

The people at the lower left of this photograph, taken in downtown Ashland during the 1913 flood, seem more interested in the photographer and his camera than in the floodwaters. The photographer was facing north along Sixteenth Street. Signs identify two of the shops in the background as the Toggery, a clothing store, and the Bybee Dry Goods Company. (Courtesy Charles R. Nichols.)

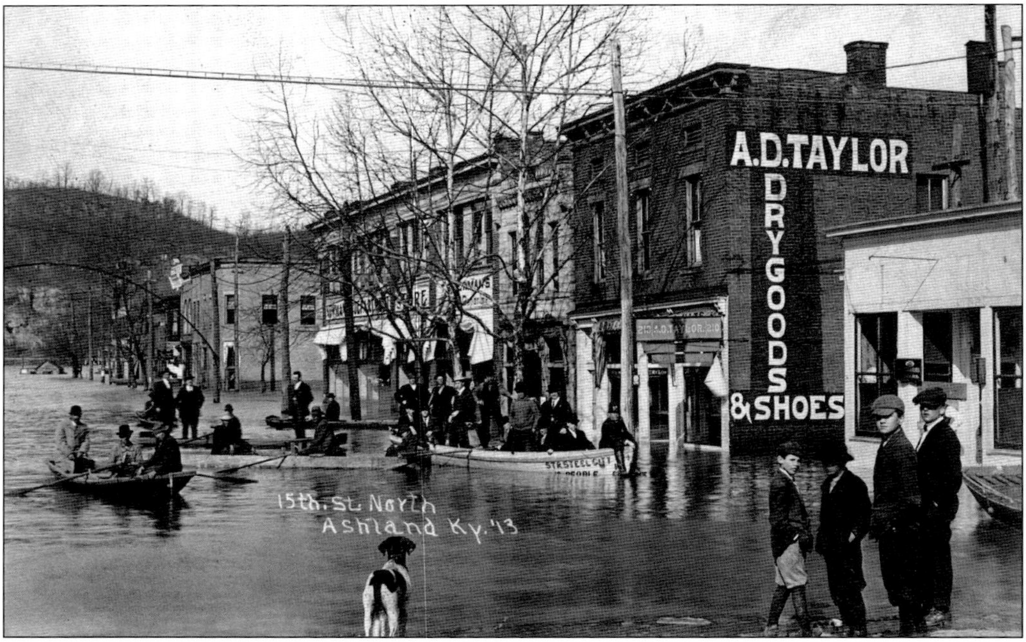

Again in this 1913 photograph in Ashland, the photographer was facing north, with the hills of Ohio visible in the background on the other side of the swollen river. Several small boats can be seen making their way along a flooded Fifteenth Street. A lettered name on the bow of the boat at the center of the picture identifies it as a launch from the steamer *Steel City*, which regularly traveled the Ohio River between Pittsburgh and Cincinnati. (Courtesy Charles R. Nichols.)

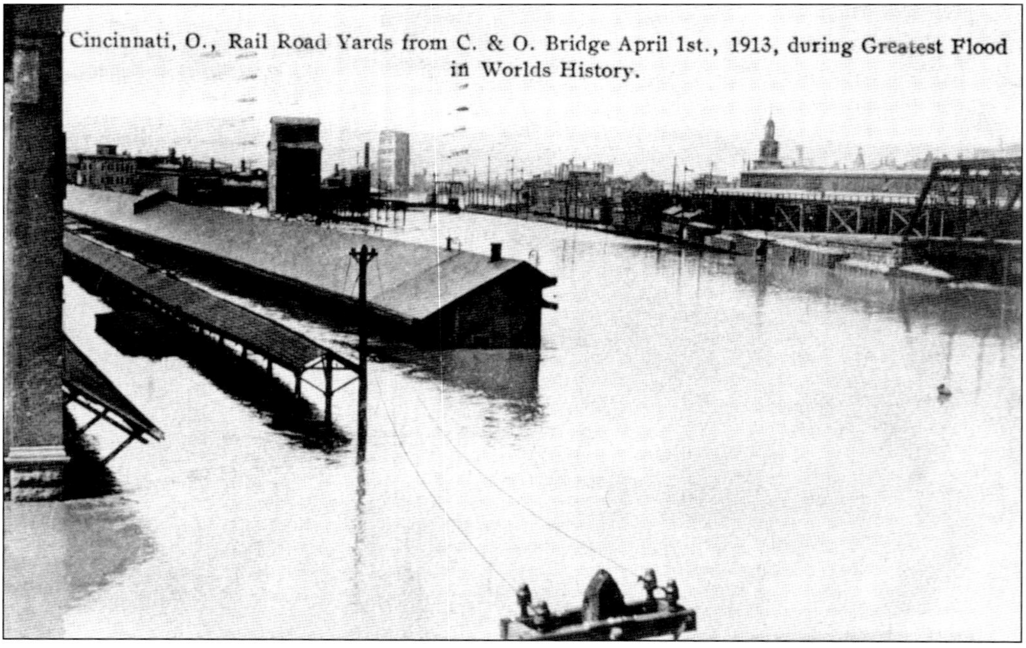

When the 1913 flood reached Cincinnati, Ohio, the river rose 21 feet in 24 hours, flooding homes, businesses, and factories. The damage was enormous. Nevertheless, the anonymous writer of the caption on this postcard of the city's flooded railroad yards clearly got carried away when he or she labeled it the "Greatest Flood in Worlds History."

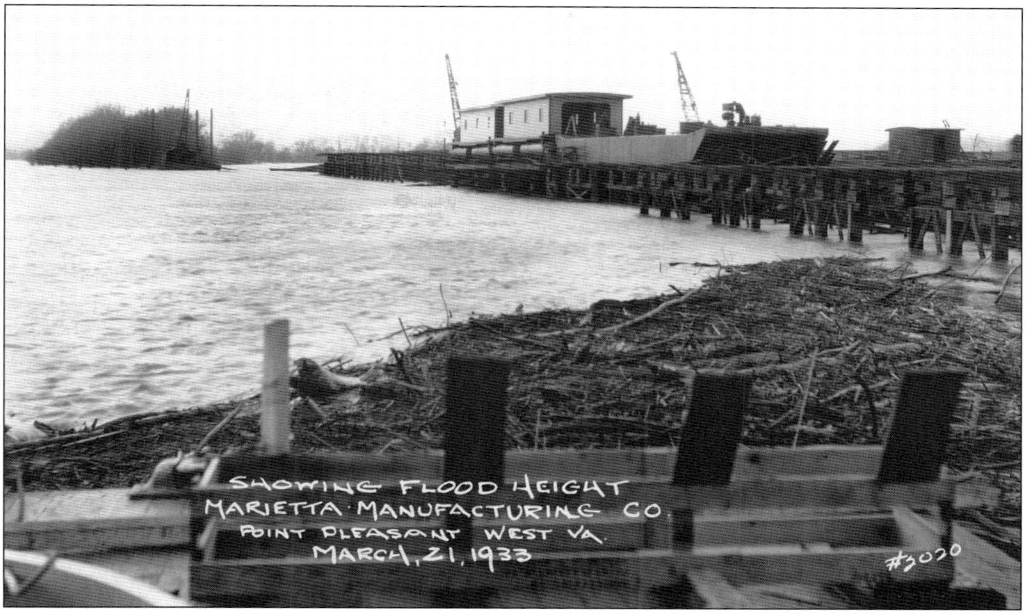

As its name suggests, the Marietta Manufacturing Company originally was located in Marietta, Ohio, but after it was badly damaged by the 1913 flood, it moved downstream to Point Pleasant, West Virginia, where it was located on high ground. That kept the boatbuilder dry during most floods. But, as seen here, the 1933 flood partially submerged it. For a view of Marietta Manufacturing during the 1937 flood, see page 50. (Courtesy Point Pleasant River Museum.)

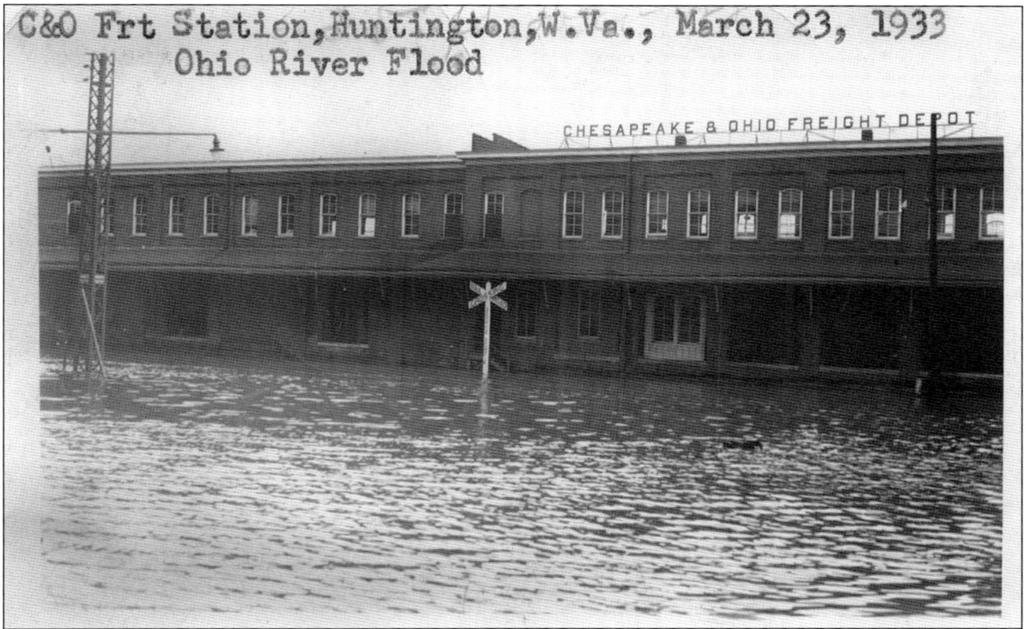

In March 1933, the Ohio River again left its banks. Here is a view of the inundated Chesapeake and Ohio Railway (C&O) Freight Station in Huntington, West Virginia. The station stood little more than a stone's throw from the Ohio River in the city's downtown and so was frequently flooded. A familiar white cross-armed sign marks a railroad crossing, but the only traffic moving today will be by boat. (Courtesy the C&O Historical Society.)

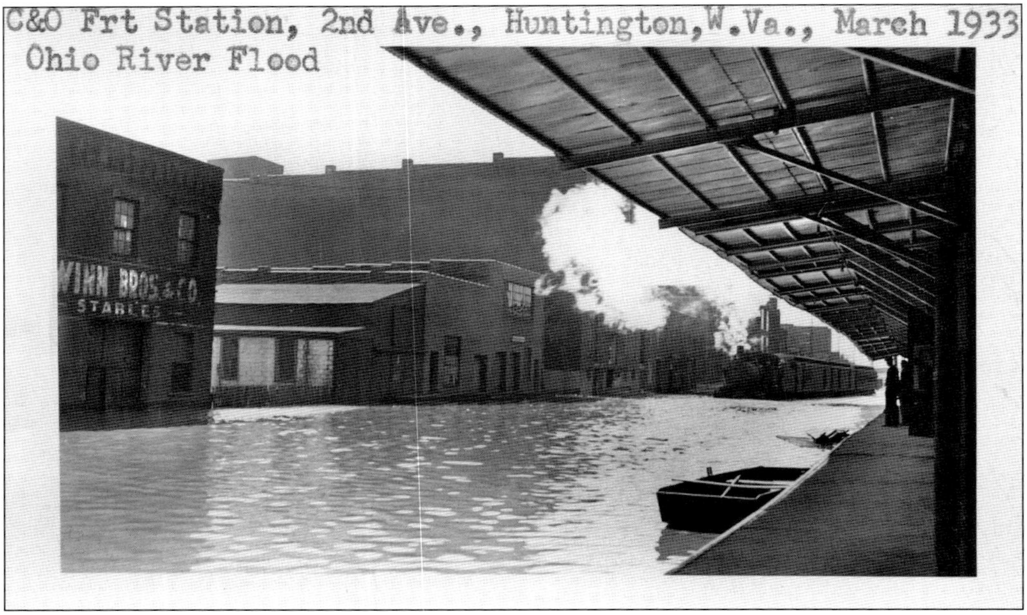

This view of the 1933 floodwaters in Huntington was taken from the platform of the old C&O Freight Station. Ordinarily, the Ohio River would be behind the station, but the floodwaters surround the station and extend on to the neighboring warehouses. A train can be seen slowly approaching in the distance, a thick cloud of white smoke pouring from the locomotive. Note the sign at far left for Winn Brothers and Company Stables. (Courtesy the C&O Historical Society.)

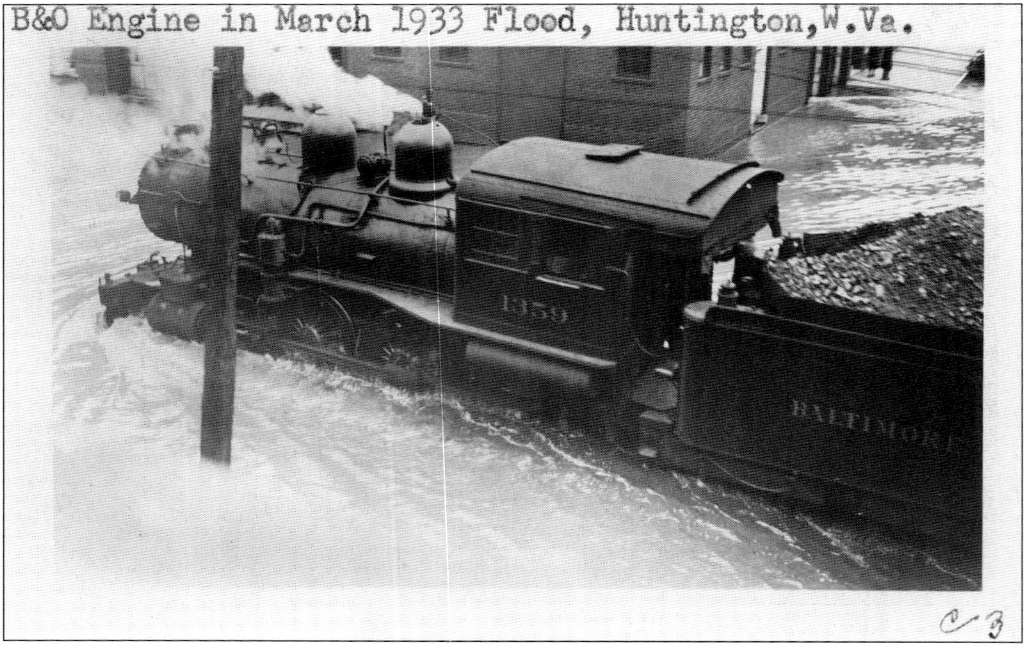

A Baltimore and Ohio Railroad (B&O) locomotive inches its careful way along the flooded track in downtown Huntington during the 1933 flood. In the 1930s, Huntington was served by both the C&O and the B&O, and the two railroads each maintained freight stations near the river's edge, convenient to the city's busy warehouse district and wholesale produce market. Today both the C&O and B&O are part of rail giant CSX. (Courtesy the C&O Historical Society.)

Two

THE 1936 FLOOD

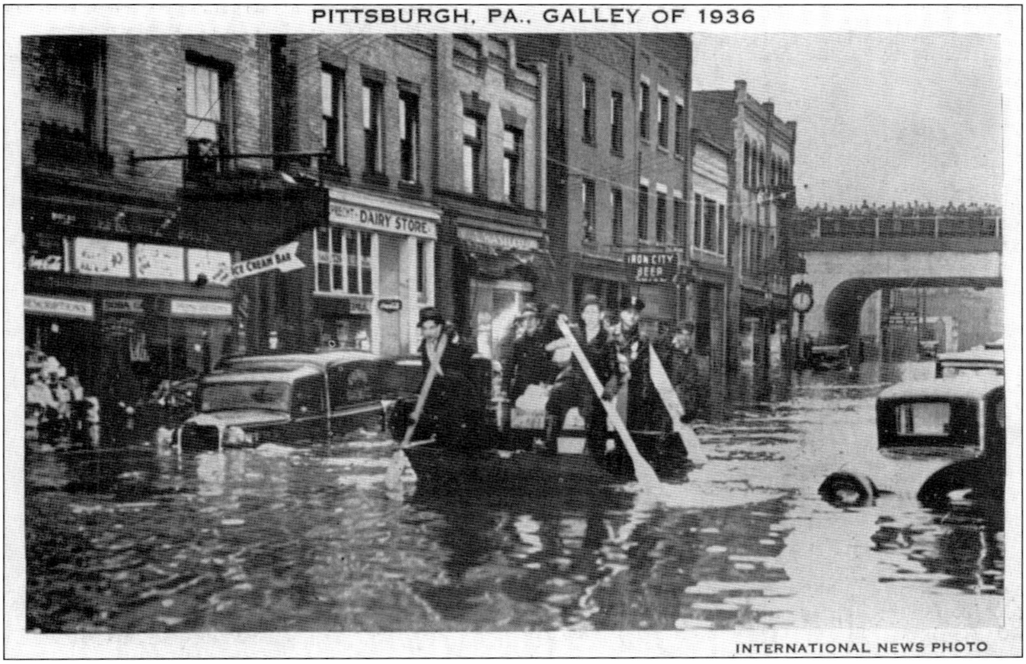

More than 60 inches of snow fell in the Pittsburgh, Pennsylvania, area during the winter of 1935–1936, and when temperatures quickly warmed, the stage was set for a massive flood. The headlines on the front page of the *Pittsburgh Post-Gazette* for March 18 gave readers the grim news: "River at 34 Feet, Still Rises; Downtown Area Under Water." Here a hardy crew of Pittsburghers can be seen paddling a scow down a water-covered street. Their cargo: food for hungry victims of the flood.

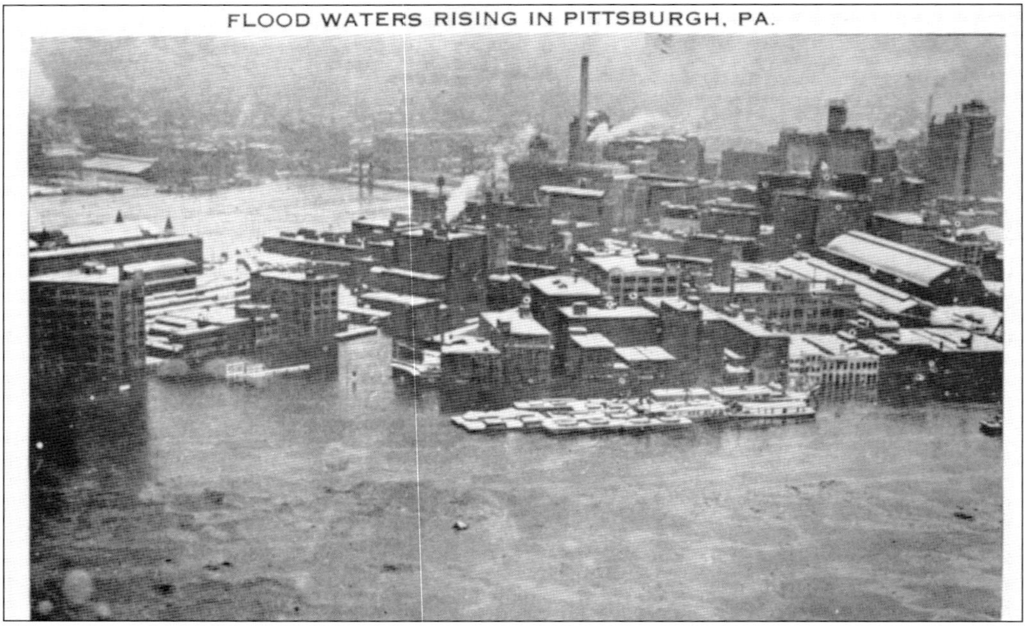

What many Pittsburgh residents still call "the Great St. Patrick's Day Flood" crested at 46.4 feet—nearly 22 feet above flood level. That 1936 mark has never been equaled, not even in 1937 when most cities downstream on the Ohio experienced record flood levels. The flood submerged everything that is now Point State Park, swamping much of the North Side, the Strip, McKees Rocks, and low-lying areas all around.

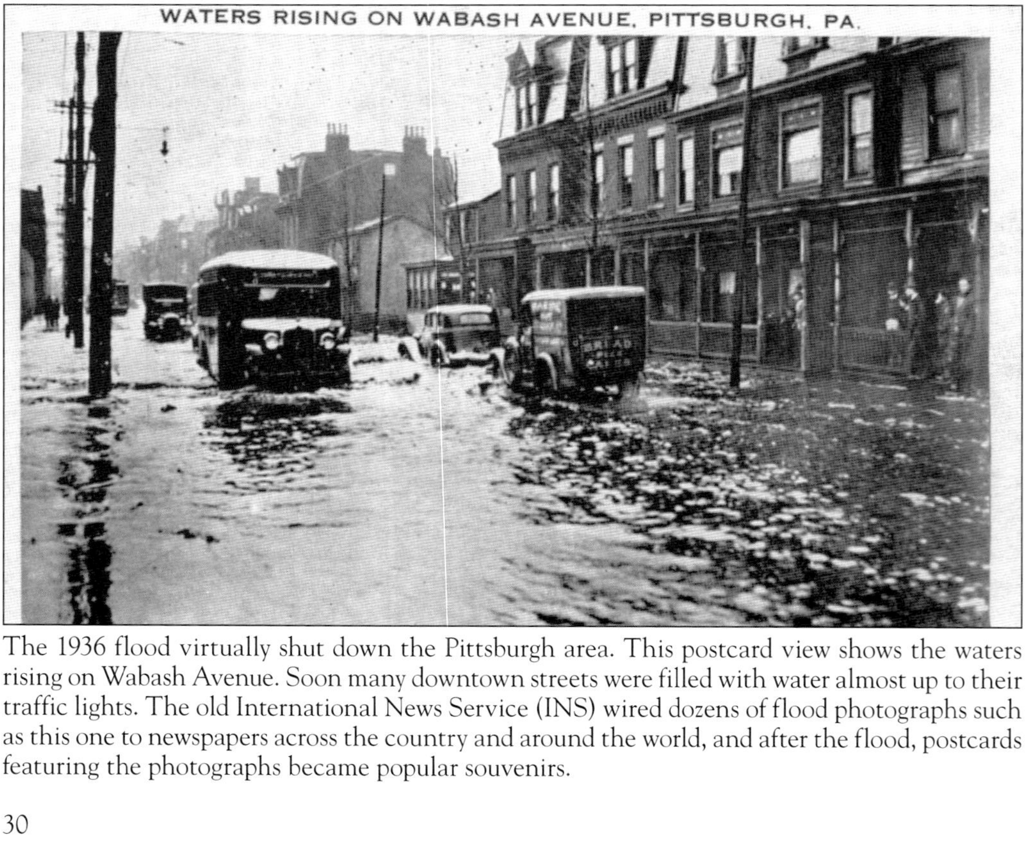

The 1936 flood virtually shut down the Pittsburgh area. This postcard view shows the waters rising on Wabash Avenue. Soon many downtown streets were filled with water almost up to their traffic lights. The old International News Service (INS) wired dozens of flood photographs such as this one to newspapers across the country and around the world, and after the flood, postcards featuring the photographs became popular souvenirs.

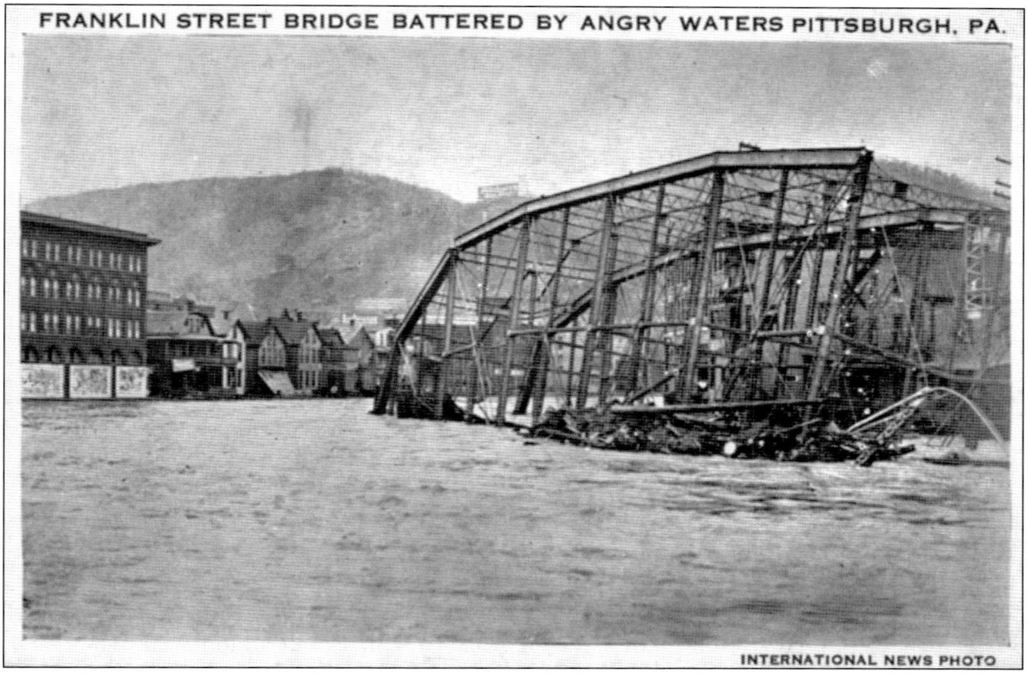

It is said Venice is the only city in the world that boasts more bridges than Pittsburgh. The 1936 flood closed many of the spans tying the city together. In this postcard view, the angry floodwaters batter the Franklin Street Bridge. The city's electric power soon failed. So did the telephones. Ironically, with water all around, many of the city's faucets went dry as the water system's pumps stopped working.

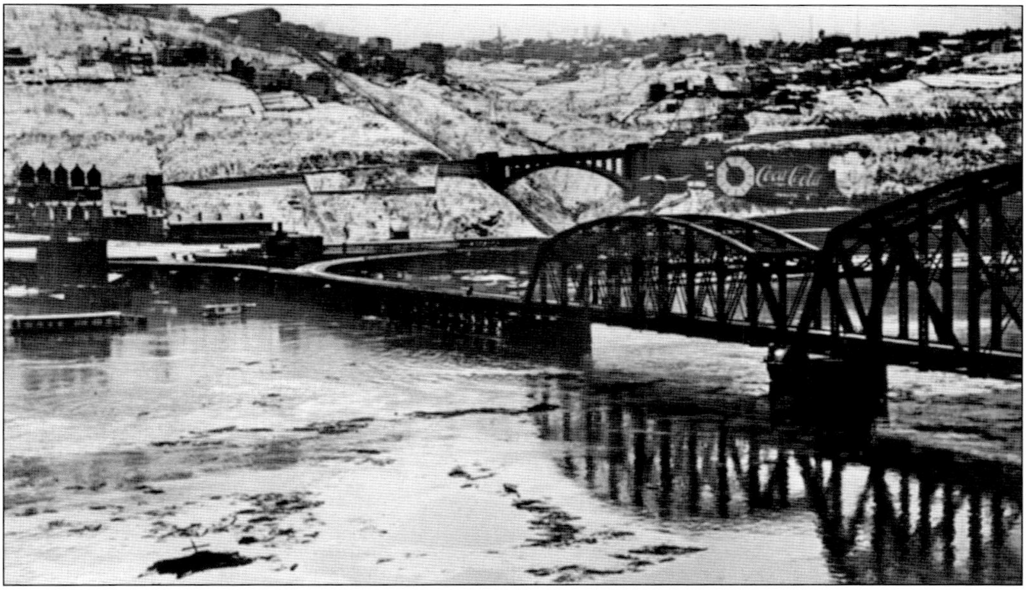

River levels fluctuated after cresting, dropping below flood stage on March 24 and then rising again before finally receding March 30. This view of the Panhandle Bridge, which carried the tracks of the old Pennsylvania Railroad's Panhandle Division over the Monongahela River, gives a good view of the flood-swollen river below. Note the ice floating in the river and the snow-covered hills in the background.

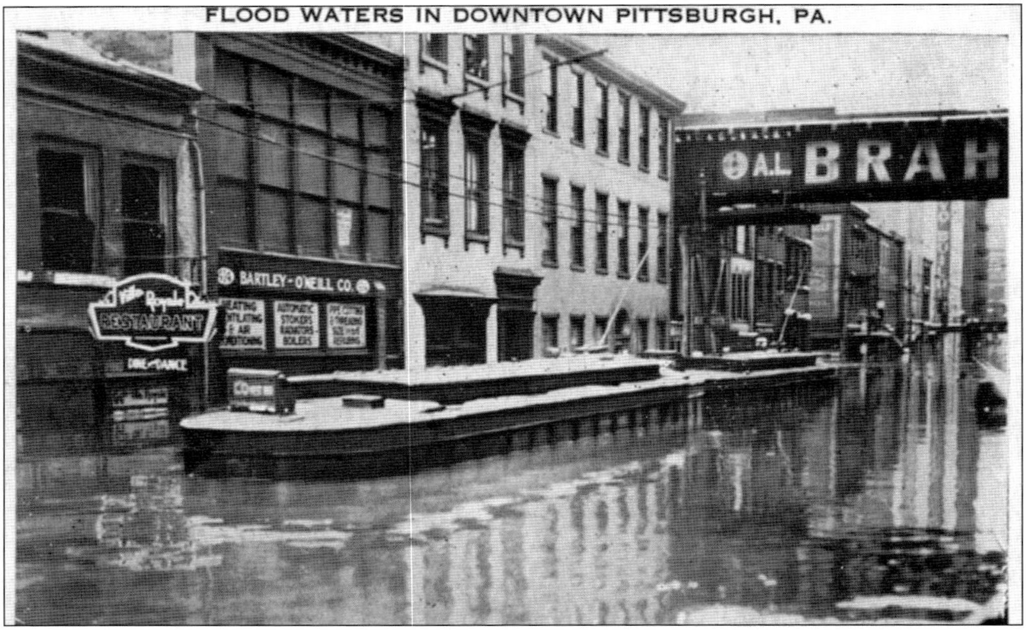

They look a bit like barges floating on this water-covered downtown Pittsburgh thoroughfare at the height of the 1936 flood. In fact, they are the roofs of trolley cars all but submerged by the floodwater. It would be several days before the system could resume even limited service. A sign on the restaurant at the left of the photograph invites patrons to "Dine and Dance." However, there won't be any dining or dancing for some time.

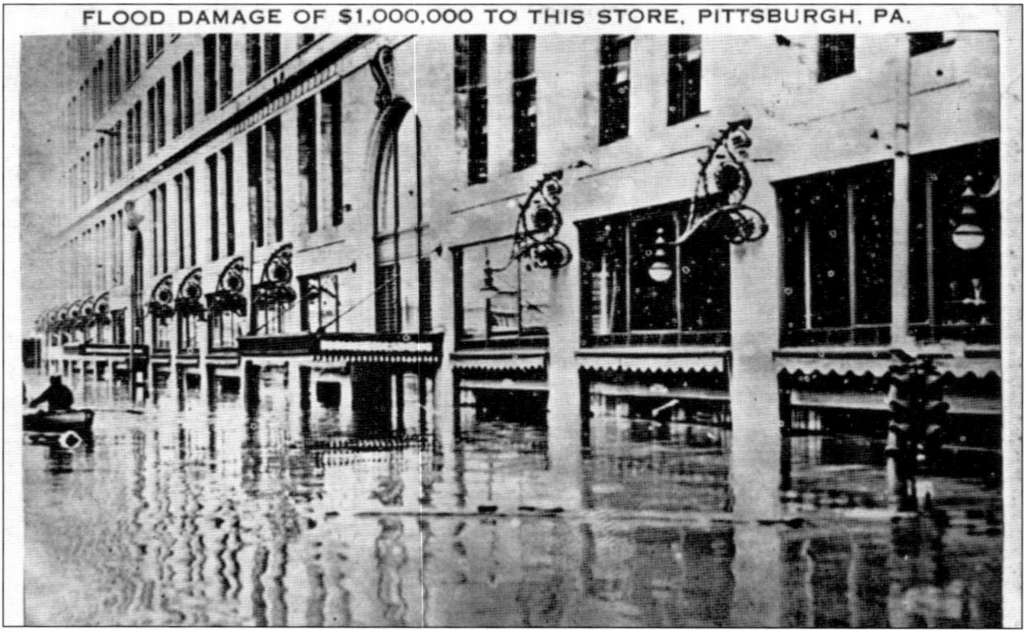

The Joseph Horne Company at Penn Avenue and Stanwick Street, for many years one of downtown Pittsburgh's largest and finest stores, is said to have suffered more than $1 million in damages when it was inundated in the city's 1936 flood. When the water went down, truck after truck of waterlogged merchandise had to be hauled away. Later a bronze marker showing how high the floodwater reached was applied to the side of the store building.

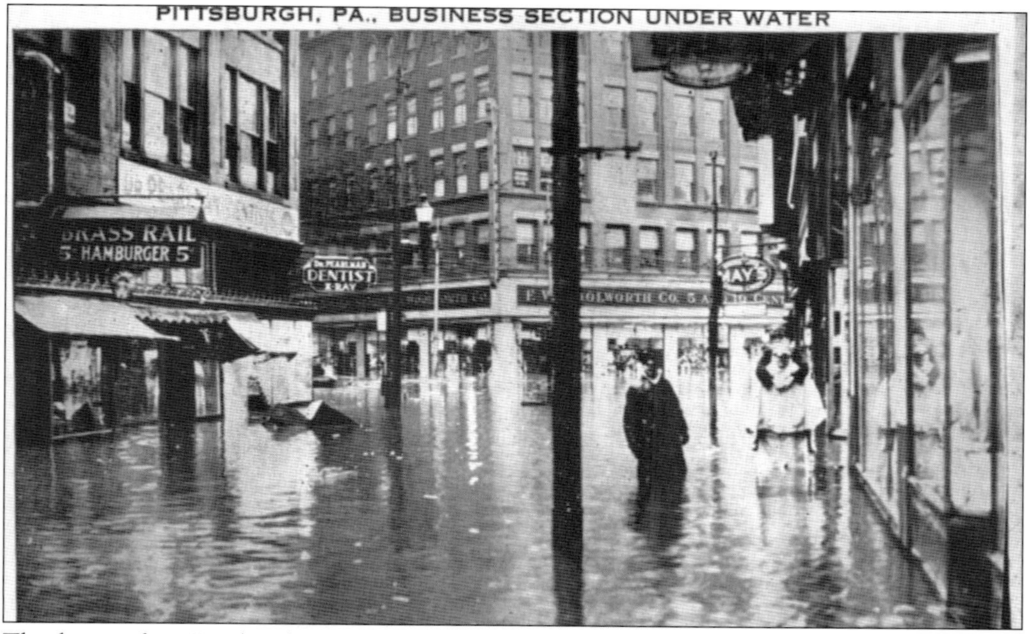

The damage from Pittsburgh's 1936 flood was little short of incredible—an estimated $250 million. That would be more than $3.5 billion in today's dollars. The flood claimed more than 60 lives, and another 500 people were injured. Thousands of buildings were destroyed or damaged. Officials said the food supply was adequate but warned that anything touched by floodwaters should be discarded. It would be weeks before the city returned to normal.

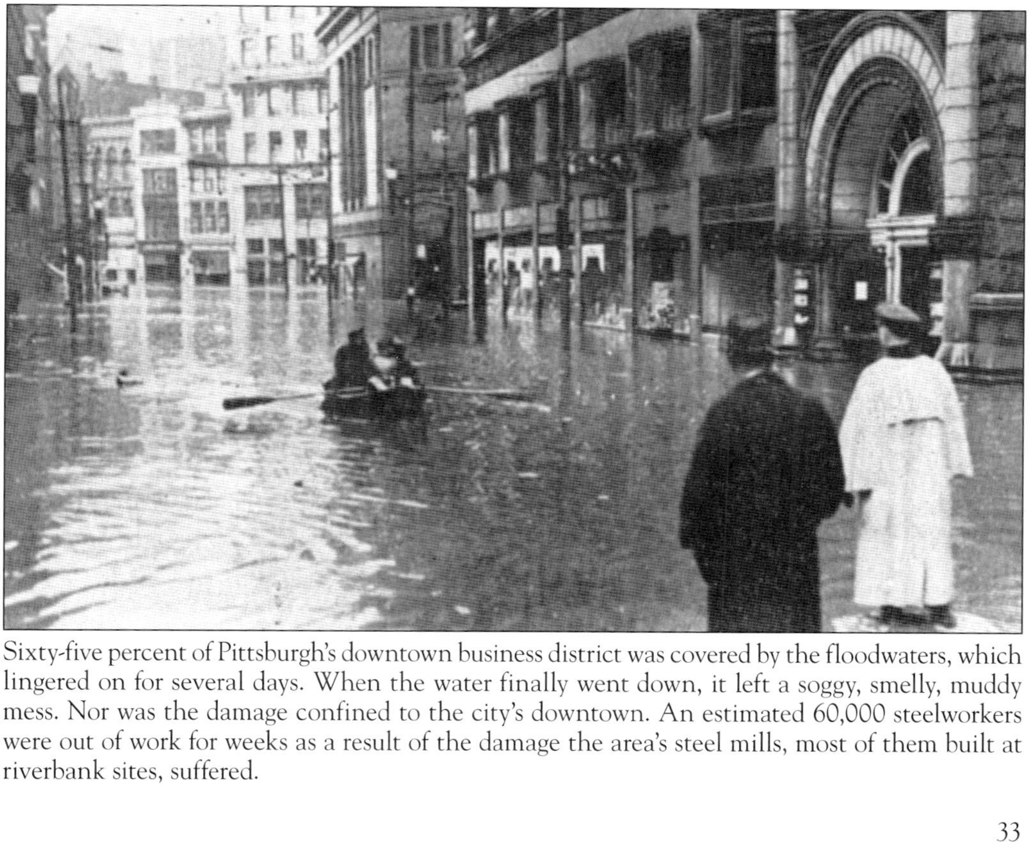

Sixty-five percent of Pittsburgh's downtown business district was covered by the floodwaters, which lingered on for several days. When the water finally went down, it left a soggy, smelly, muddy mess. Nor was the damage confined to the city's downtown. An estimated 60,000 steelworkers were out of work for weeks as a result of the damage the area's steel mills, most of them built at riverbank sites, suffered.

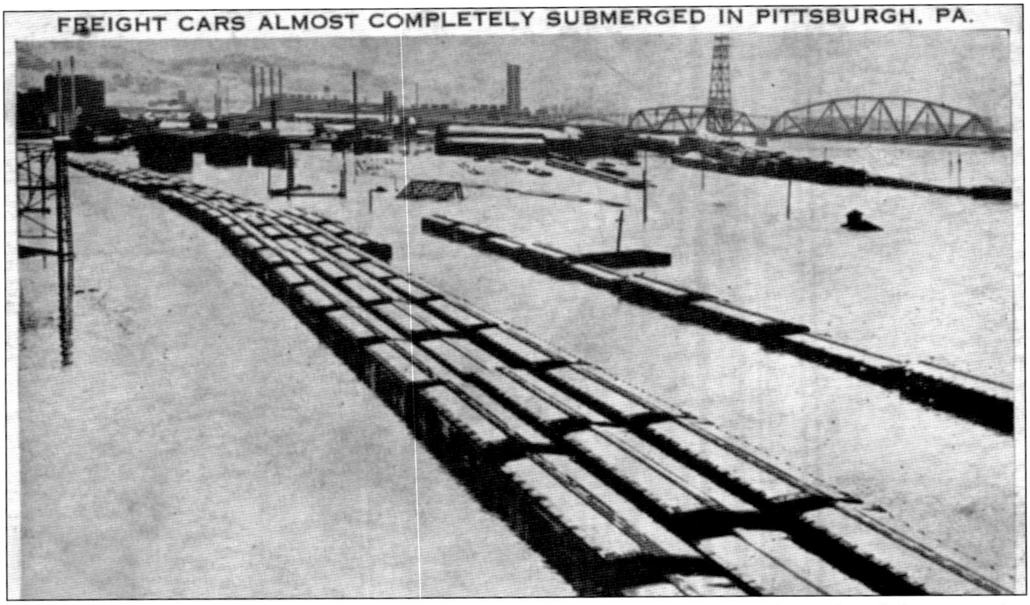

At the height of the 1936 flood, there was no train service into or out of Pittsburgh because the railroad tracks that ran along the city's three rivers—the Allegheny, Monongahela, and Ohio—were blocked or washed away by the floodwaters. This freight-yard photograph shows long strings of railroad boxcars almost completely submerged by the floodwaters. Railroad crews would be busy for weeks repairing the damage from the record-setting flood.

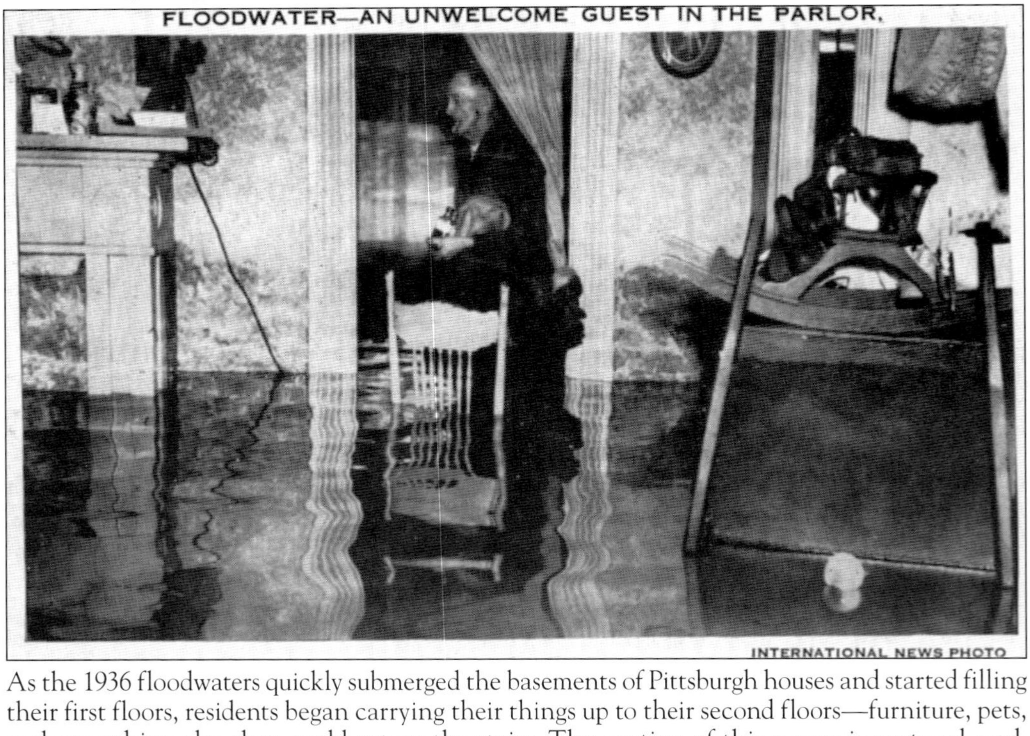

As the 1936 floodwaters quickly submerged the basements of Pittsburgh houses and started filling their first floors, residents began carrying their things up to their second floors—furniture, pets, and everything else they could get up the stairs. The caption of this souvenir postcard read, "Floodwater—An Unwelcome Guest in the Parlor." With no electricity, candles furnished the only light in thousands of homes.

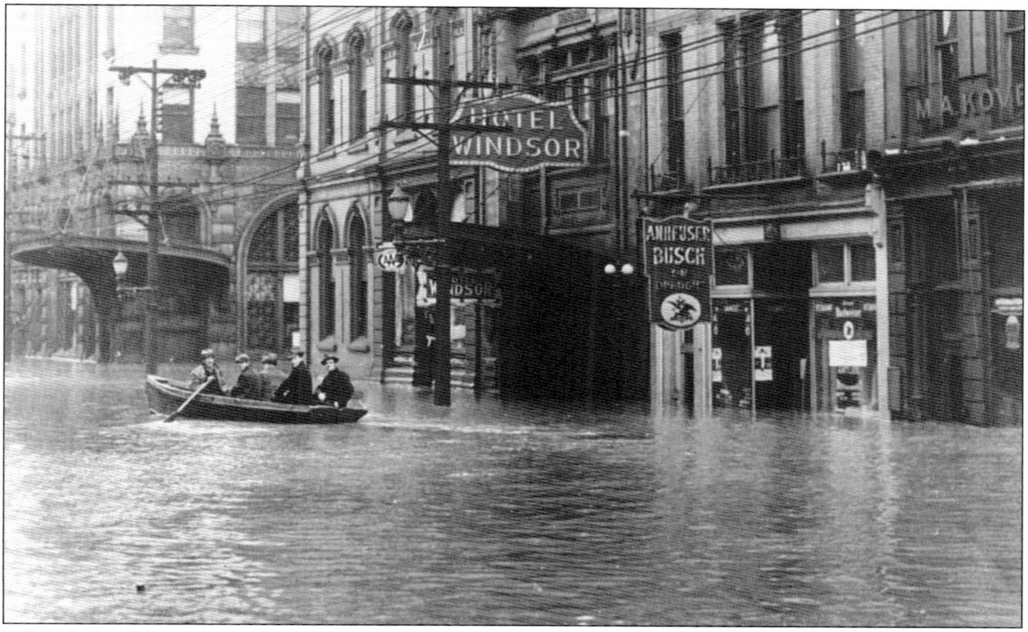

Wheeling, West Virginia, is especially vulnerable to flooding because it is built on an island and a narrow strip of land along a few miles of the riverbank. The flood of March 1936 covered Wheeling Island and much of the downtown, putting three feet of muddy water in these buildings on Main Street, including the Windsor Hotel and the National Bank of West Virginia (the ornate building at left rear with the distinctive semicircular marquee).

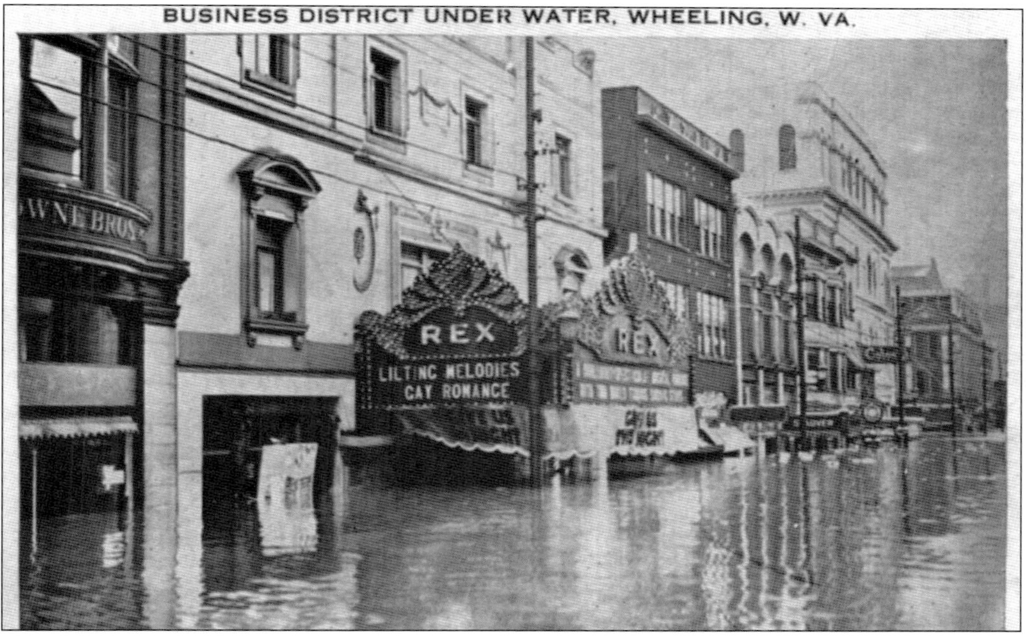

In this 1936 International News Service photograph, the rising water can be seen nearly reaching the ornate marquee of the Rex Theater on Wheeling's Market Street. The flood forced 20,000 Wheeling area residents from their homes, cut off utilities, and took at least 17 lives. Some of the victims perished when they were trapped in their homes. Others drowned in accidents involving the makeshift armada of rescue boats.

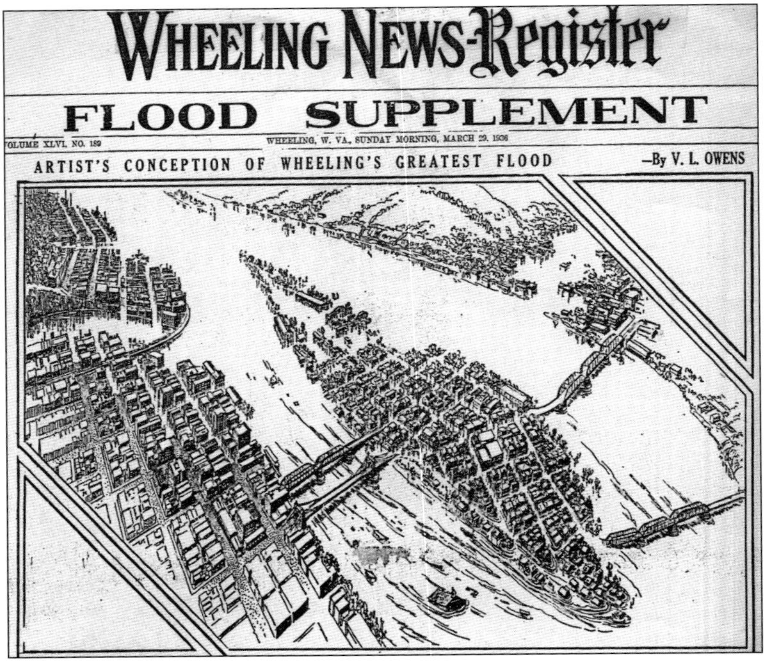

On March 29, 1936, when the *Wheeling News Register* published a special supplement commemorating the flood, it offered an artist's sketch of what it called "Wheeling's Greatest Flood." That description is still accurate. Like Pittsburgh, Wheeling would find the flood of 1936 far more damaging than that of 1937. In 1936, the Ohio crested at 55.5 feet, nearly 10 feet higher than the 46.2 feet that would be recorded in 1937.

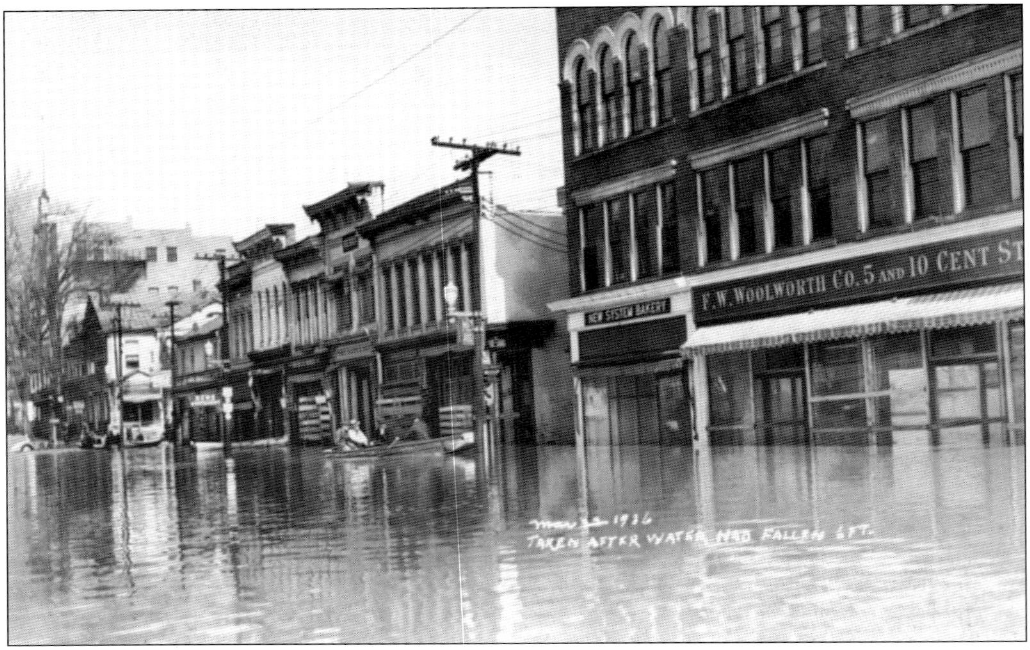

As the March 1936 flood moved down the Ohio River from Pittsburgh, Pennsylvania, and Wheeling, West Virginia, businesses and homeowners in the cities downriver began preparing for the worst. On March 20, the water in the streets of Marietta, Ohio, reached a 48-foot crest. A handwritten note on this postcard indicates the photograph was taken March 22 after the water had fallen by six feet. Flooded Putnam Street businesses seen here include the New System Bakery and the F. W. Woolworth Company.

Opened in 1926, Huntington's Sixth Street Bridge was the city's first—and for many years only—bridge across the Ohio River. It was closed in 1993 and later demolished, replaced by the new Robert C. Byrd Bridge. Here the old bridge provides the backdrop for a 1936 flood photograph of the Chesapeake and Ohio Railway Freight Station. Look closely at the photograph's center section to see a man wading through the water. (Courtesy the C&O Historical Society.)

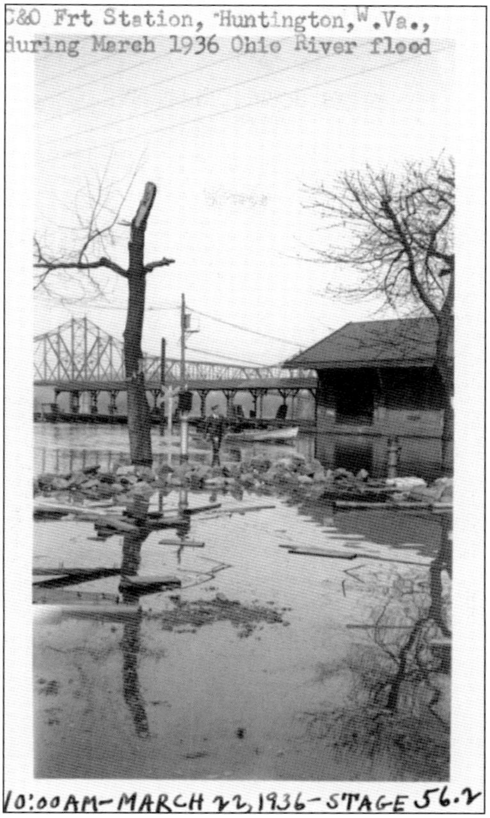

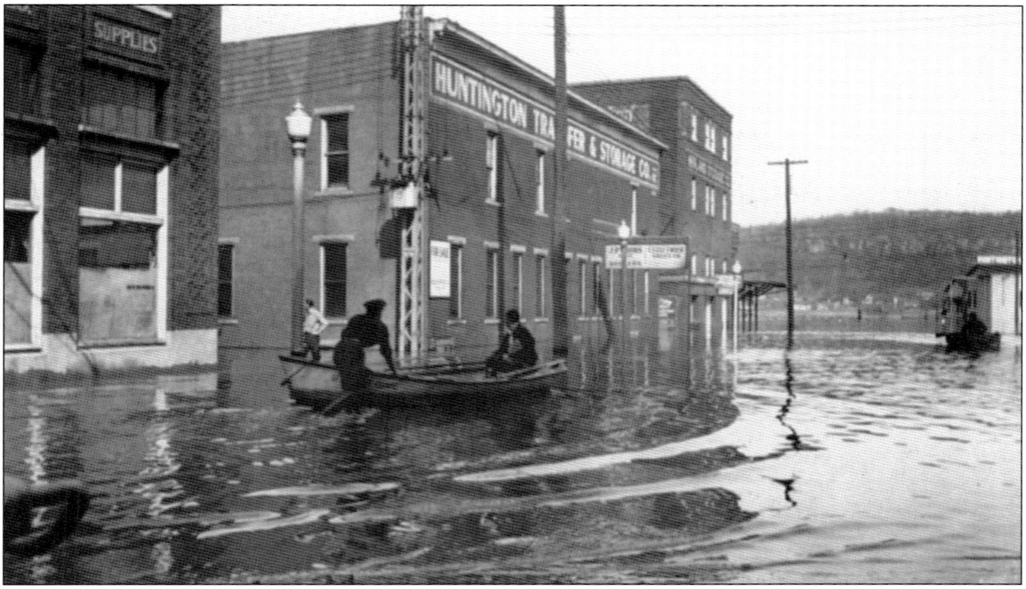

Two boats—one at left center, the other at right rear—make their way through the flooded Huntington, West Virginia, warehouse district at the edge of the Ohio River on March 22, 1936. A sign on one of the buildings identifies it as the home of the Huntington Transfer and Storage Company. Most of the buildings in the city's warehouse district were leveled as a result of downtown urban renewal in the 1960s. (Courtesy the C&O Historical Society.)

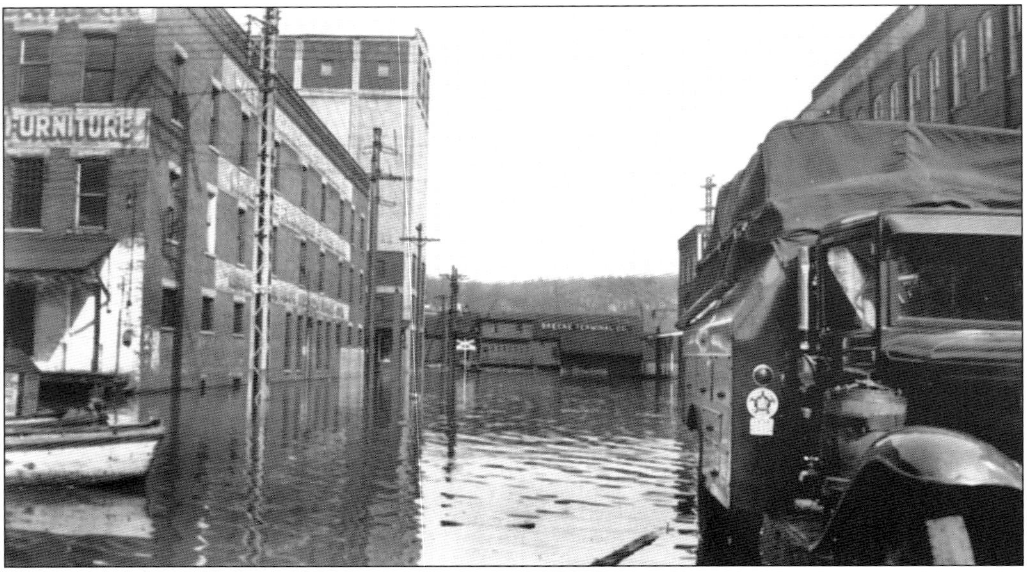

Here is another 1936 photograph of Huntington's flooded warehouse district. Just visible in the distance are the hills of Ohio on the other side of the flooded river. Below them, a sign identifies the Greene Terminal Company. There is a furniture warehouse at the left, with the bow of a small boat just visible at the photograph's edge. The truck at right is parked just at the edge of the floodwaters. (Courtesy the C&O Historical Society.).

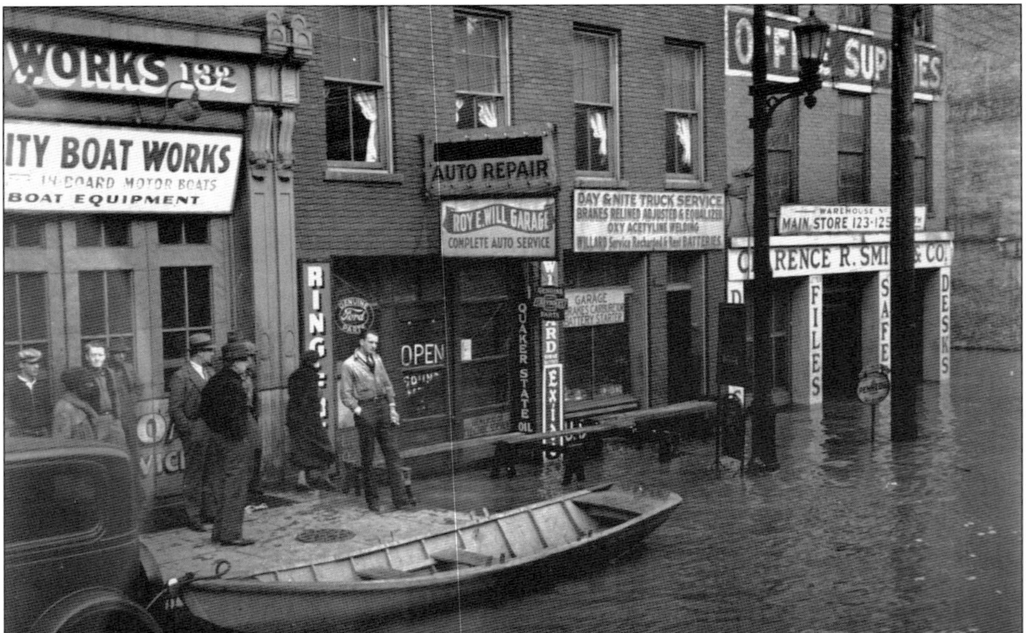

Photographers working for the Farm Security Administration (FSA), a federal New Deal program initiated by U.S. president Franklin Roosevelt, documented much of the nation's Depression-era misery. Many of the FSA photographers went on to iconic careers in photography. Among them was Carl Mydans, who took this striking flood photograph in Louisville, Kentucky, in March 1936. Later that year, Mydans would leave the FSA to join the staff of the fledgling *Life* magazine. (Courtesy the Library of Congress.)

Three

PENNSYLVANIA 1937

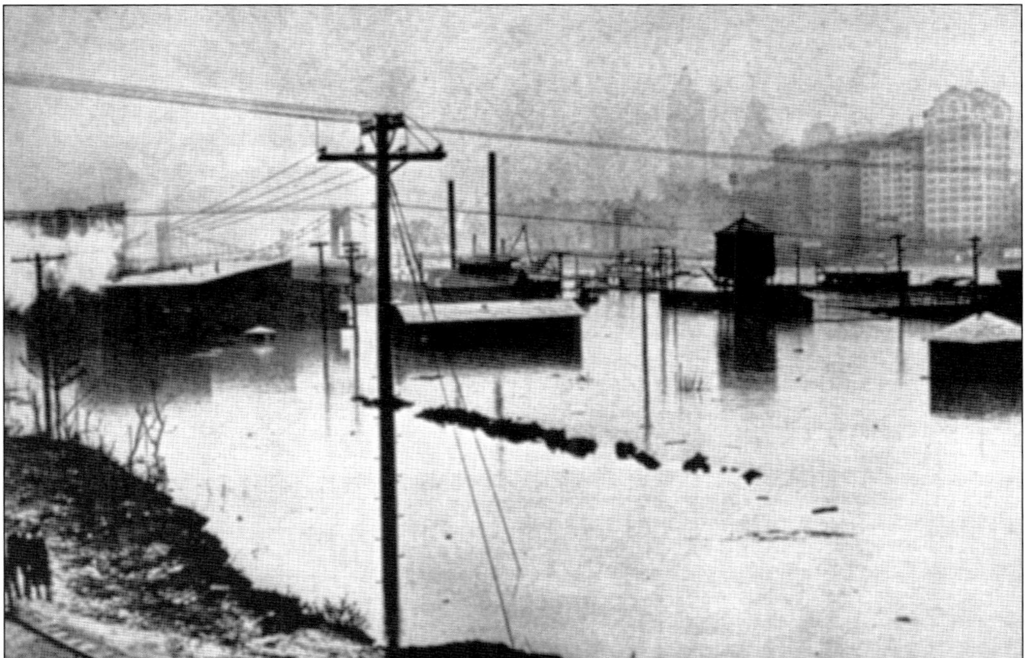

With the St. Patrick's Day Flood of March 1936 still fresh in the public's memory, Pittsburgh again faced the threat of flood in January 1937 when the Allegheny and Monongahela Rivers began rising. Flood stage at the famous point where the two rivers join to form the Ohio River is 24 feet. Quickly the water reached 25 feet and was still rising. Pittsburgh residents feared the worst and began preparing for another watery onslaught.

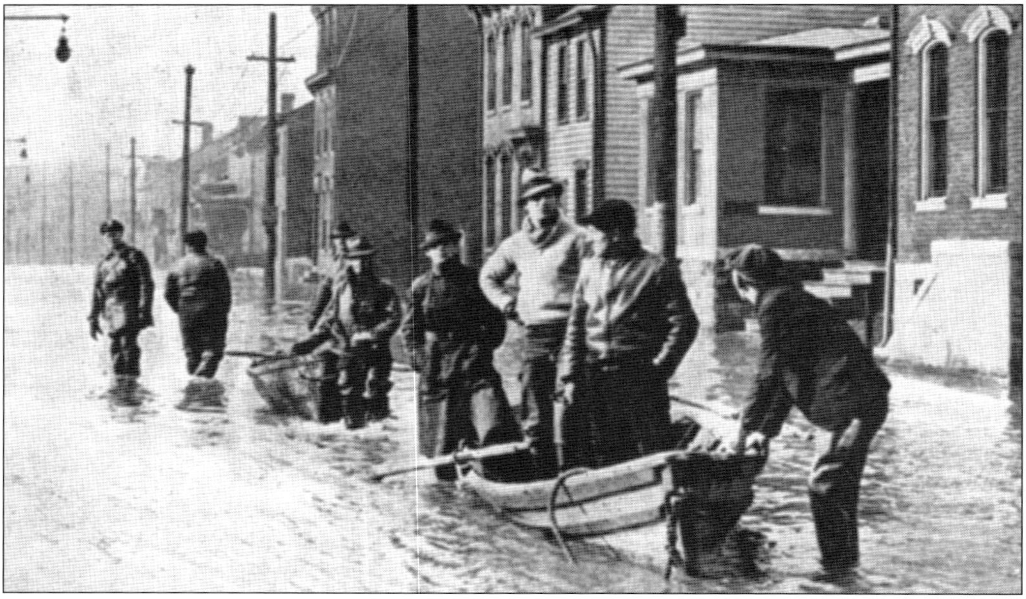

Sharpsburg is a borough in Allegheny County, Pennsylvania, about five miles northeast of Pittsburgh on the Allegheny River. In this January 1937 view of Sharpsburg's Main Street, the water is little more than ankle deep. Nevertheless, the men have their rowboats ready and are preparing for flood duty. The police officer standing at the far left seems ready to direct traffic, although the only traffic moving this day will be by boat.

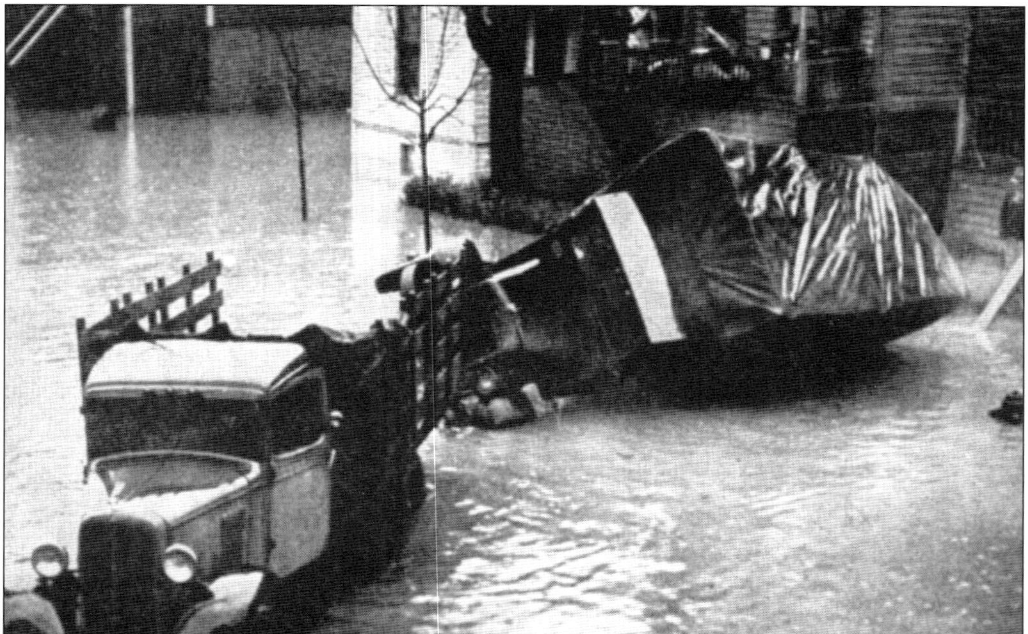

Although it was little consolation for those who saw their homes and businesses flooded, the 1937 flood in Pittsburgh was no match for that of 1936. The crest in 1937 was 35 feet. That was 11 feet over flood stage but another 11 feet short of the 46.4 feet recorded on March 18, 1936, which remains the city's worst flood ever. Here the 1937 floodwaters have capsized a truck at Etna, another borough just outside Pittsburgh.

Four

West Virginia 1937

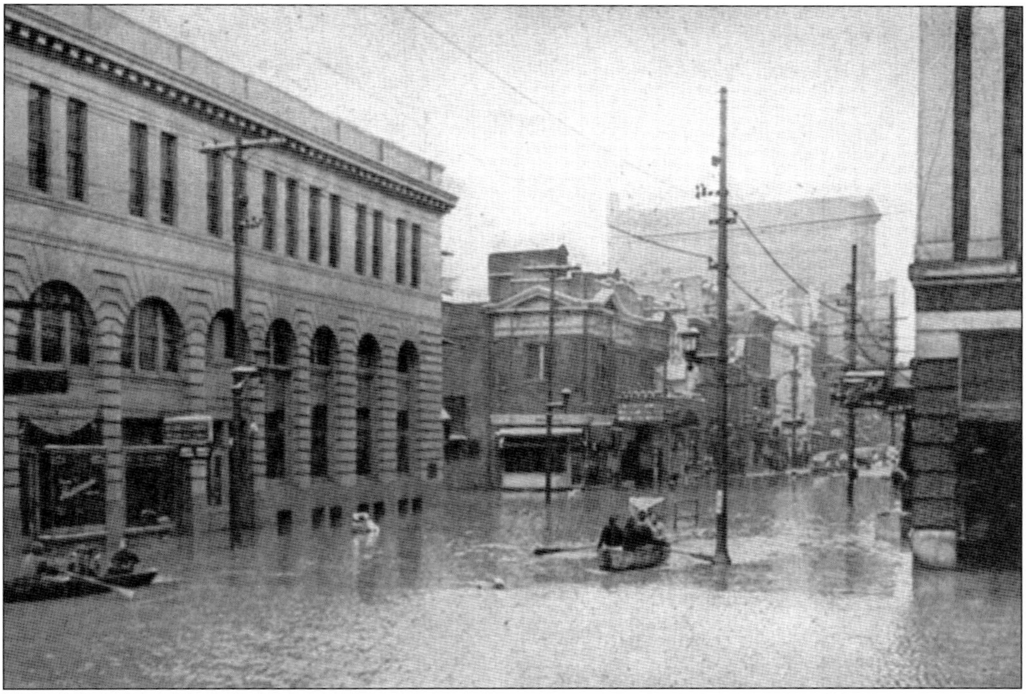

It is Wheeling, West Virginia, not Venice, and that is a rowboat, not a gondola. As was the case in Pittsburgh, residents of Wheeling would find the flood of January 1937 no match for the record-setter of March 1936. That is not to say it was not damaging. Rising two inches an hour toward a crest of nearly 47 feet, the floodwaters soon covered much of the city. Once again, Wheeling Island was submerged, and authorities ordered its 10,000 inhabitants evacuated.

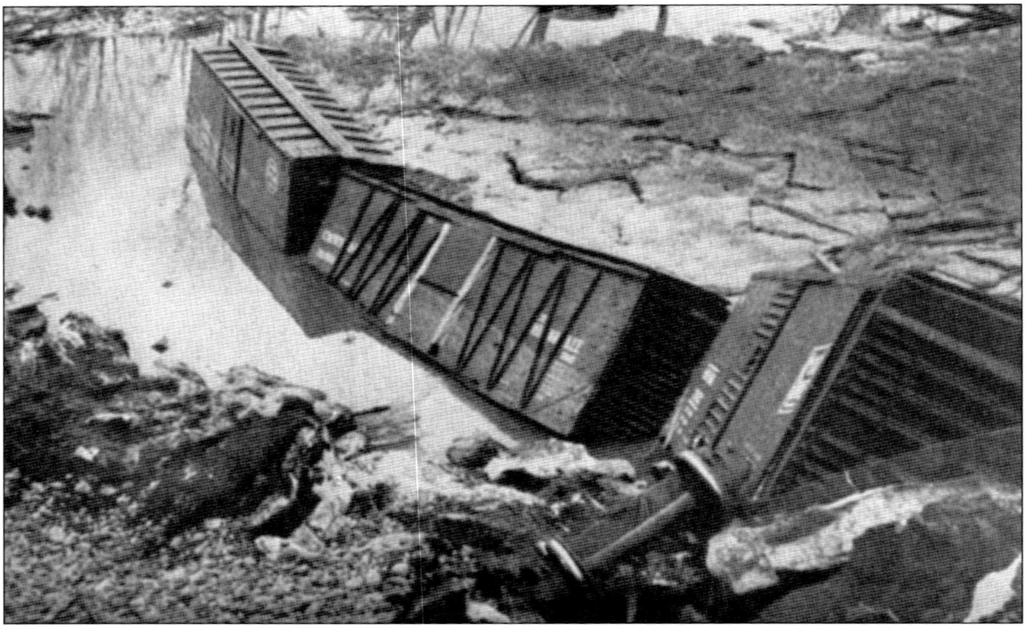

The 1937 flood devastated railroads throughout the length of the Ohio Valley. When a river-weakened stretch of track at Moundsville, West Virginia, collapsed, it sent this trio of freight cars crashing into the mud. Accidents such as this one ultimately forced the Baltimore and Ohio Railroad (B&O, now CSX) to suspend its operations along the Ohio River. Damage to the B&O and other railroads that served the valley would take weeks to repair.

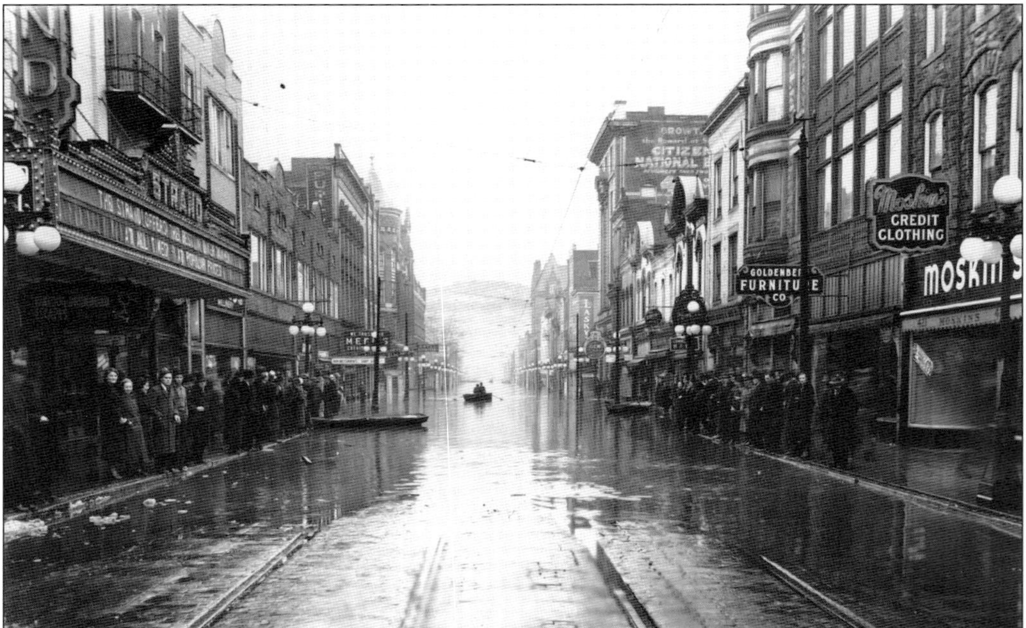

The 1937 floodwaters are still coming up in this Parkersburg, West Virginia, photograph taken on Market Street between Fourth and Fifth Streets. Curious onlookers stand on the sidewalk under the marquee of the Strand Theater and across the street in front of Moskin's Credit Clothing. In the distance can be seen two men paddling a rowboat. (Photograph by Artcraft Studio.)

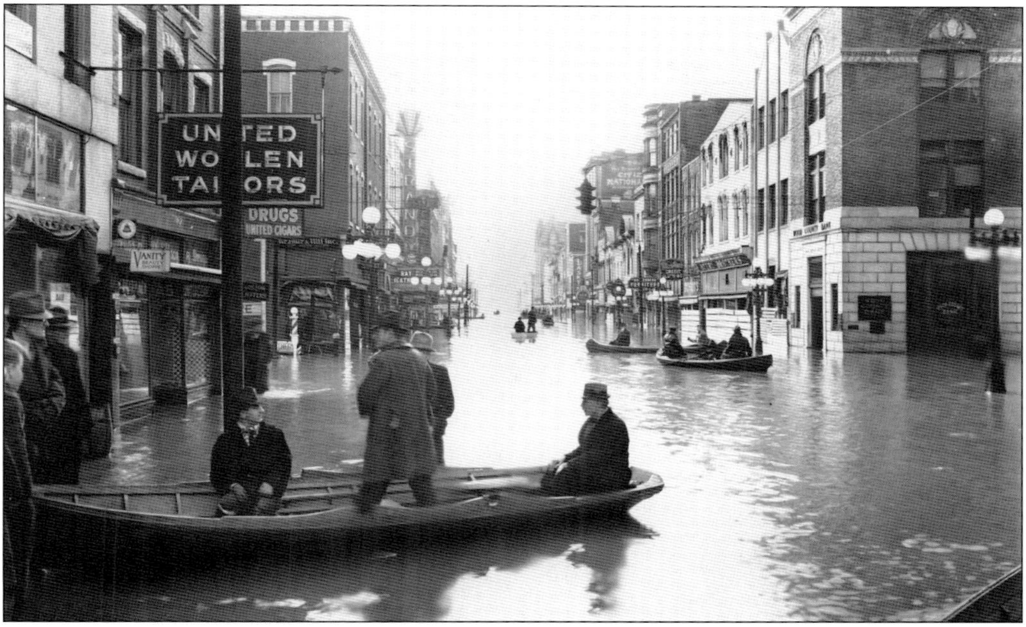

Here is another view of Parkersburg's Market Street at Fifth Street, this one looking in the opposite direction. The Strand's vertical sign can be seen at the left rear. The floodwaters have deepened, and boats now crowd the street. The 1937 flood in Parkersburg crested at 55.4 feet—19.4 feet above flood stage but 3.5 feet short of the city's record crest of 58.9 feet, set in 1913. (Photograph by Artcraft Studio.)

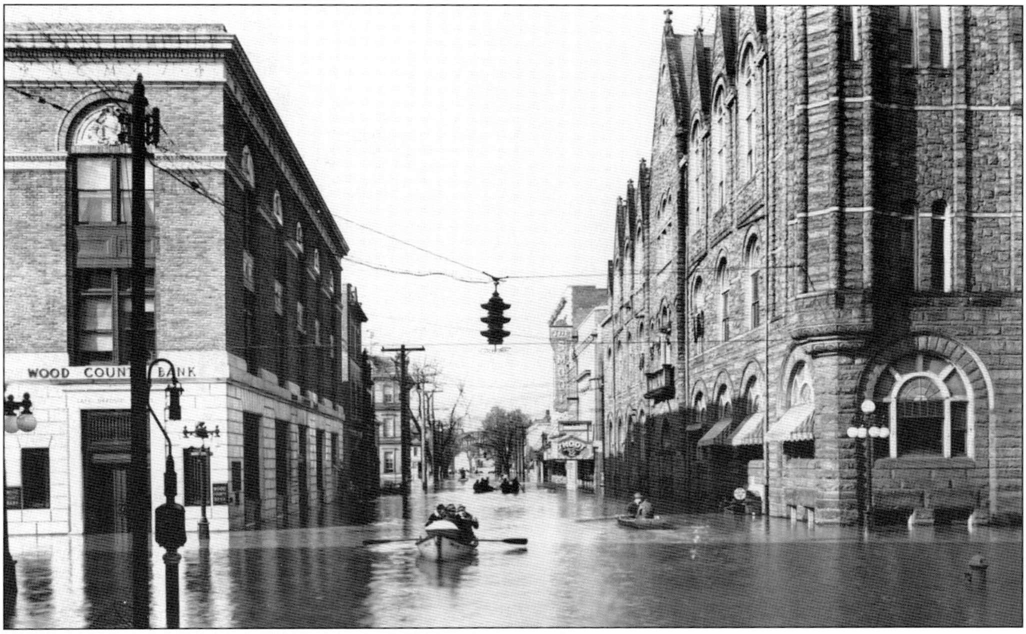

The Wood County Bank and Parkersburg City Hall are shown when the flood was at its crest. A useless traffic light hangs over the intersection. Although city hall was entirely surrounded by the floodwater, the police department maintained its headquarters there, operating from makeshift offices on the second floor. The only access to the building was by boat. (Photograph by Artcraft Studio.)

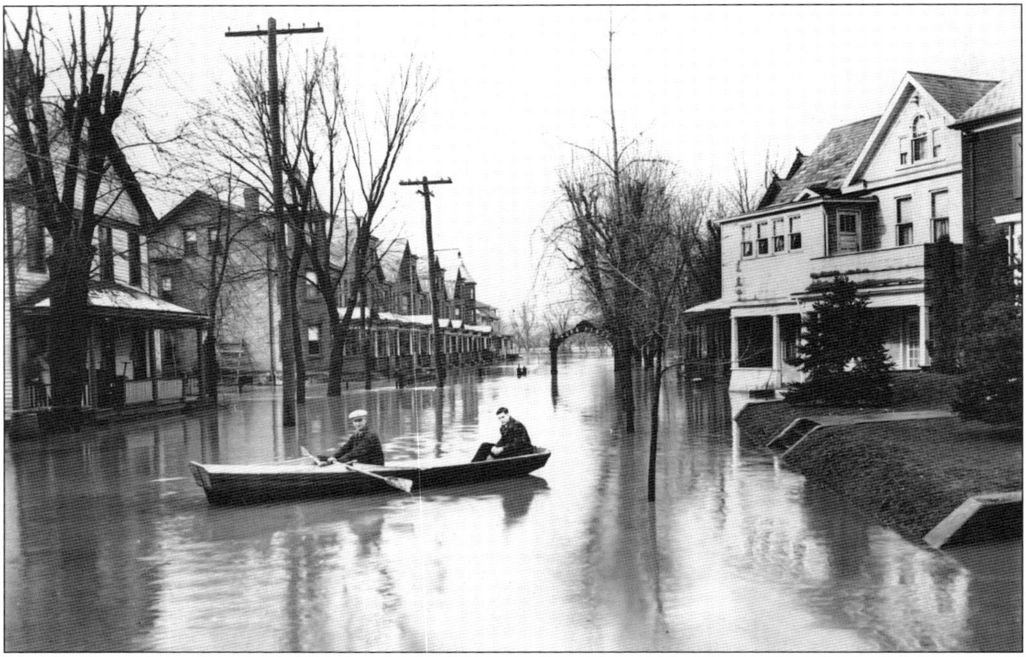

Two boaters pose for the camera near the arched metal sign marking the flooded entrance to Park Place, a tree-lined residential section located just off Parkersburg's Garfield Avenue near Eighth Street. The last buildings in Park Place were demolished in the 1970s to make room for an expanding Camden-Clark Hospital. (Photograph by Artcraft Studio.)

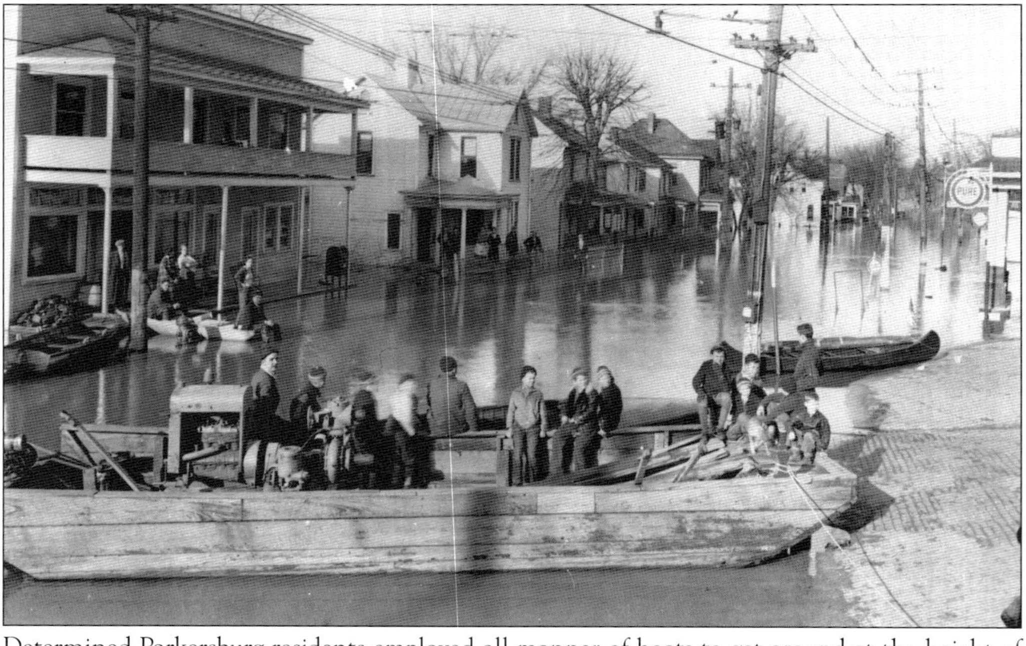

Determined Parkersburg residents employed all manner of boats to get around at the height of the flood. In this photograph, taken at Murdoch Avenue and Nineteenth Street, can be seen rowboats, canoes, and, in the foreground, an improvised barge with a number of men and boys aboard. At least some of the youngsters no doubt viewed the flood as a welcome treat, as it meant the schools were closed. (Photograph by Artcraft Studio.)

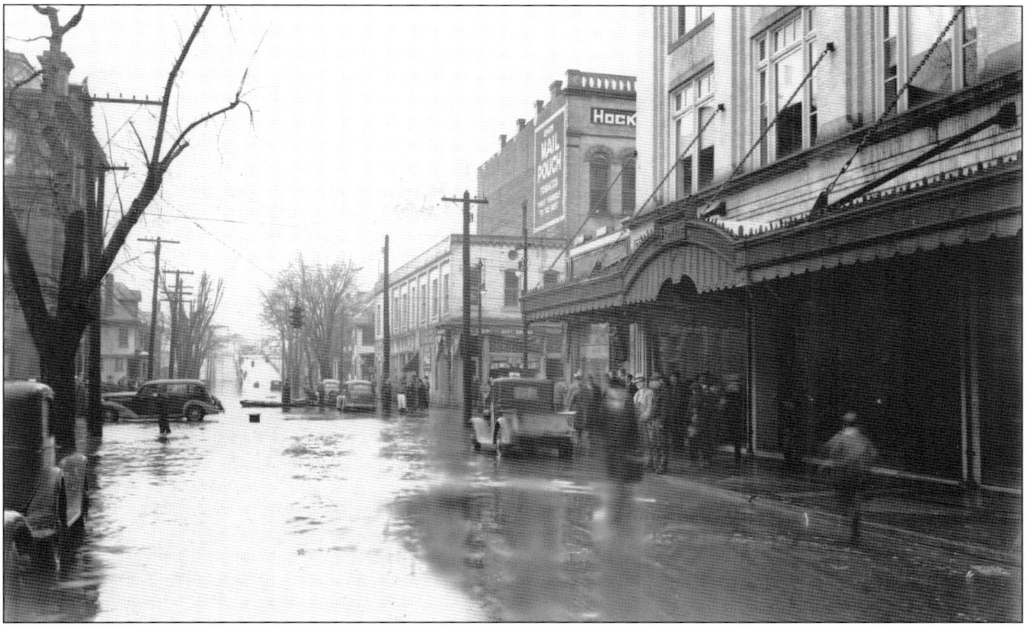

It is not clear whether the water is coming up or going down in this 1937 Parkersburg flood photograph, as it is not dated. The scene is Fifth and Julian Streets looking toward the old Belpre Bridge. Parkersburg residents took the flooding in stride. Water and telephone service were maintained, though limited. Refugees were evacuated and housed in various buildings on high ground. (Photograph by Artcraft Studio.)

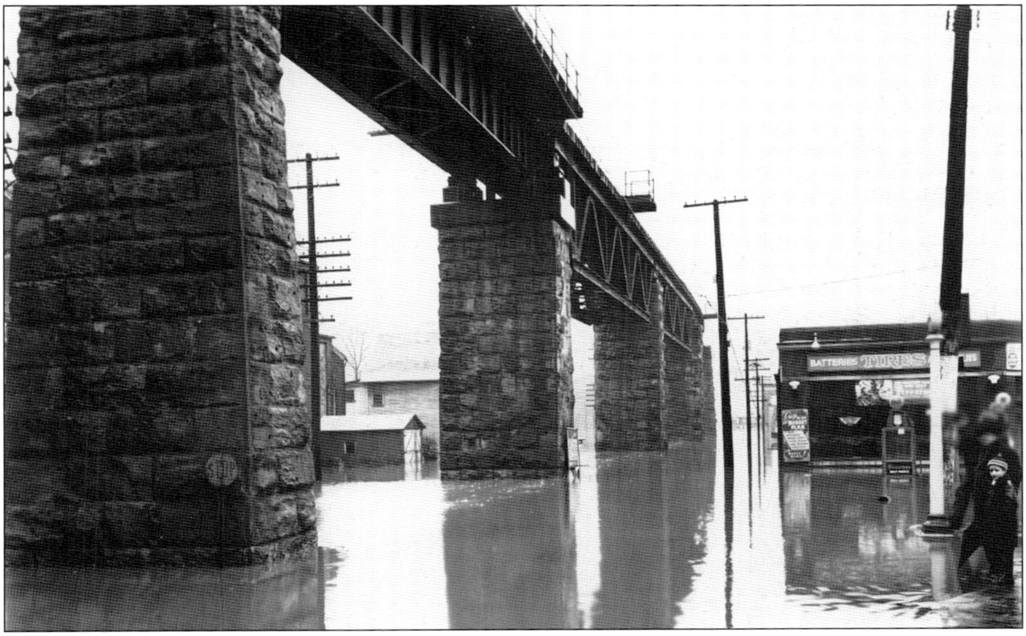

The elevated tracks of the Baltimore and Ohio Railroad bisect Parkersburg at Sixth Street, then cross the river to Ohio. Self-taught professional photographer Vincent "Jimmy" Borelli took this flood shot of the massive stone track piers at Sixth and Ann Streets. At right is his young son Paul, who grew up to follow in his father's footsteps as a photographer. His Artcraft Studio supplied the Parkersburg flood photographs used in this book.

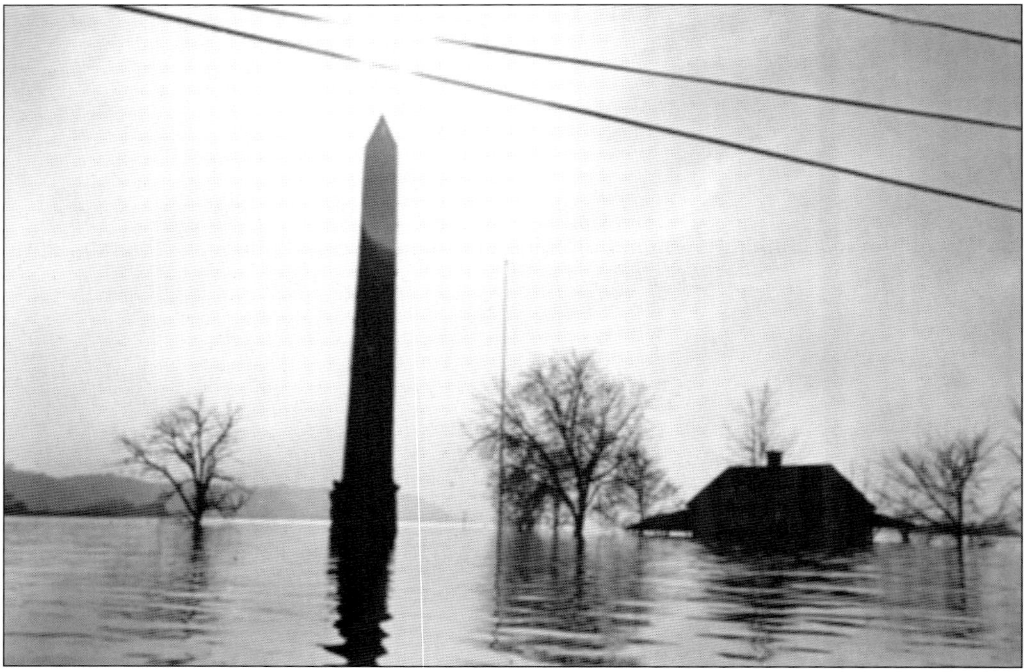

Point Pleasant, West Virginia, built on an arrowhead of land where the Kanawha River meets the Ohio River, was the scene of a historic battle between the Virginia militia and Shawnee warriors. The 1774 battle broke the power of the Native Americans in the Ohio Valley. A tall monument and a log house stand on the battle site where the two rivers meet. The 1937 floodwaters inundated the monument's base and the house. (Courtesy Point Pleasant River Museum.)

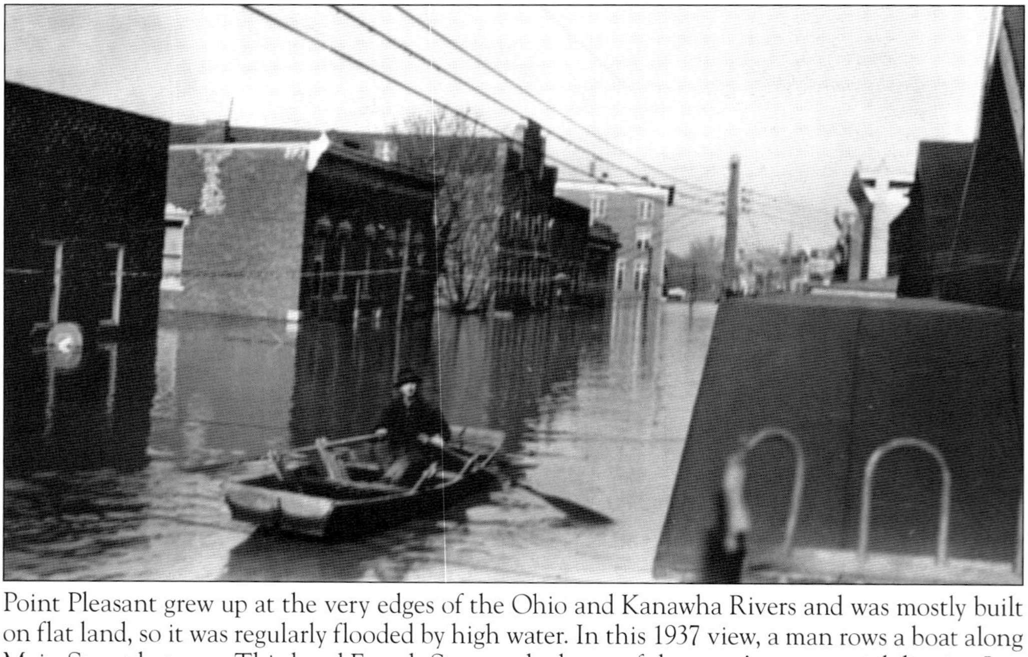

Point Pleasant grew up at the very edges of the Ohio and Kanawha Rivers and was mostly built on flat land, so it was regularly flooded by high water. In this 1937 view, a man rows a boat along Main Street between Third and Fourth Streets, the heart of the town's commercial district. Just visible in the far background can be seen the Lowe Hotel, a showplace when it opened in 1903. (Courtesy Point Pleasant River Museum.)

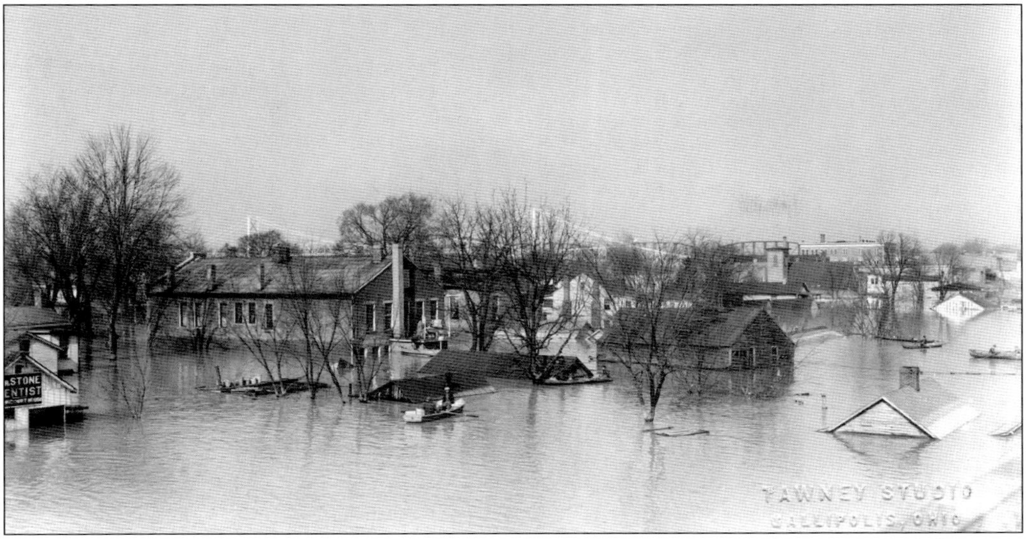

Today the Point Pleasant River Museum is housed in the brick store building seen at left center in this 1937 flood view, taken from the Shadle Bridge crossing the Kanawha River. Seen here is the rear of the store building, marked by a tall chimney. Just visible in the background are the twin spires of the Silver Bridge, which linked the town with Ohio until it fell in 1967, a tragedy that claimed 46 lives. (Courtesy Point Pleasant River Museum.)

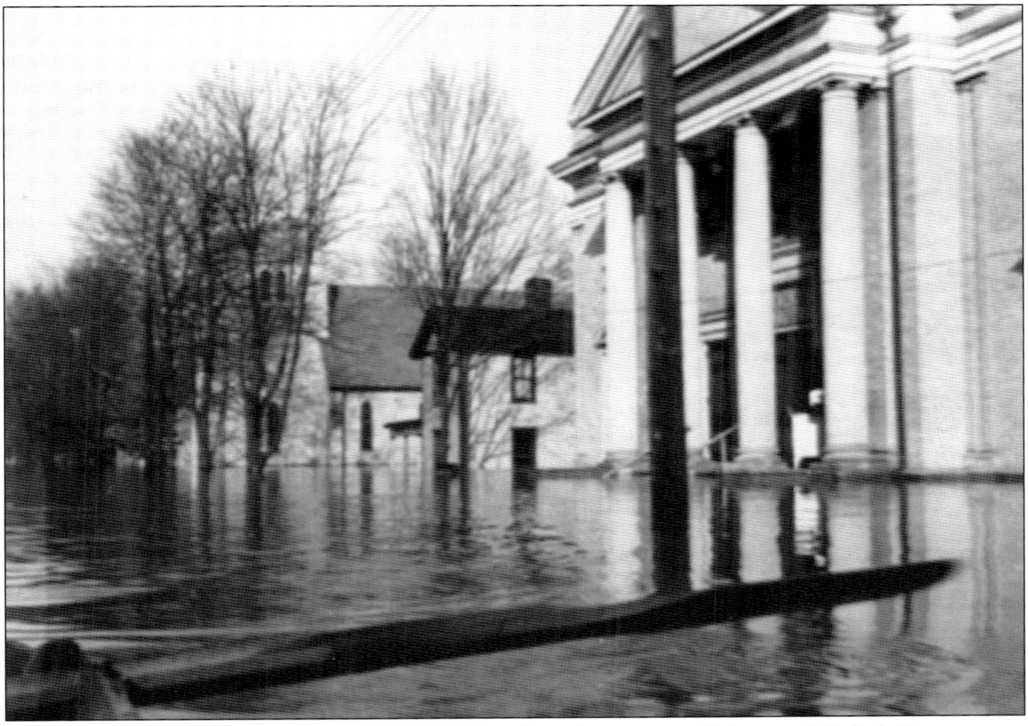

The Point Pleasant Presbyterian Church, located on the corner of Main and Eighth Streets, was one of several Point Pleasant churches visited by the 1937 floodwaters. But the members of the various congregations were undiscouraged. Once the water receded, they quickly cleared away the mud and resumed services. Many of the town's businesses, too, were closed for only a brief while. (Courtesy Point Pleasant River Museum.)

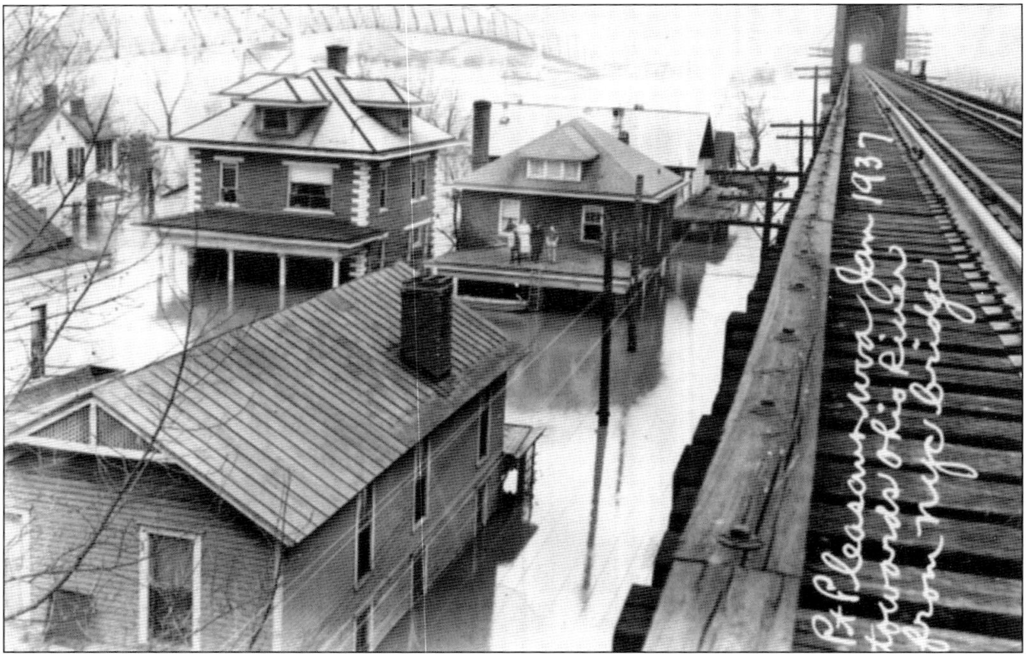

A photographer who climbed up onto the elevated tracks leading to the New York Central Railroad bridge across the Ohio River took this striking view of Point Pleasant's flooded Main Street between Sixth and Seventh Streets. Note the people standing on the roof of their front porch. At their feet is a ladder that extends down from the roof to a waiting boat tied below. (Courtesy Point Pleasant River Museum.)

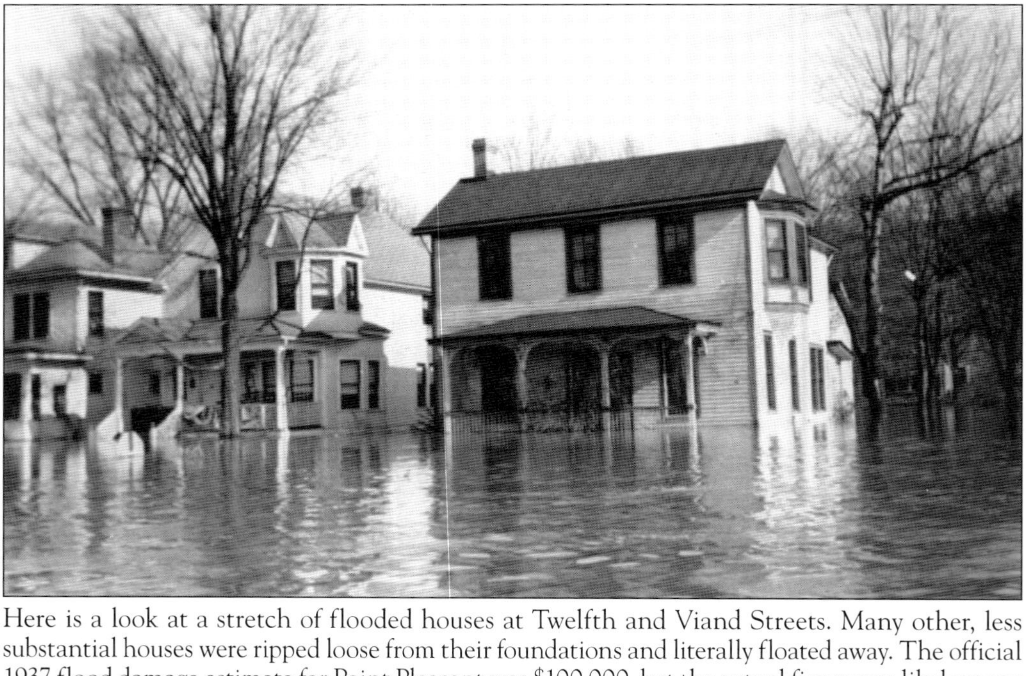

Here is a look at a stretch of flooded houses at Twelfth and Viand Streets. Many other, less substantial houses were ripped loose from their foundations and literally floated away. The official 1937 flood damage estimate for Point Pleasant was $100,000, but the actual figure was likely many times that. Some businesses were able to get federal loans for flood repairs, but homeowners were left to fend for themselves. (Courtesy Point Pleasant River Museum.)

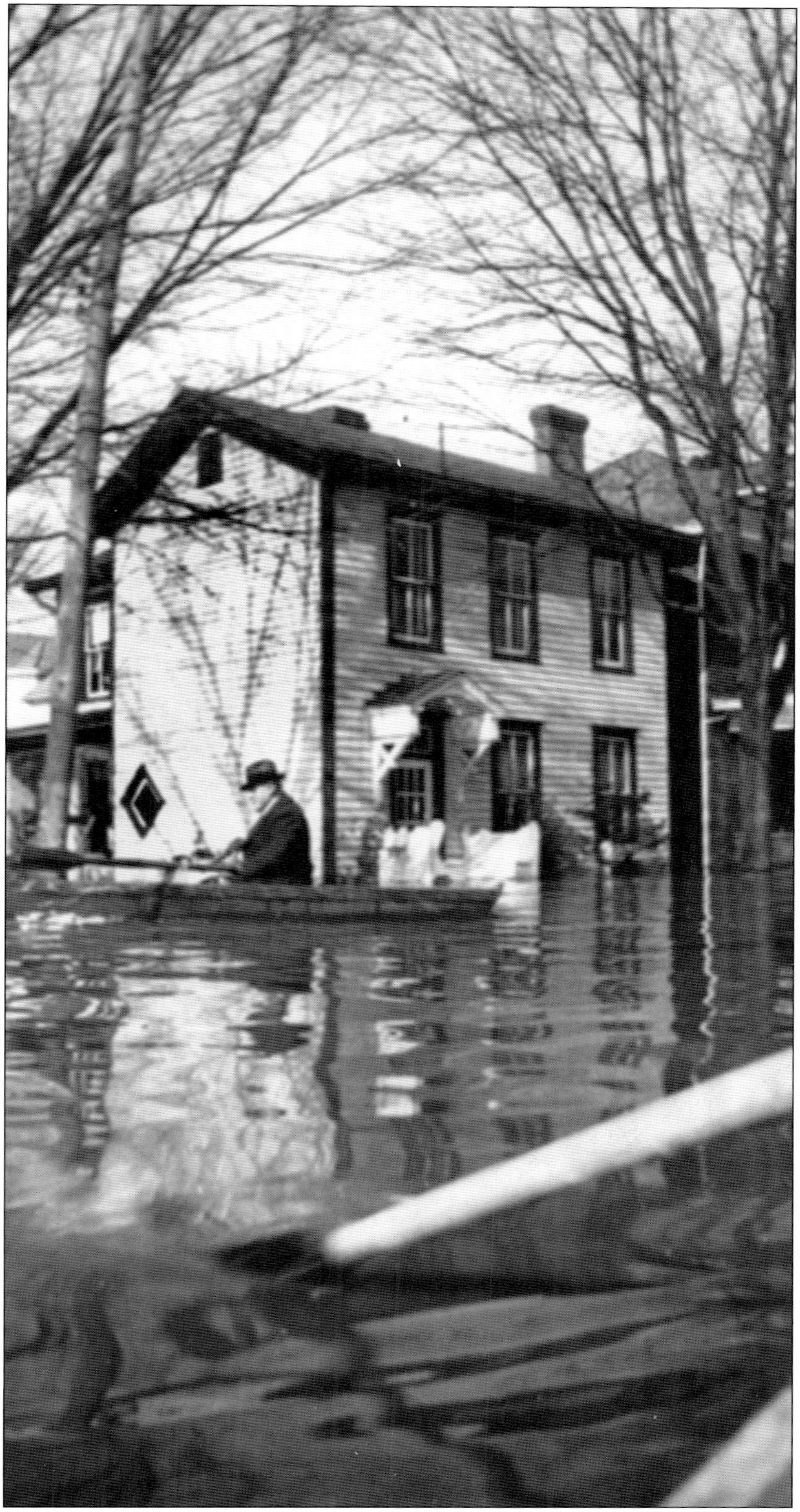

A man rows through the 1937 floodwaters at Twelfth and Viand Streets in a scene that was all too familiar for Point Pleasant residents. The 1937 flood, the town's worst ever, prompted calls for construction of a floodwall. But it was not until after World War II and more damaging floods in 1943 and 1945 that the federal government complied. The completed wall was turned over to the city in 1951. (Courtesy Point Pleasant River Museum.)

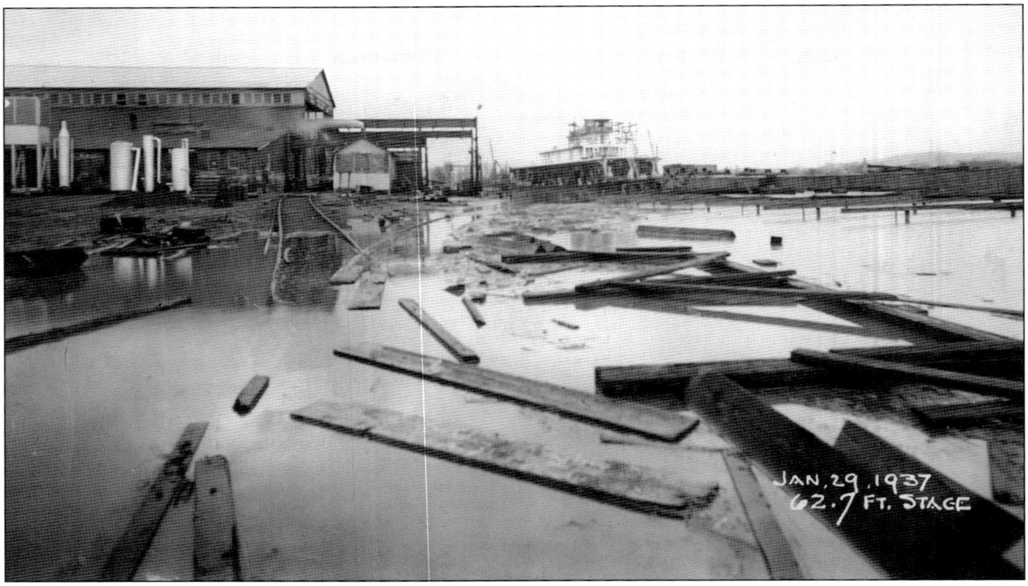

At 62.7 feet, the 1937 flood was so high that it submerged many Point Pleasant sections high enough to escape previous floods. Included was the Marietta Manufacturing Company. During World War II, the boatbuilder employed a small army of workers producing hundreds of boats for the military. But after the war, the company struggled and finally went out of business in 1970. (Courtesy Point Pleasant River Museum.)

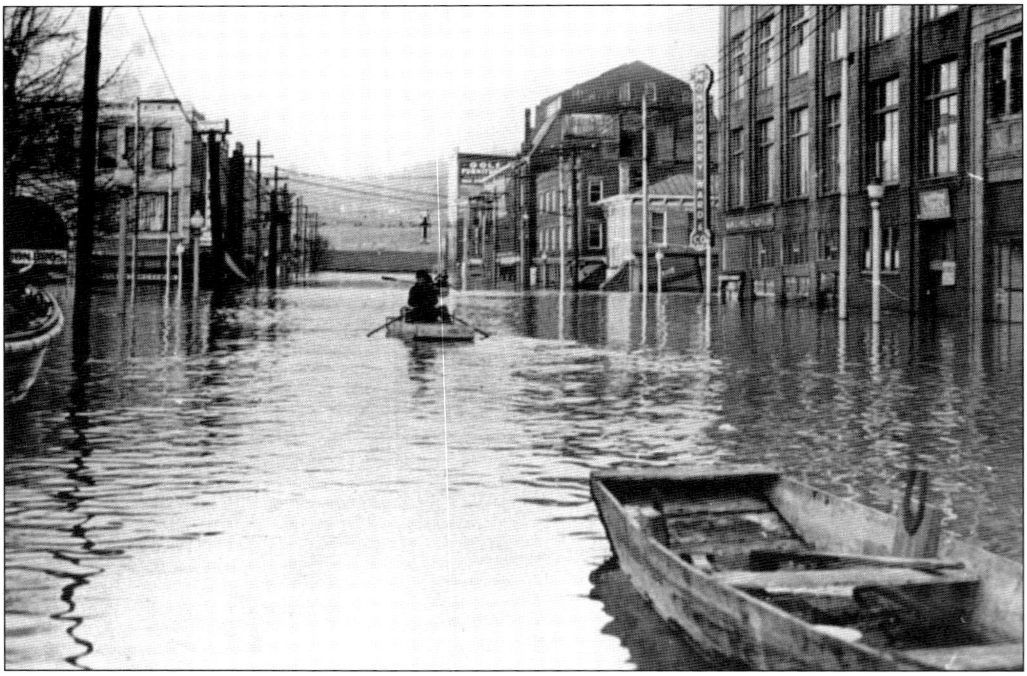

The January 1937 flood was the worst ever in Huntington, West Virginia. It inundated most of the city's downtown and forced thousands of residents from their homes. In this photograph, rowers in a skiff survey the city's Eighth Street as the water rises to the roofline of the old City Market, visible under the Fourth Avenue traffic signal. The Montgomery Ward store is at the right and the Dickinson Brothers furniture store at left.

This close-up view of the Dickinson Brothers furniture store, located on the northwest corner of Fourth Avenue and Eighth Street, vividly shows the depth of the floodwaters that stretched up and down Fourth Avenue, one of the downtown's main thoroughfares. There is a gradual grade between Fourth and Fifth Avenues, which halted the water's spread, keeping it from extending past Fifth Avenue.

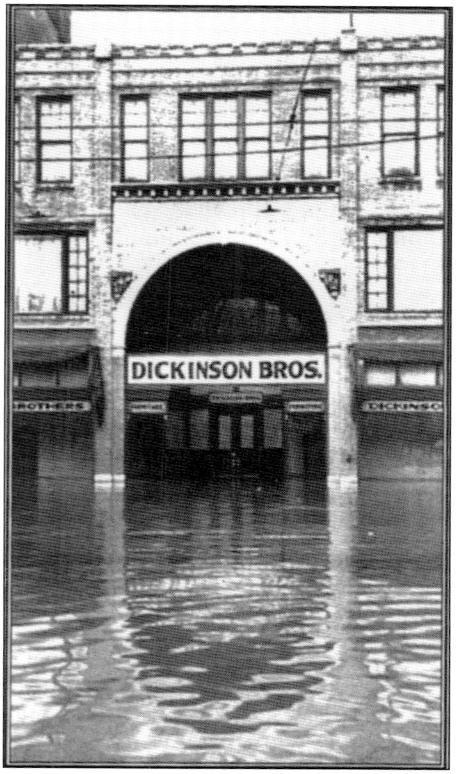

The Cabell County Courthouse, which occupies a full block between Fourth and Fifth Avenues and Seventh and Eighth Streets, became an improvised port for U.S. Coast Guard boats brought to Huntington city for rescue work. The courthouse grounds became a virtual lake, making it ideal for mooring the boats.

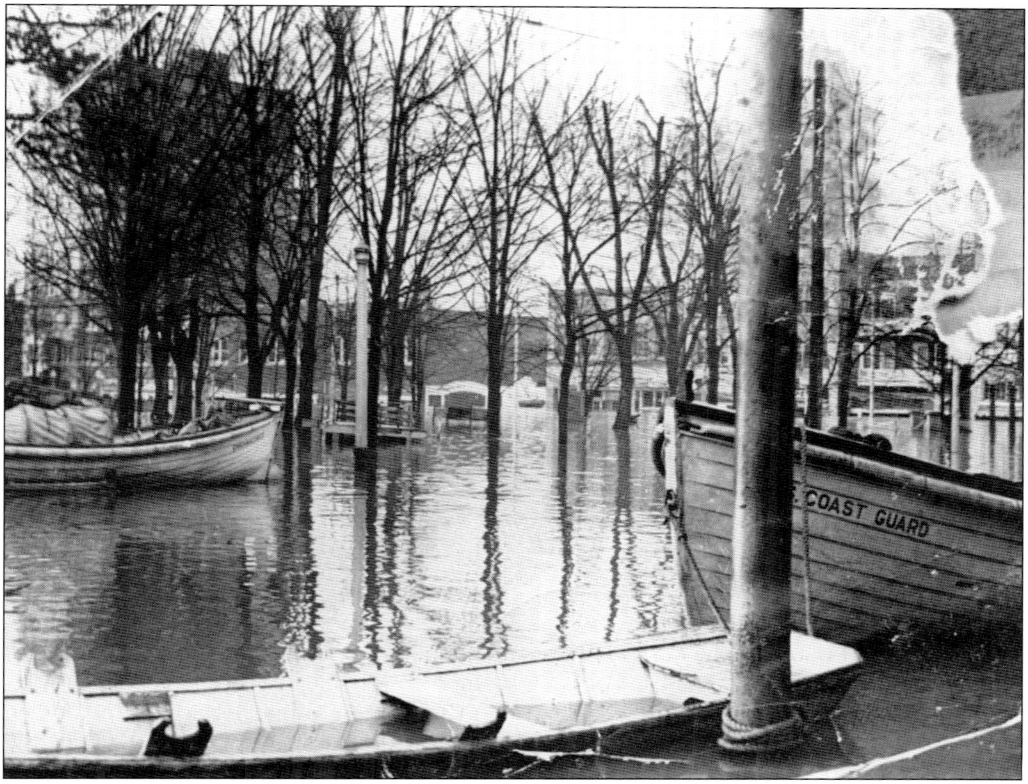

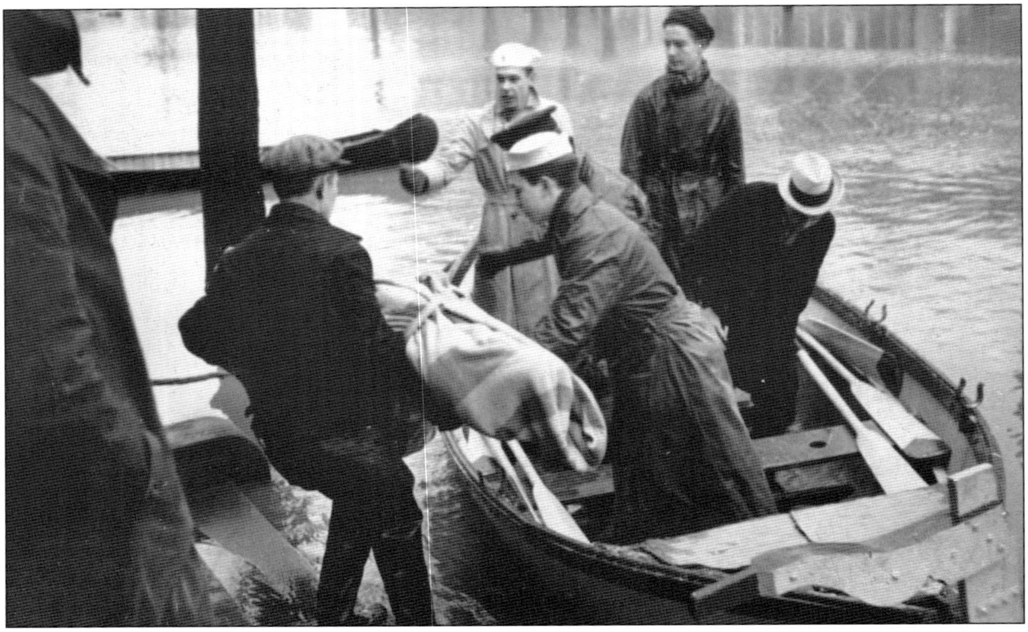

This is a dramatic view of a rescue crew in action at an unidentified Huntington location during the 1937 flood. U.S. Coast Guard crews worked day and night during the flood, aided by Naval Reservists, Boy Scouts, American Legion members, Red Cross volunteers, and others. Some of those rescued were taken to shelters located on high ground. Others went to nearby Charleston by special C&O trains.

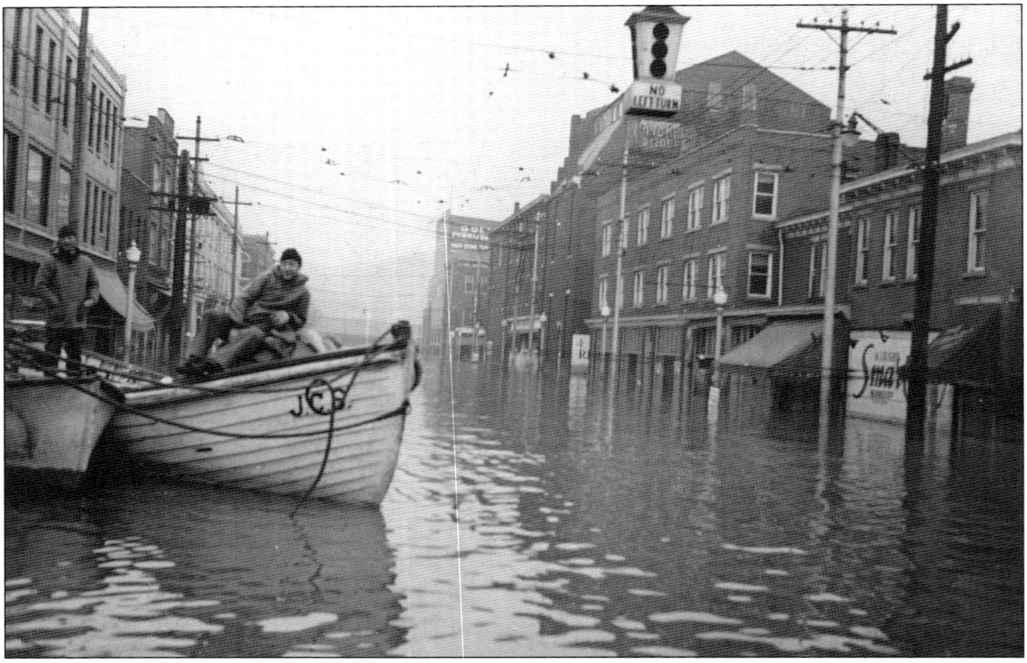

Two boat crew members catch a few minutes of rest while their boats are tied up on the west side of Eighth Street between Third and Fourth Avenues. A sign attached to the bottom of the traffic signal warns motorists there is "No Left Turn" at the busy intersection—not a problem today. It will be several days before the water recedes enough for cars and trucks to travel downtown again.

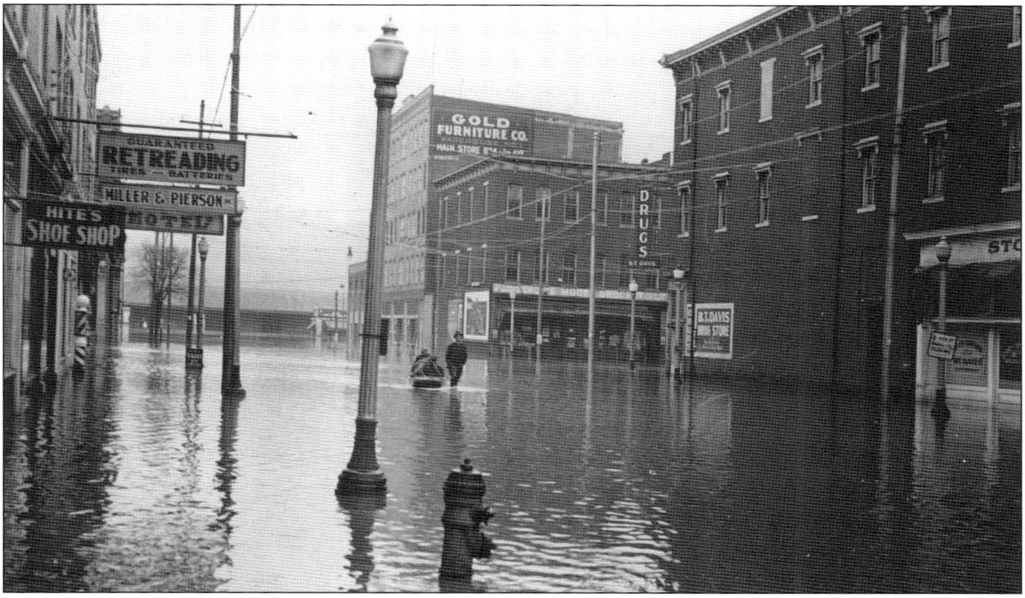

This view of a flooded Third Avenue and Eighth Street may bring back memories for some longtime Huntington residents because it offers glimpses of several long-vanished businesses. A hanging sign at the left marks Hite's Shoe Shop. Just visible at the right of the photograph is the front of the Stop and Shop Market. On the corner is the B. T. Davis Drug Store, and in the background is the Gold Furniture Company warehouse.

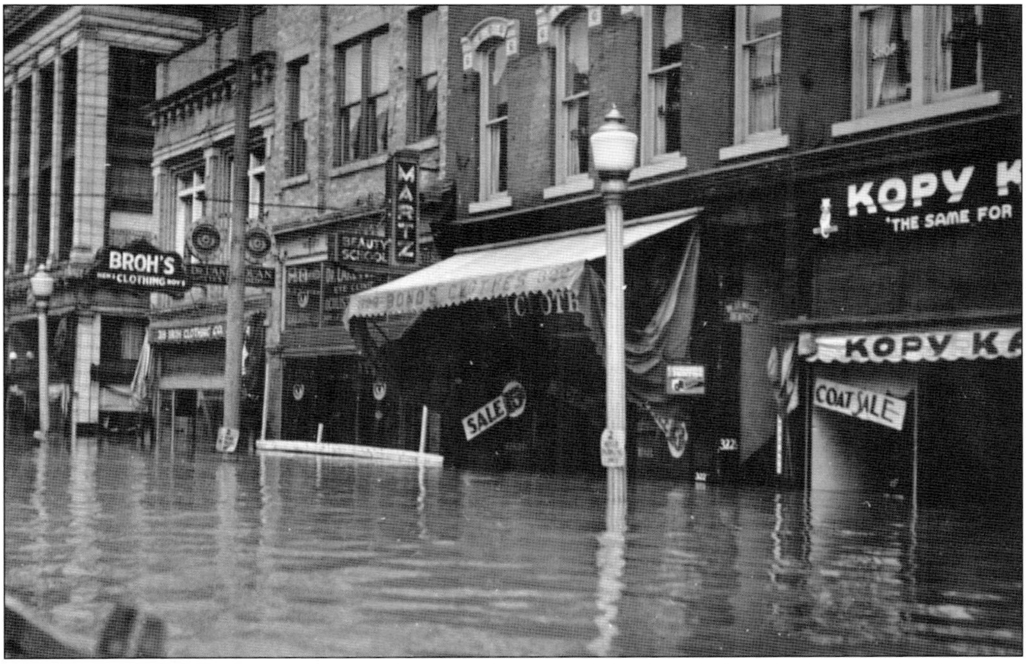

The east side of Huntington's Ninth Street between Third and Fourth Avenues looked like this at the crest of the 1937 flood, with signs advertising Broh's Clothing, Dr. Lake Polan's Eye Clinic, the Martz Beauty School, and the Kopy Kat clothing store. Certainly, Dr. Polan's sign is the most distinctive of the group. Partially hidden by a tall light pole, it is shaped like a giant pair of eyeballs.

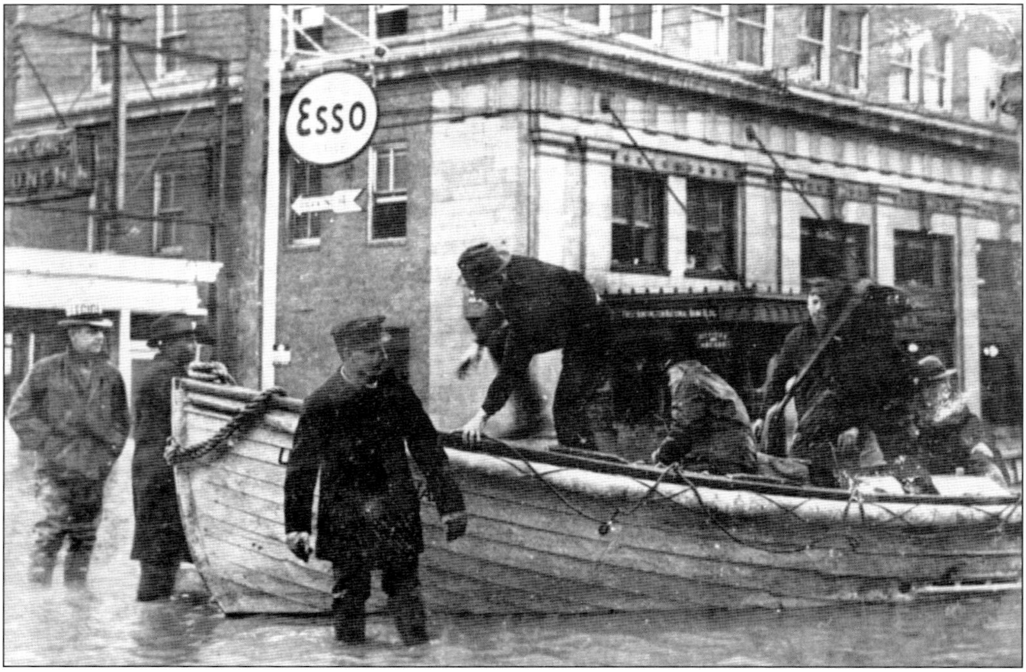

Snow is falling on this rescue boat crew, photographed heading south on Tenth Street between Fourth and Fifth Avenues. The former First Huntington National Bank building is visible behind the boat. The marquee covers the Tenth Street entrance to the offices on the bank's upper floors. In the 1930s, the bank's office floors were occupied by many of the city's leading doctors and lawyers. Note the sign pointing the way to a nearby Esso service station.

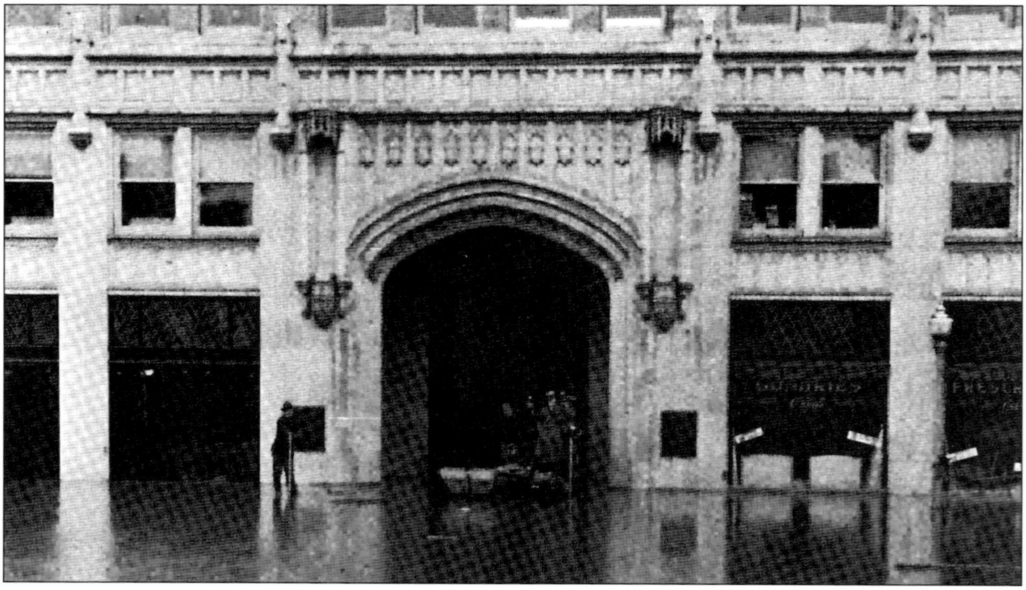

This handsome Huntington building on the southwest corner of Fourth Avenue and Eleventh Street was christened the Coal Exchange Building when it was built in 1925. By 1937, the Chesapeake and Ohio Railway had purchased it and renamed it the C&O Building. In 1937, the building also housed the Huntington District offices of the U.S. Army Corps of Engineers. After the C&O moved out and sold the structure, its name was changed back to the Coal Exchange Building.

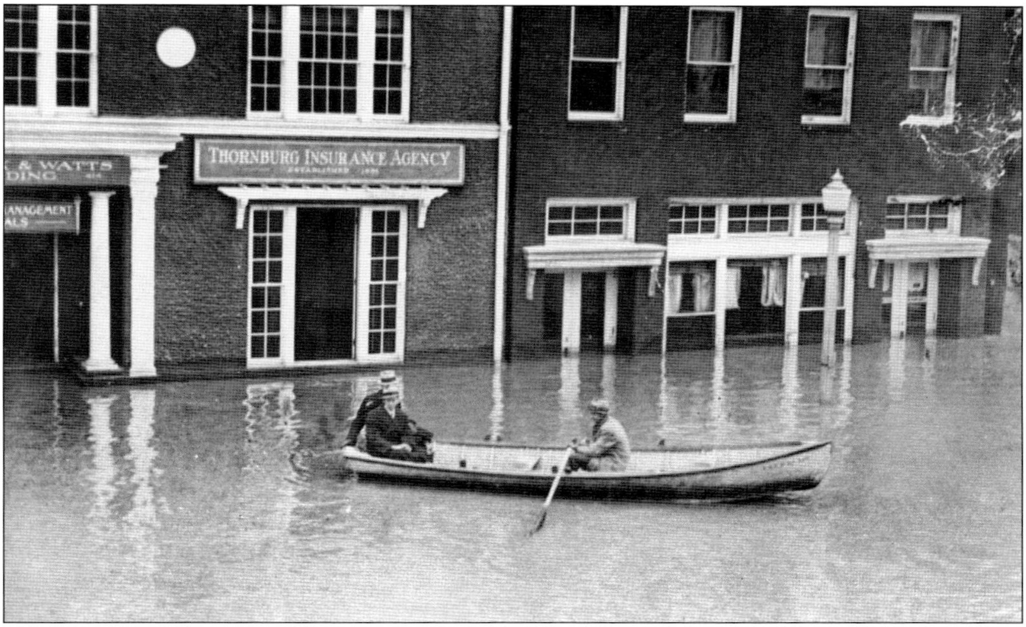

The 1937 floodwaters inundated several offices located on the east side of Eleventh Street between Fourth and Fifth Avenues. Among them was the Thornburg Insurance Agency. As the agency's sign proudly notes, it was established in 1881, making it almost as old as the city itself. Note how well dressed the gentlemen in the boat are. Did they dress that morning thinking it would be just another routine day at the office?

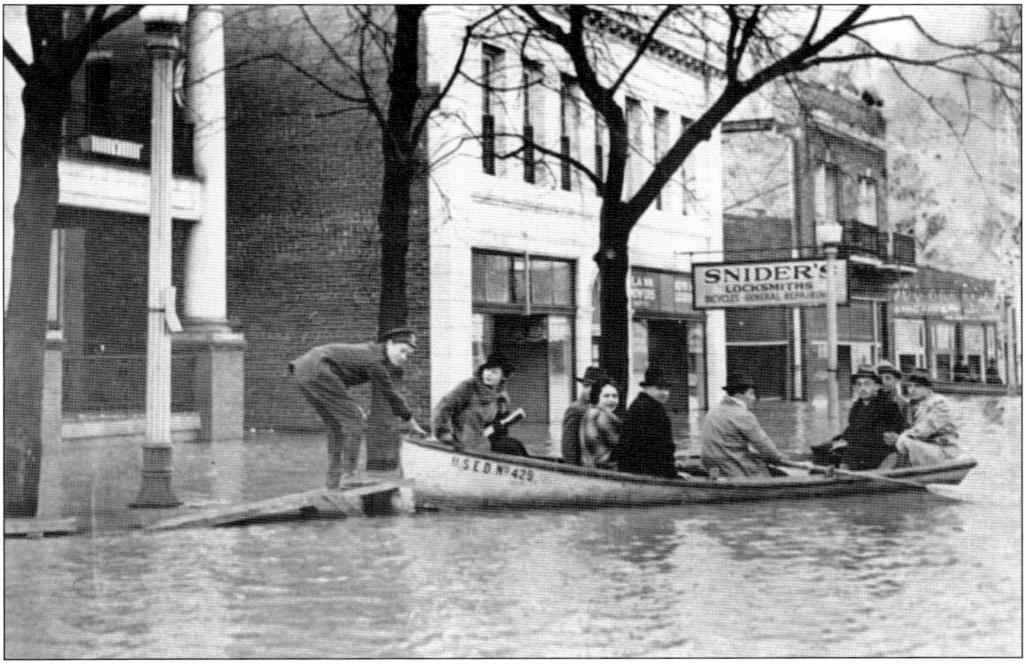

A police officer gets ready to push off a boat loaded with people in front of Snider's Locksmiths on the west side of Eleventh Street between Fourth and Fifth Avenues. The officer has a big grin on his face, but the folks in the boat apparently don't see much to smile about. In addition to locksmithing, Snider's did a brisk business selling and repairing bicycles.

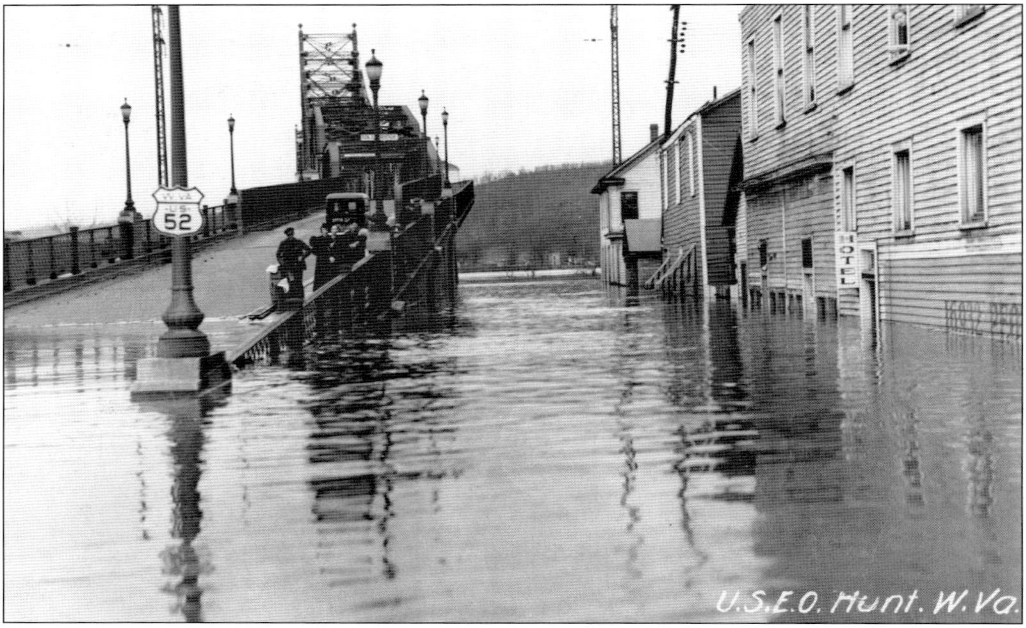

Huntington's Sixth Street Bridge across the Ohio River stood high and dry during the 1937 flood, but the bridge saw no traffic because the bridge ramps on both the Ohio and West Virginia sides were covered by the floodwaters. Just behind the old frame hotel that stood beside the bridge was the city's busy Produce Market, also submerged by the flood. (Courtesy U.S. Army Corps of Engineers.)

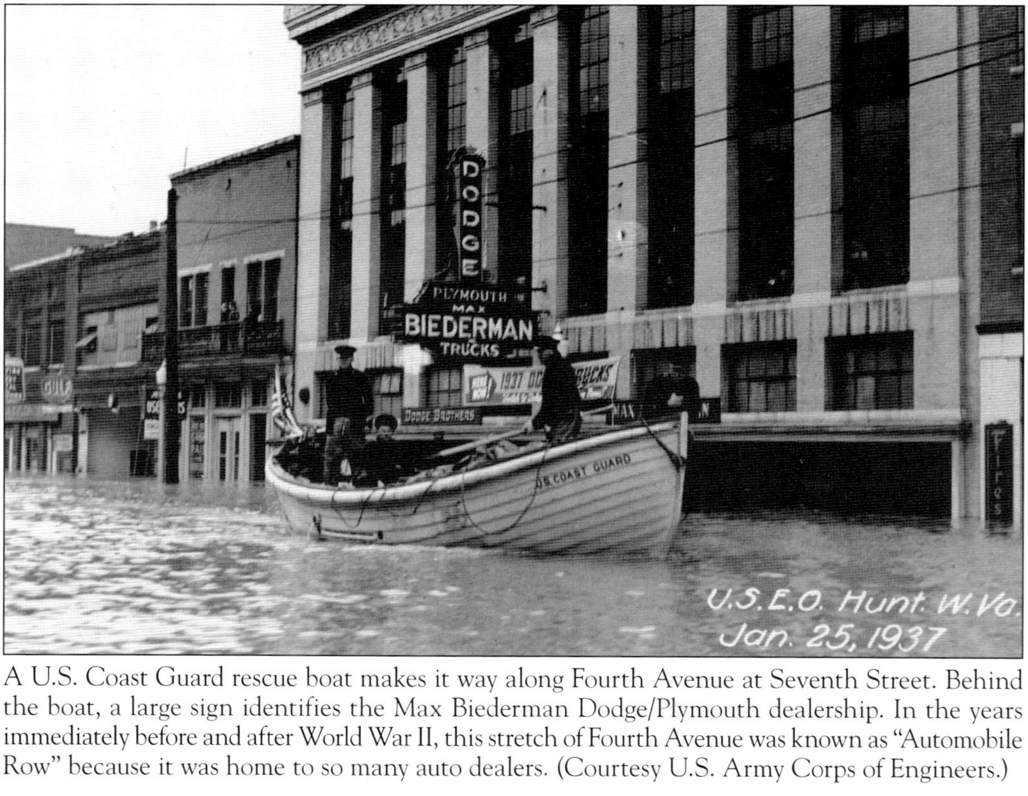

A U.S. Coast Guard rescue boat makes it way along Fourth Avenue at Seventh Street. Behind the boat, a large sign identifies the Max Biederman Dodge/Plymouth dealership. In the years immediately before and after World War II, this stretch of Fourth Avenue was known as "Automobile Row" because it was home to so many auto dealers. (Courtesy U.S. Army Corps of Engineers.)

The marquee at the Palace Theater, located on Huntington's downtown Fourth Avenue, advertises the always popular Charles Laughton in *His Last Rembrandt*. But it will be a while before the theater again can welcome moviegoers. As can be seen here, workers fashioned a wall of sandbags and sheets of wood in an effort to keep the water out.

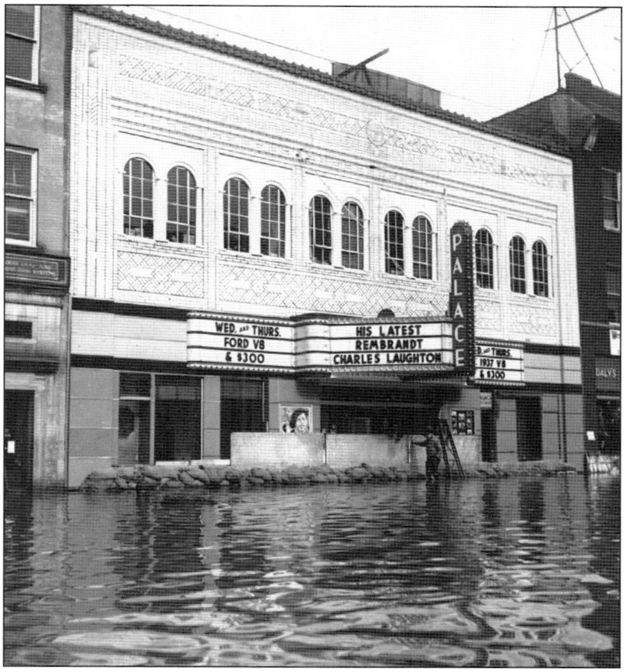

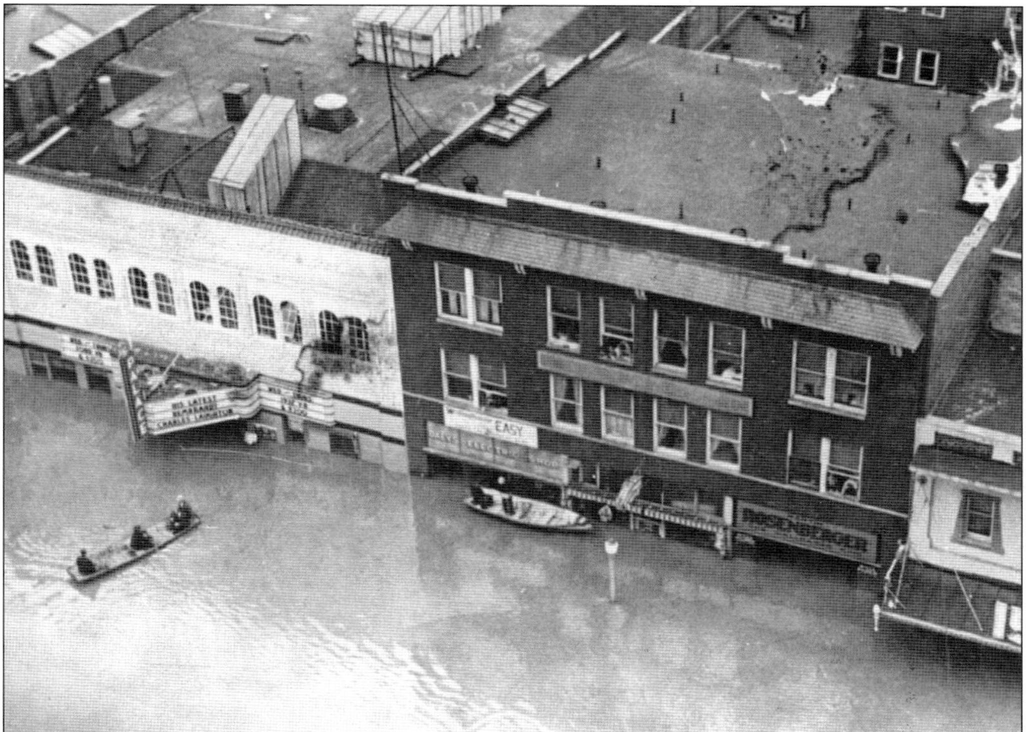

As this unusual aerial view of the Palace shows, the effort to keep out the floodwaters proved for naught. The water has topped the improvised wall of sandbags and wood. Long a showplace (note the fancy arched windows and decorative tile on the front), the theater was later renamed the Camelot. No longer a movie theater, it now houses a dance studio.

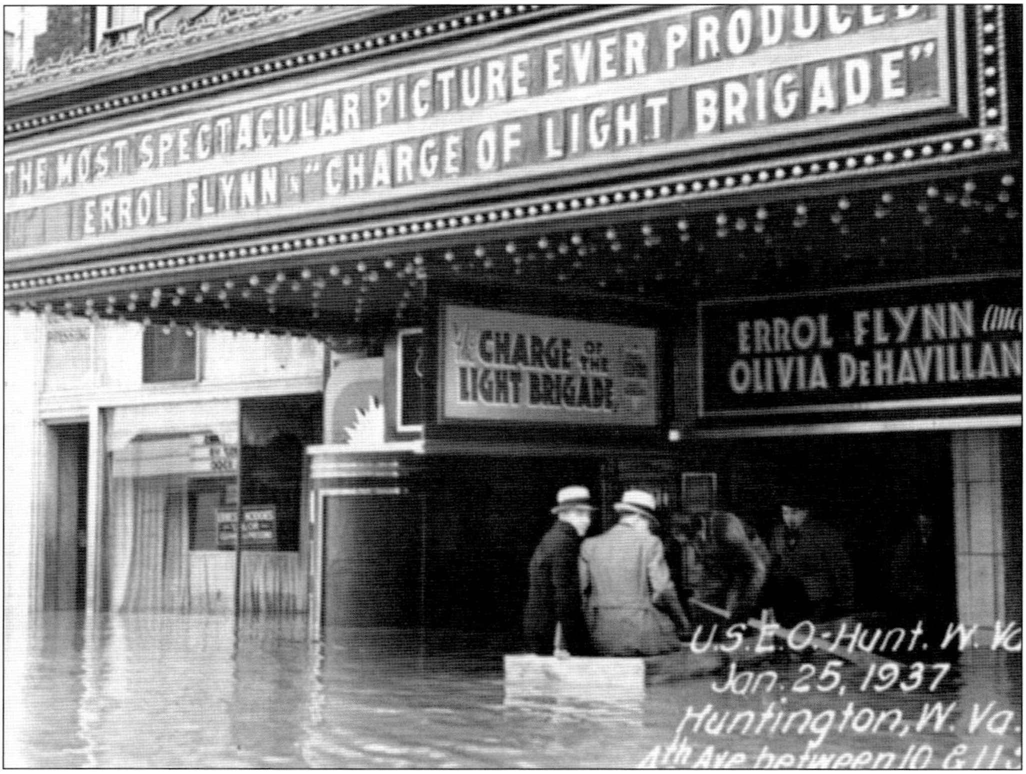

Huntington's Orpheum Theater stood just across from the Palace between Tenth and Eleventh Streets on Fourth Avenue. The men in the rowboat under the marquee seem to be thinking about floating on into the theater's flooded lobby. Maybe they are Errol Flynn fans. The theater advertises his *Charge of the Light Brigade*. Later renamed the Cinema, the theater now operates as a second-run house. (Courtesy U.S. Army Corps of Engineers.)

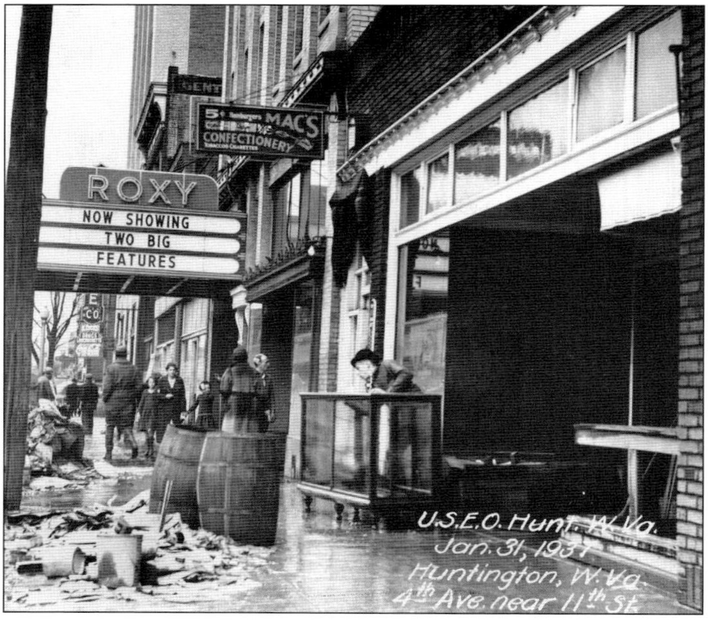

One of five movie theaters then located in a two-block stretch of Huntington's Fourth Avenue, by 1937, the Roxy already was reduced to showing double features and would not survive for many more years. Later it would be home to a loan office. Today it is a parking lot. This photograph was taken nearly a week after the photograph of the flooded Orpheum. It gives a good idea of the mess left behind when the floodwaters receded. (Courtesy U.S. Army Corps of Engineers.)

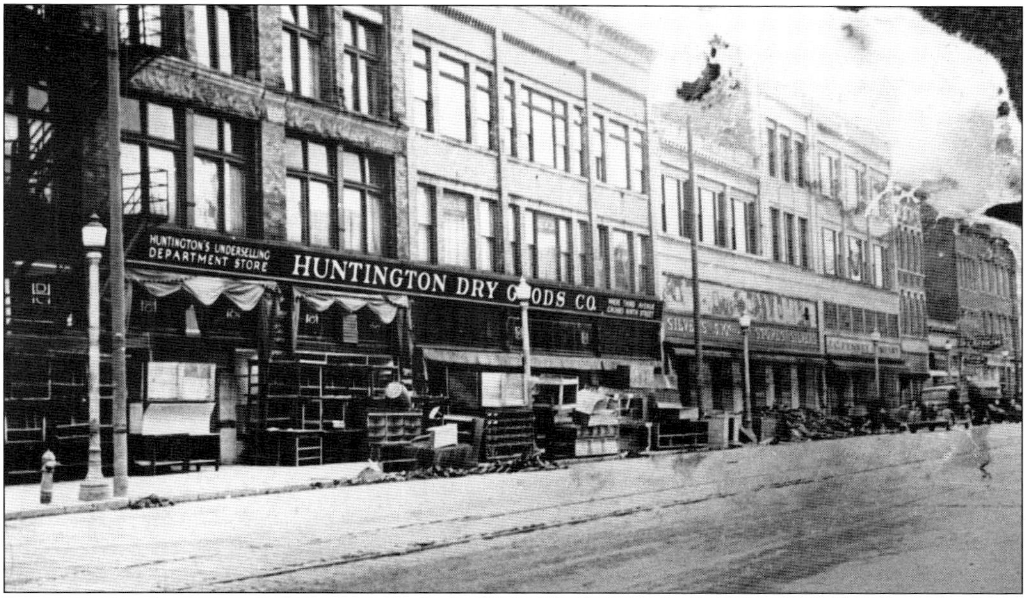

Located on the southwest corner of Third Avenue and Ninth Street, the Huntington Dry Goods Company—later renamed the Huntington Store—was a busy department store in the 1930s. Here is a post-flood shot of the store with debris piled high for cleanup crews to haul away. Most of what is piled at the curb appears to be display counters, likely from the basement sales area, which would be been underwater. The neighboring Silver's 5-and-10-Cent Store and J. C. Penney Company also have piled flood-damaged items at the curb.

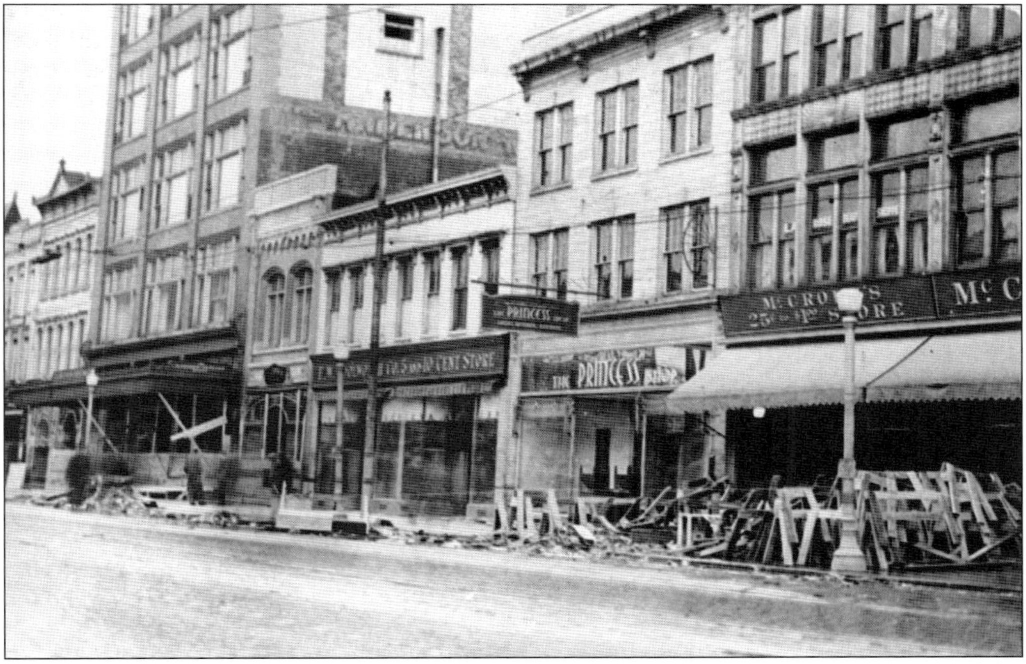

The big post-flood cleanup continues in downtown Huntington in this photograph of the south side of Third Avenue between Ninth and Tenth Streets. Stores shown—all of them long gone—include the Anderson-Newcomb department store, F. W. Woolworth's, the Princess Shop (a fashionable dress store), and McCrorey's.

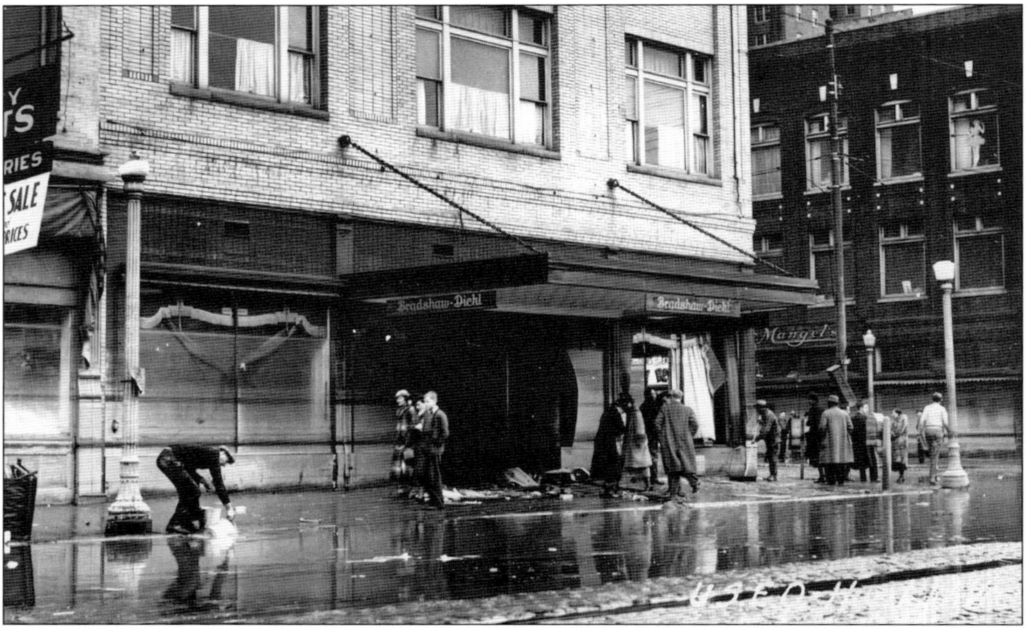

Pedestrians step with care as they make their way past the Bradshaw-Diehl department store on the southeast corner of Third Avenue and Tenth Street as workers continue their post-flood cleanup. Like the other department stores once found in Huntington, Bradshaw-Diehl closed its doors years ago. The Pullman Plaza Hotel now occupies the block where it once stood. (Courtesy U.S. Army Corps of Engineers.)

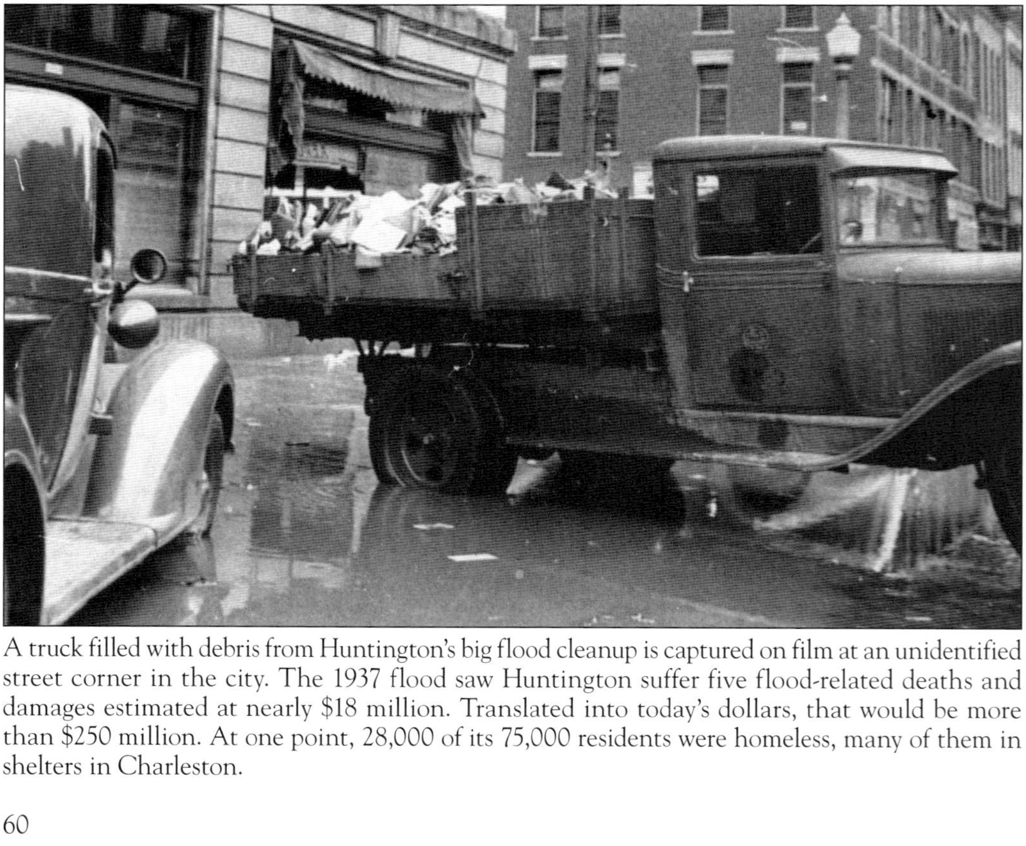

A truck filled with debris from Huntington's big flood cleanup is captured on film at an unidentified street corner in the city. The 1937 flood saw Huntington suffer five flood-related deaths and damages estimated at nearly $18 million. Translated into today's dollars, that would be more than $250 million. At one point, 28,000 of its 75,000 residents were homeless, many of them in shelters in Charleston.

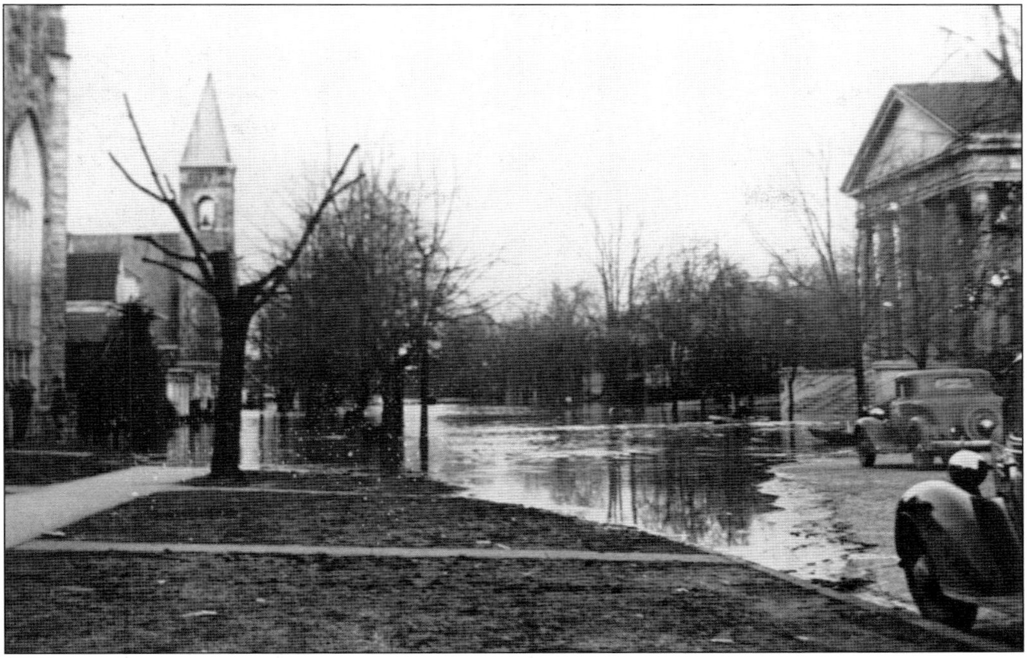

Huntington is often called a "City of Churches," and nowhere is that more evident than downtown Fifth Avenue, home to a half dozen congregations. Fifth Avenue Baptist, at far right in this photograph, was right on the edge of the 1937 flood's reach. Even so, pumps had to be employed to keep the water out of the church basement. For several days, the church fed and sheltered neighboring residents who had been driven from their homes.

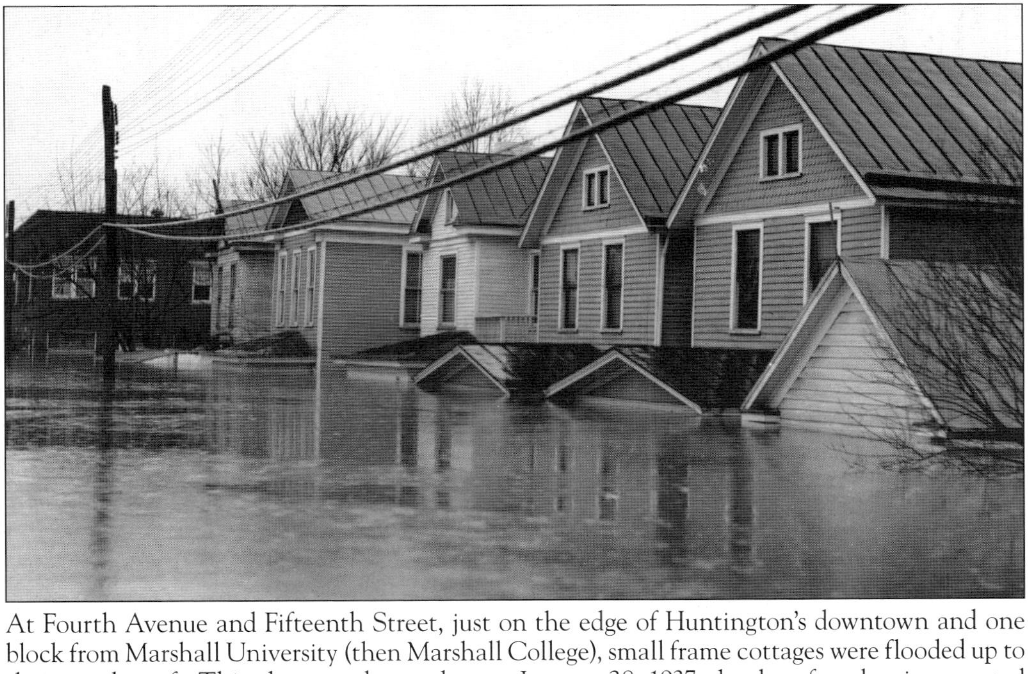

At Fourth Avenue and Fifteenth Street, just on the edge of Huntington's downtown and one block from Marshall University (then Marshall College), small frame cottages were flooded up to their porch roofs. This photograph was shot on January 28, 1937, the day after the river crested at Huntington at 69.45 feet. "Huntington was one big lake," a flood survivor recalled in a 1987 interview with the *Herald-Dispatch*.

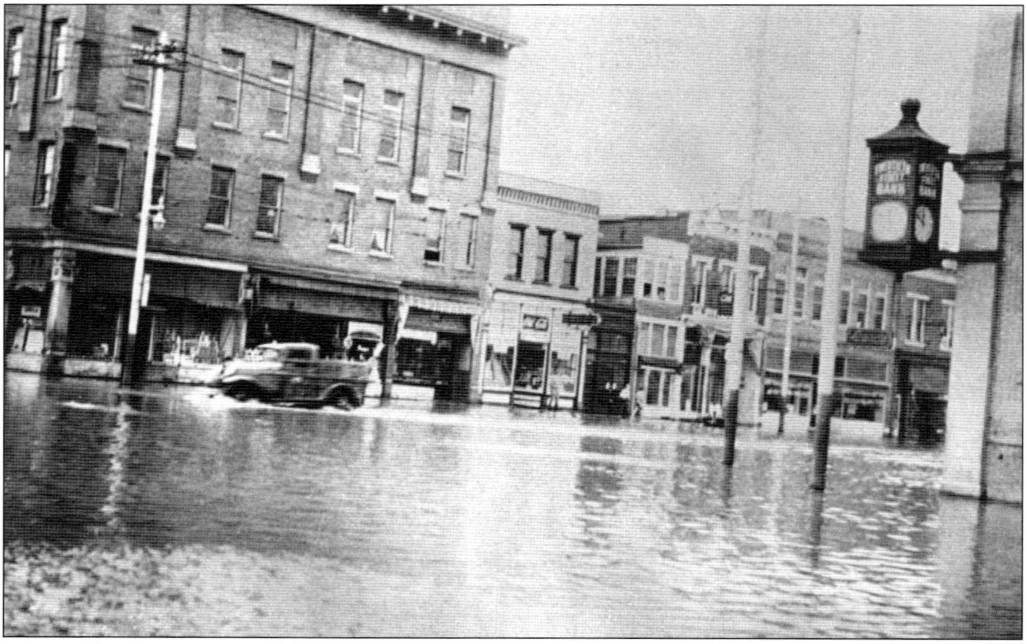

Many older Huntington residents will recognize this scene. For many years, the Twentieth Street Bank on the busy corner of Third Avenue and Twentieth Street was a local landmark and its big clock perched high overhead a familiar sight. The old bank survived a number of floods, including that of 1937, but in 1978, it was demolished, replaced by a new, modern building. Today the bank is a branch of City National Bank.

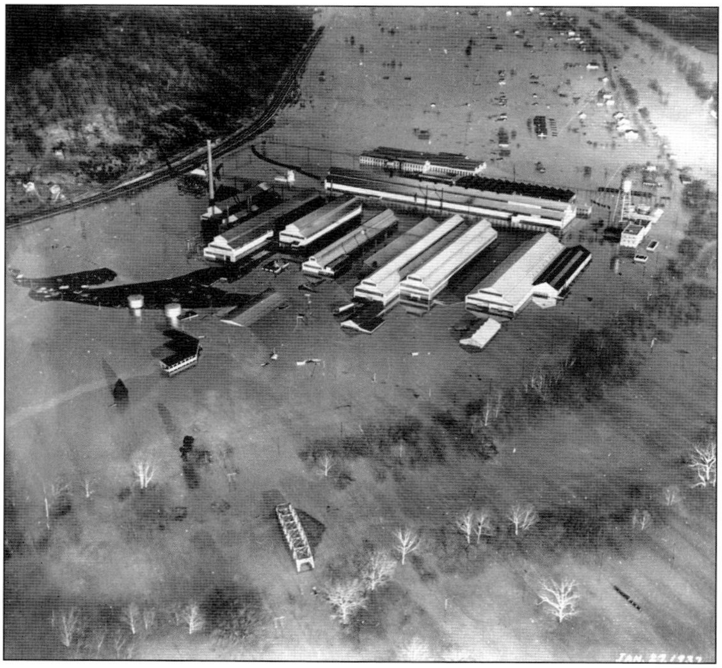

East of downtown Huntington, the 1937 flood inundated the sprawling plant of the International Nickel Company (INCO), halting production. Construction of Huntington's protective floodwall began in 1938 and continued even after World War II broke out. Wartime shortages brought most construction to a standstill, but the Huntington floodwall was deemed a priority project; one reason was that INCO was deemed essential to the war effort.

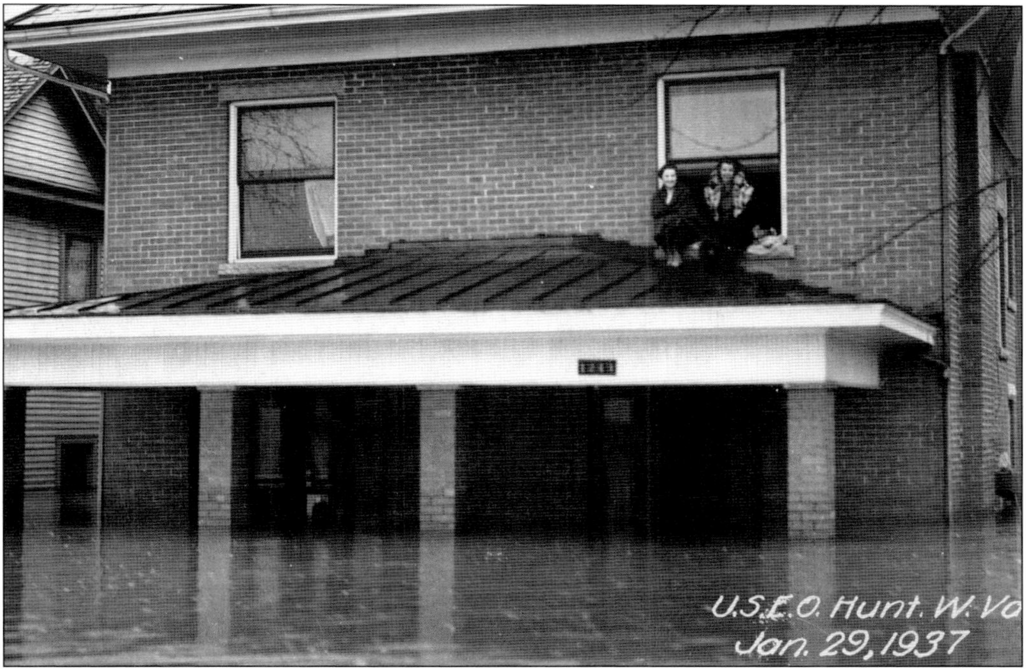

Although they are bundled up against the cold, these smiling young women perched on a second-floor windowsill on Huntington's Washington Avenue near West Twelfth Street do not seem especially concerned about their plight. This photograph was taken on January 29, and by that point, the floodwaters had started to recede. A photograph taken two days earlier might have captured the young women in a very different mood. (Courtesy U.S. Army Corps of Engineers.)

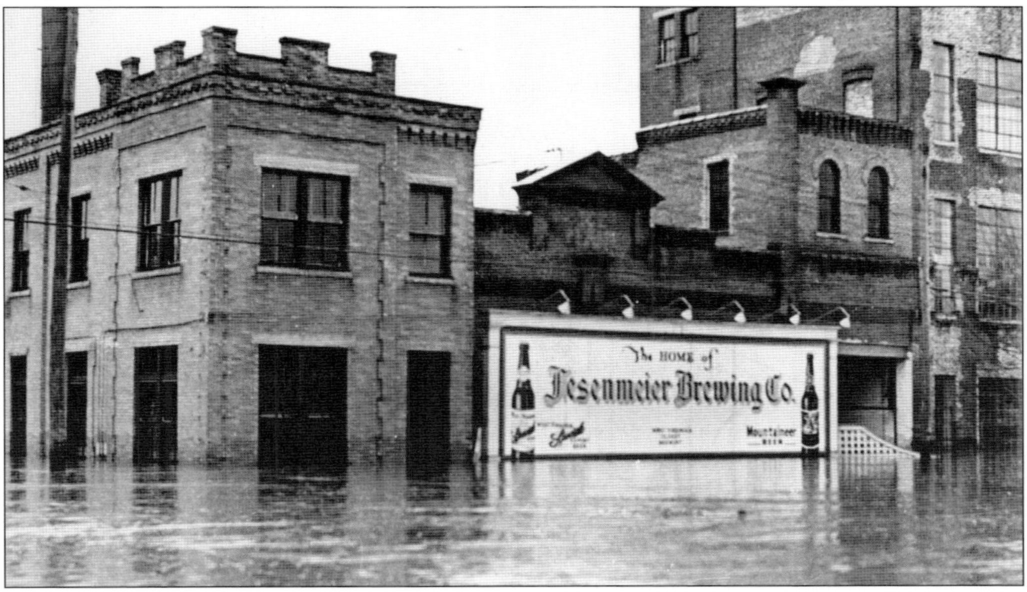

A January 28, 1937, photograph shows the floodwaters lapping around the Fesenmeier Brewing Company on the southwest corner of Huntington's Madison Avenue and West Fourteenth Street, in the neighborhood once known as Central City. The old brewery dated back to 1891 and was once West Virginia's largest. It closed in 1971, and the next year it was demolished to make way for a shopping center.

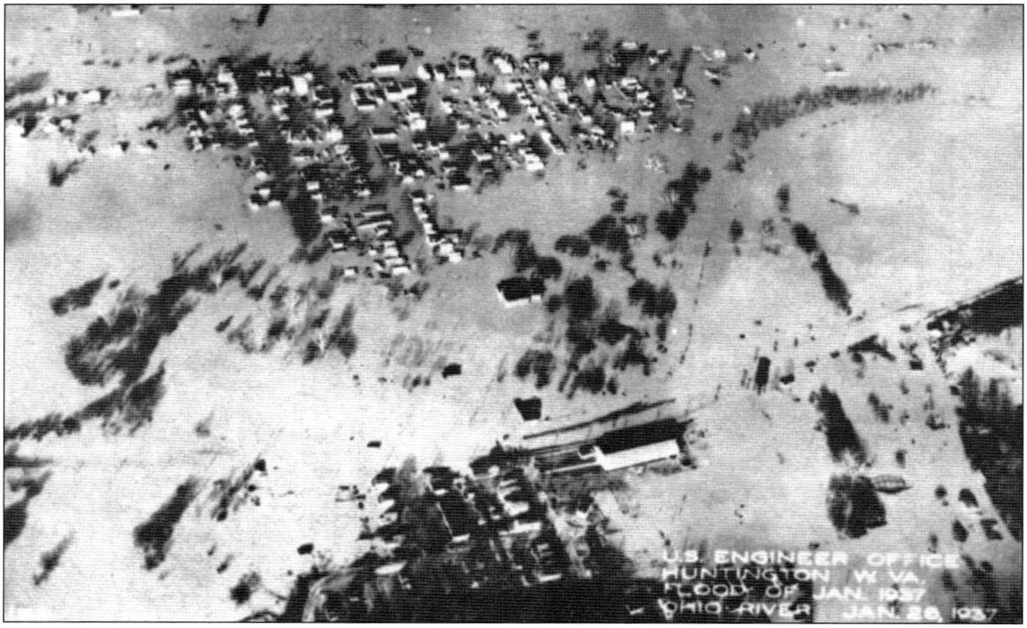

Founded by abolitionist Eli Thayer in 1857 and a Union stronghold during the Civil War, the village of Ceredo is located on the Ohio River just west of Huntington and is today primarily a residential community. As this aerial view shows, the January 1937 flood inundated much of the village. The photographer was facing north, with the Ohio River at the top of the photograph. (Courtesy U.S. Army Corps of Engineers.)

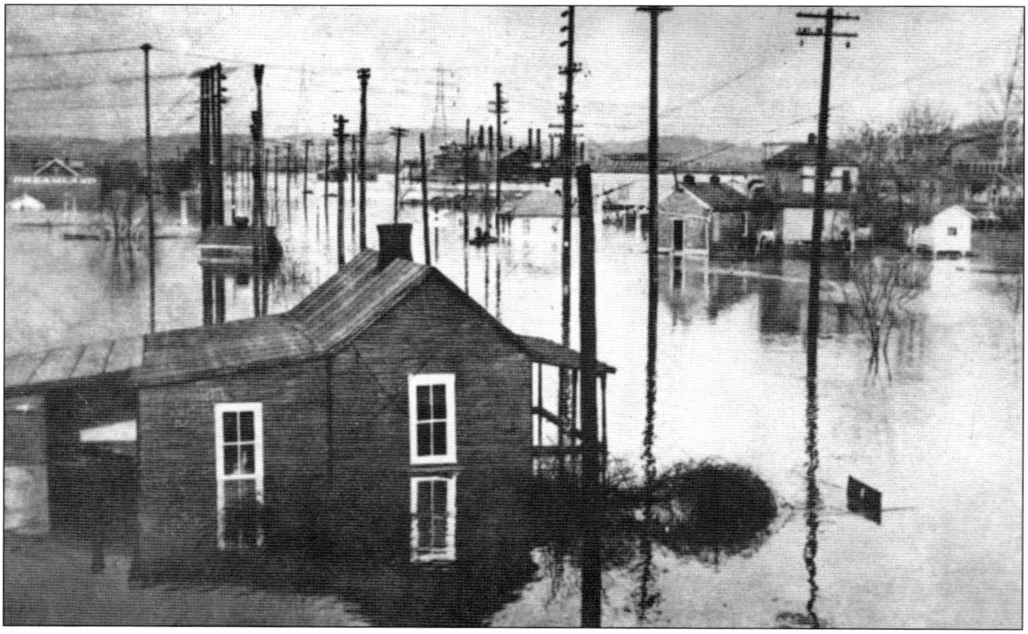

Kenova is the westernmost community in West Virginia. It is located across the Ohio River from Ohio and across the Big Sandy River from Kentucky. Its name is derived from those of the three states. From its founding in 1889, Kenova was primarily a railroad town, and that was still the case when the 1937 flood hit. Here is a view of a flooded Twenty-third Street taken from the Chesapeake and Ohio Bridge over the Big Sandy.

Five

Ohio 1937

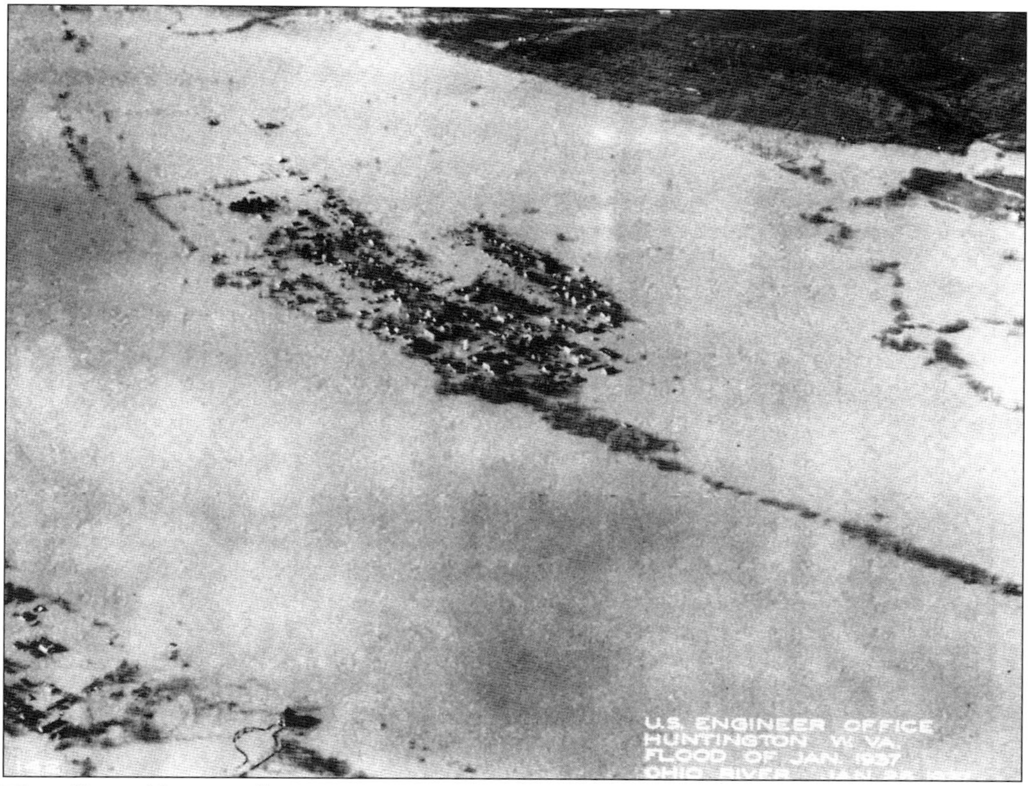

The village of Proctorville in Lawrence County, Ohio, was incorporated in 1878 and was named for storekeeper Jacob Proctor, who did a thriving business with the Ohio's riverboats. The village was totally submerged by the 1937 flood. A Proctorville road sign was swept away and deposited on the doorstep of a house in Portsmouth, 50 miles downstream. Today Proctorville is primarily a bedroom community for Huntington, West Virginia, which lies just across the river. (Courtesy U.S. Army Corps of Engineers.)

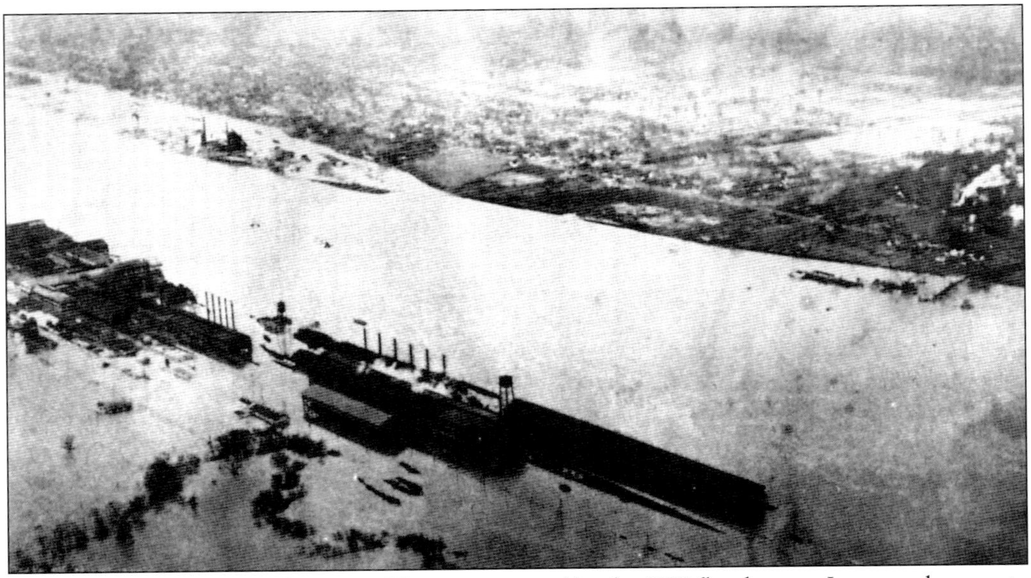

An estimated 90 percent of Ironton, Ohio, was covered by the 1937 floodwaters. Ironton, the county seat of Lawrence County, is on the far side of the Ohio in this aerial view. A flooded Ashland, Kentucky, can be seen at the bottom left of the photograph. The flood completely isolated Ironton from highway and rail travel, and drove more than 600 people from their homes.

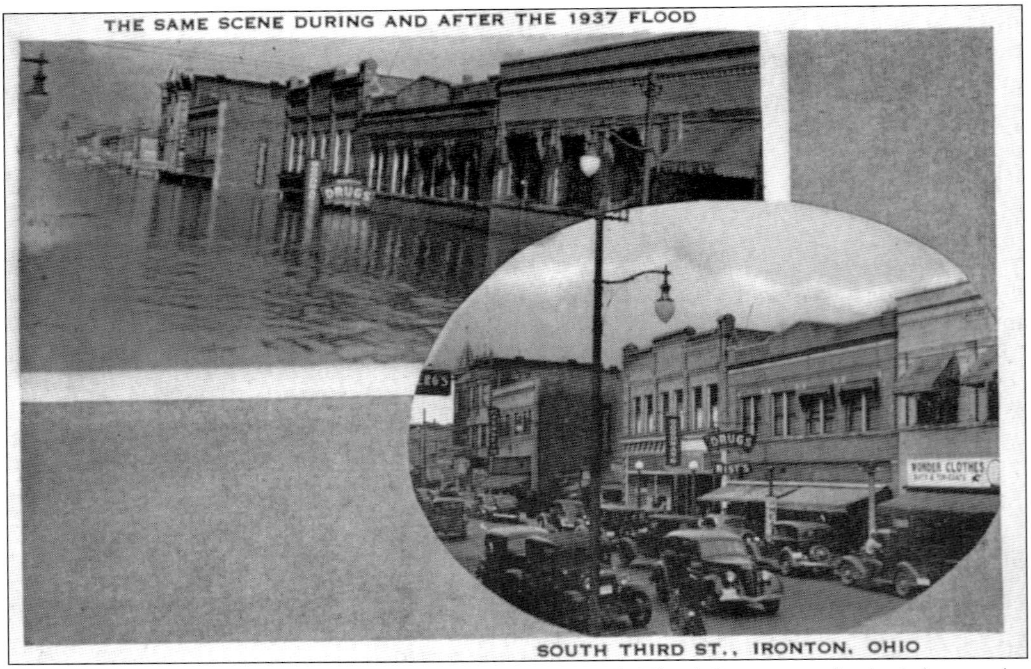

This souvenir postcard shows a stretch of Ironton's South Third Street as it looked during the 1937 flood and then as it looked after the water receded, the mud was cleared away, and things restored to normal. Note the hanging "Drugs" sign. In the flood photograph, the rising water has all but reached it. The card itself was issued by Rist's, the drugstore shown.

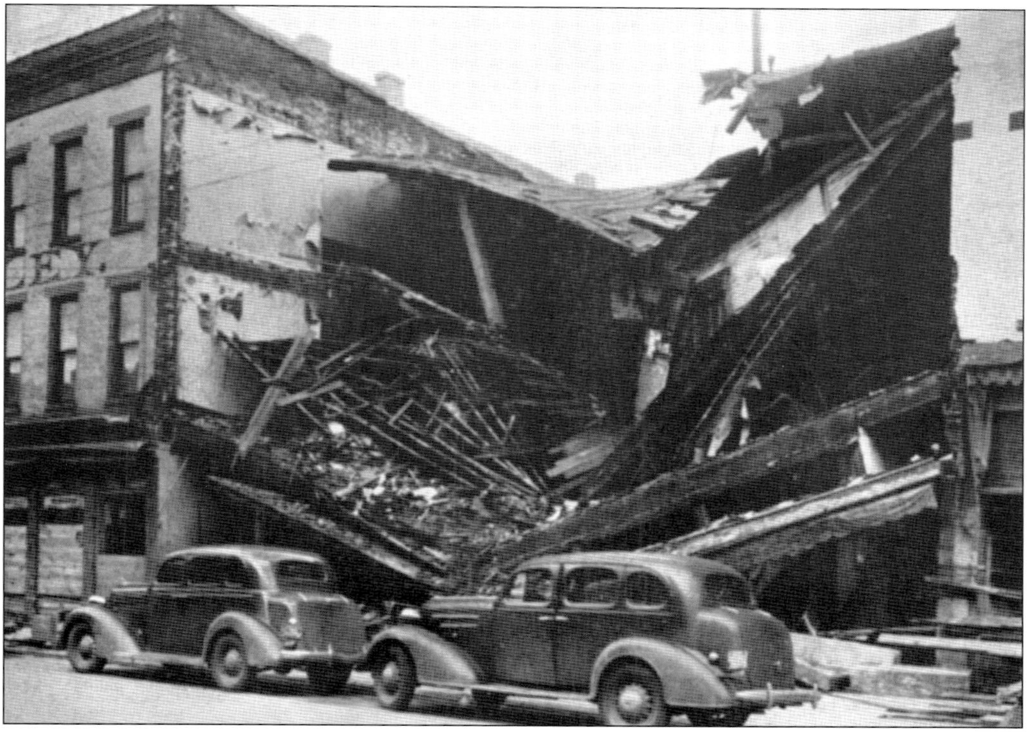

At least five buildings in downtown Ironton were so weakened by the 1937 flood that they collapsed. Another, the Hudon-Pillar Hardware at Second and Lawrence Streets, was a mass of brick and burned timber after a midnight fire at the height of the flood. This building at Second and Center Streets housed the Kiddie Shop before it collapsed. The sidewalk and street are dry, so it appears this photograph was taken several days after the water went down.

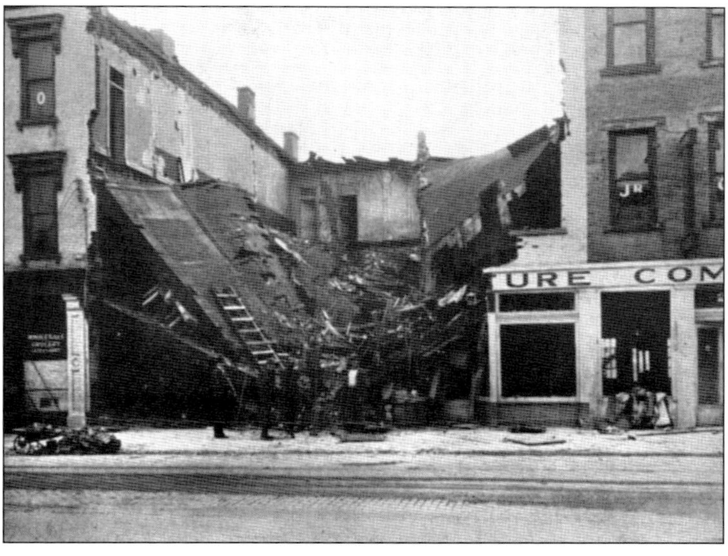

Ironton's Bunn Building at North Second and Railroad Streets collapsed on February 2, crushing and killing Agnes Jones, Ironton's only direct fatality in the flood. Alarmed about the safety of several houses and business buildings, city officials conducted an emergency inspection and directed that 25 of them be immediately demolished. Urgent repairs were ordered for a long list of other structures.

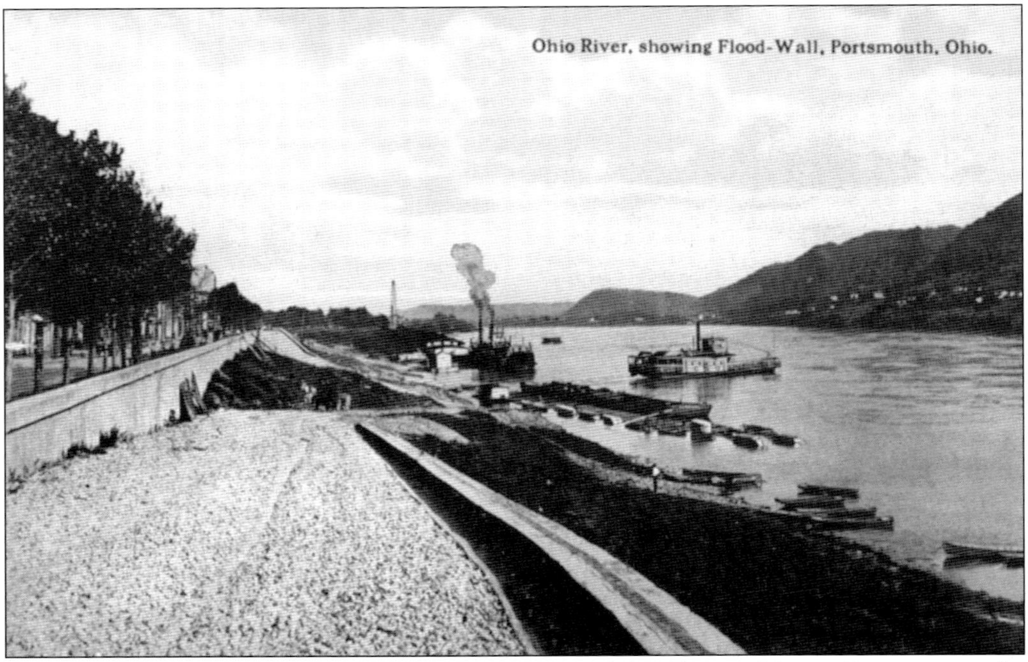

In 1931, Portsmouth, Ohio, located at the confluence of the Ohio and Scioto Rivers, erected a 3-mile floodwall, a portion of which is shown here in a souvenir postcard. Portsmouth residents felt they would be snug and dry when future floods came down the Ohio River. Their town, they boasted, was now "flood-proof." But that boast proved hollow in 1937.

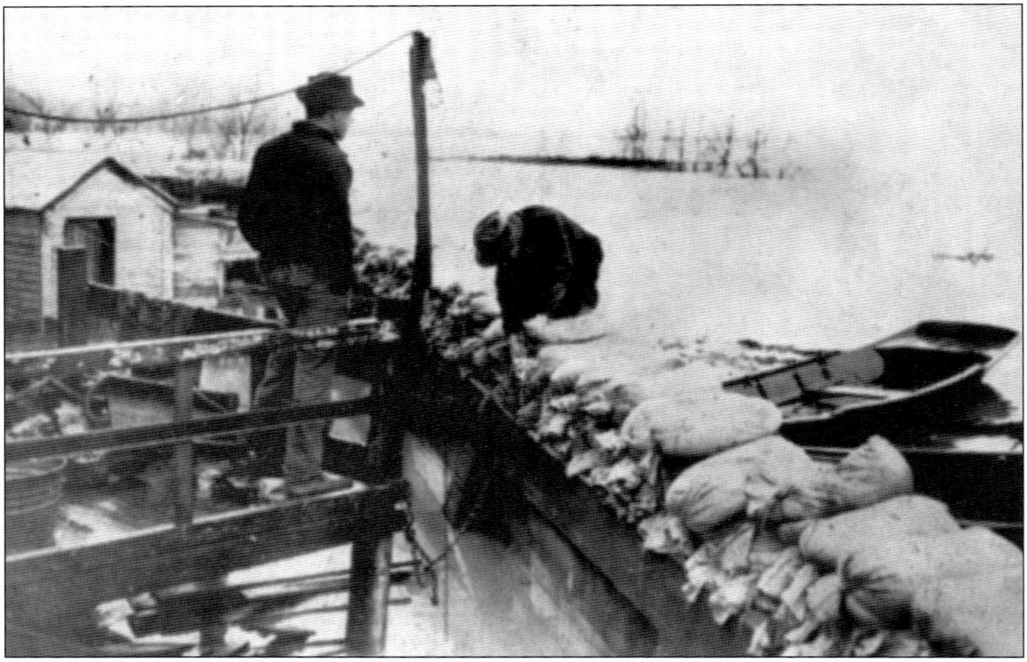

Work crews with the federal government's Depression-era Work Progress Administration (WPA) reinforced the Portsmouth floodwall with sandbags. But the wall soon sprang massive leaks. The city, hoping to save the wall from collapse, opened the sewer outlets and let the river in. Soon only a ripple in the water showed where the floodwall stood.

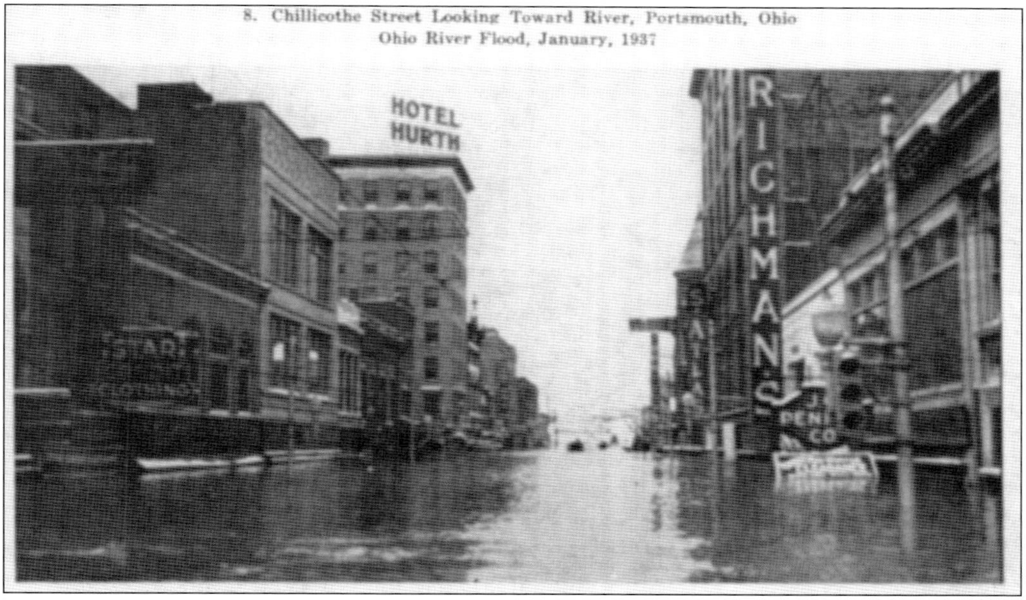

The rising floodwaters quickly inundated Portsmouth. This view of downtown Chillicothe Street was taken looking toward the Ohio River. One of the flooded stores was Richman's clothing store. The now-vanished Richman chain, which once had hundreds of stores nationwide, was founded in Portsmouth in 1853. Twenty-five years later, owner Henry Richman moved the company to Cleveland. In the photograph's background, a big rooftop sign identifies the Hotel Hurth, long a local landmark.

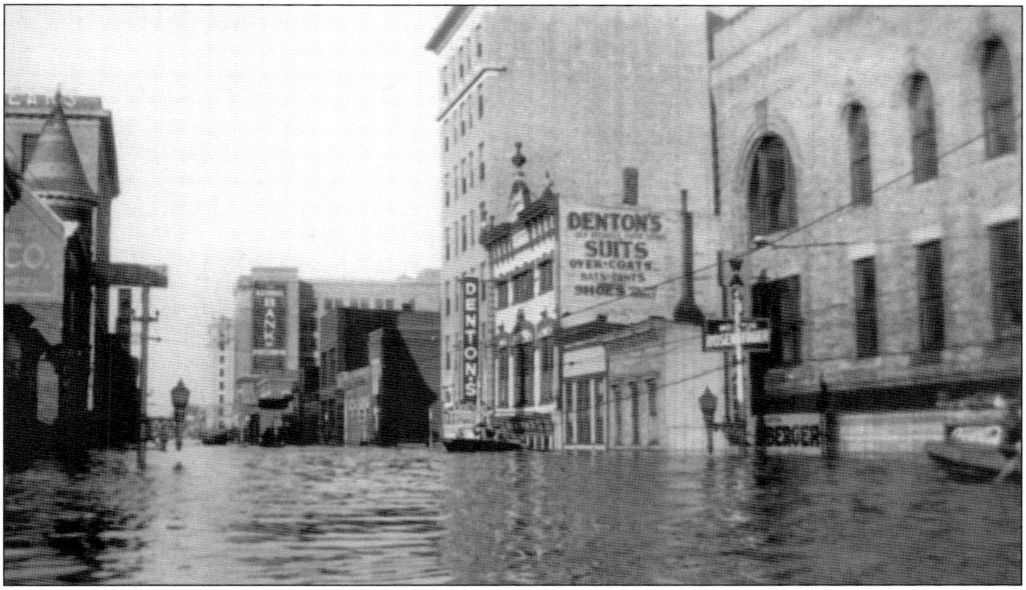

Here is another view of Portsmouth's flooded Chillicothe Street, this one taken from Second Street. Within 24 hours, the city's entire business district was submerged under 7 feet of dirty water. Police were given "shoot to kill" orders in an attempt to prevent looting. Nevertheless, thieves paddling around in boats and on makeshift rafts sneaked into flooded buildings and stole everything they could carry off.

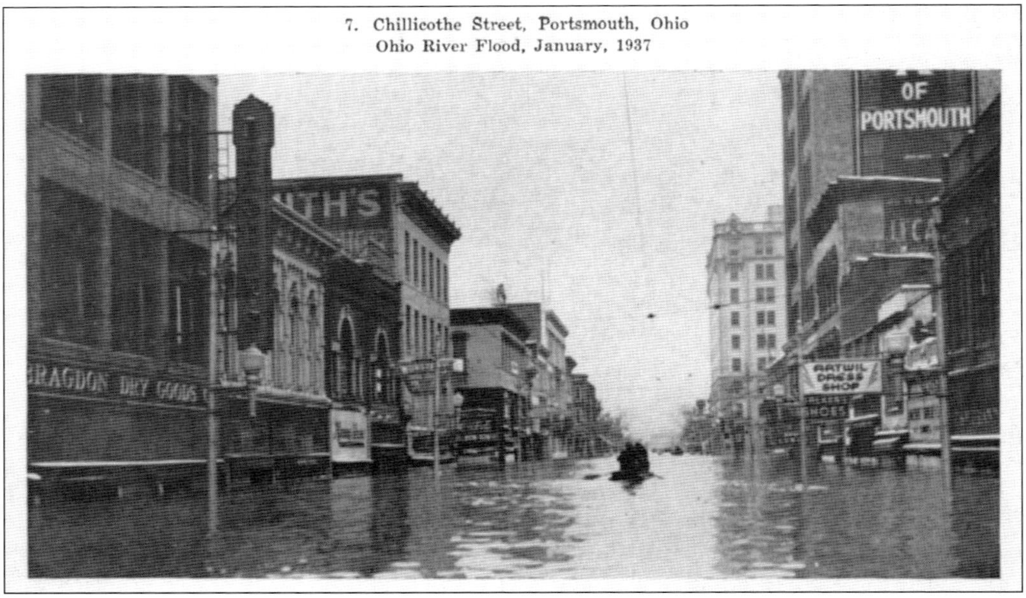

This view of Portsmouth's flooded Chillicothe Street looks north. The occupants of a lone rowboat slowly survey the watery scene. The flooded stores shown include, at far left, Bragdon's Dry Goods, a popular department store at the time. On the other side of the street is the Artwil Dress Shop. At top right can be glimpsed the bottom portion of the National Bank of Portsmouth's sign.

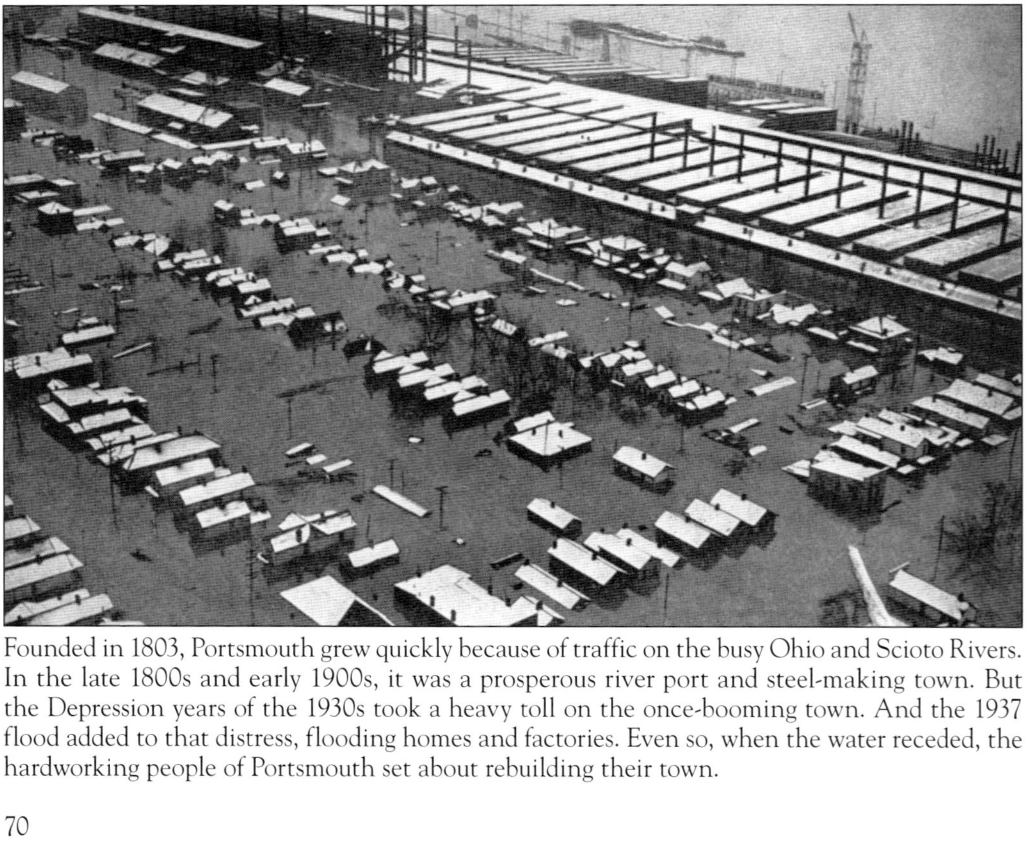

Founded in 1803, Portsmouth grew quickly because of traffic on the busy Ohio and Scioto Rivers. In the late 1800s and early 1900s, it was a prosperous river port and steel-making town. But the Depression years of the 1930s took a heavy toll on the once-booming town. And the 1937 flood added to that distress, flooding homes and factories. Even so, when the water receded, the hardworking people of Portsmouth set about rebuilding their town.

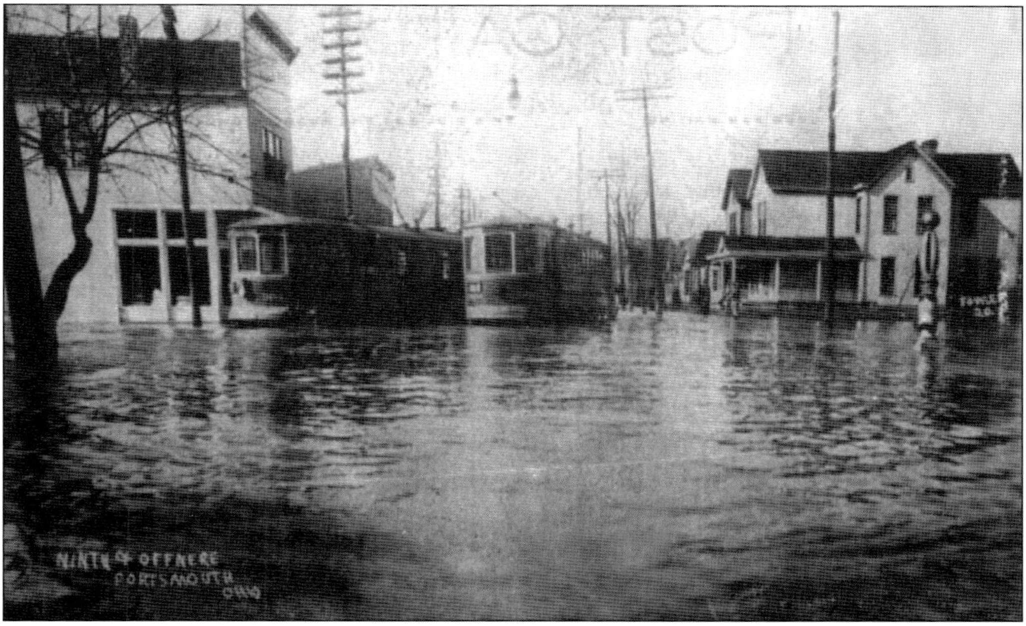

Two streetcars stand abandoned in a flooded street in Portsmouth. As the floodwaters rose, thousands of men, women, and children immediately fled the city. Thousands more followed. Countless more people remained behind, marooned on the second and third stories of houses and buildings, awaiting rescue by the small army of police, firefighters, and volunteers who worked night and day until the floodwaters receded.

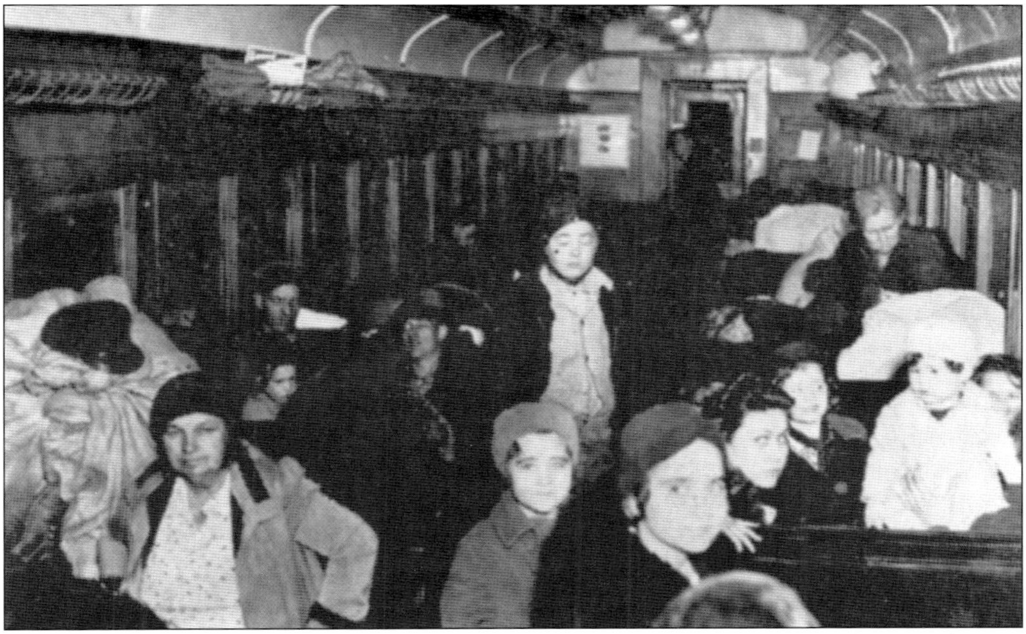

An estimated 25,000 of those evacuated from flooded Portsmouth were taken by special trains to safety in Columbus. Many of the evacuees clutched suitcases or bags hastily stuffed with a few clothes and prized possessions. Those were the lucky ones. Others had nothing more than the clothes on their backs. Arriving in Columbus, they were housed in churches, fraternal halls, and other makeshift quarters until it was deemed safe for them to return home.

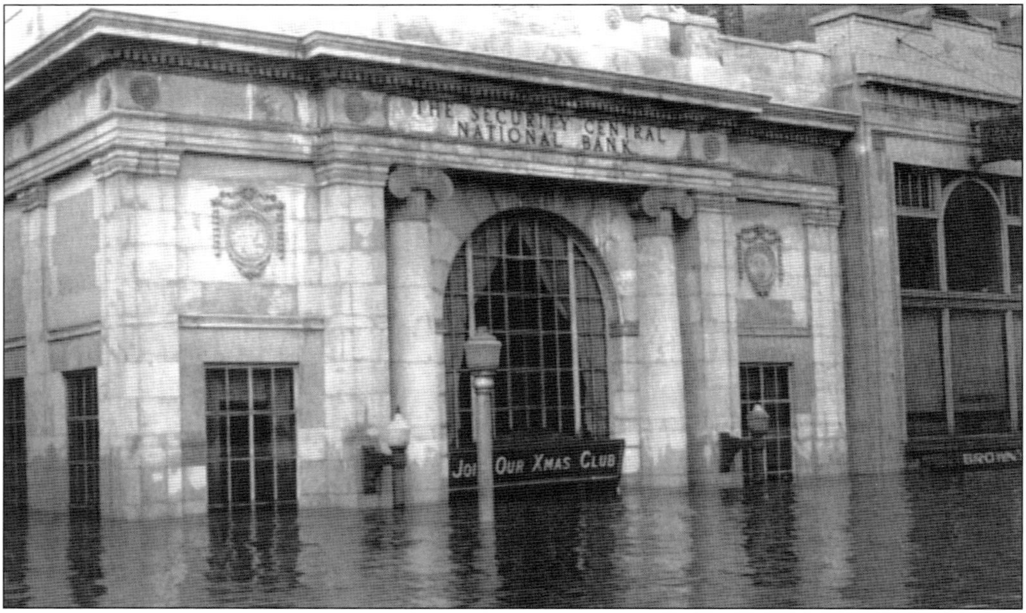

A sign over the doorway of Portsmouth's flooded Security Central National Bank urges customers to "Join Our Xmas Club," but the bank will be welcoming no customers this day. The elegant bank building at 825 Gallia Street was constructed in 1918. Since 1979, it has been the home of the Southern Ohio Museum.

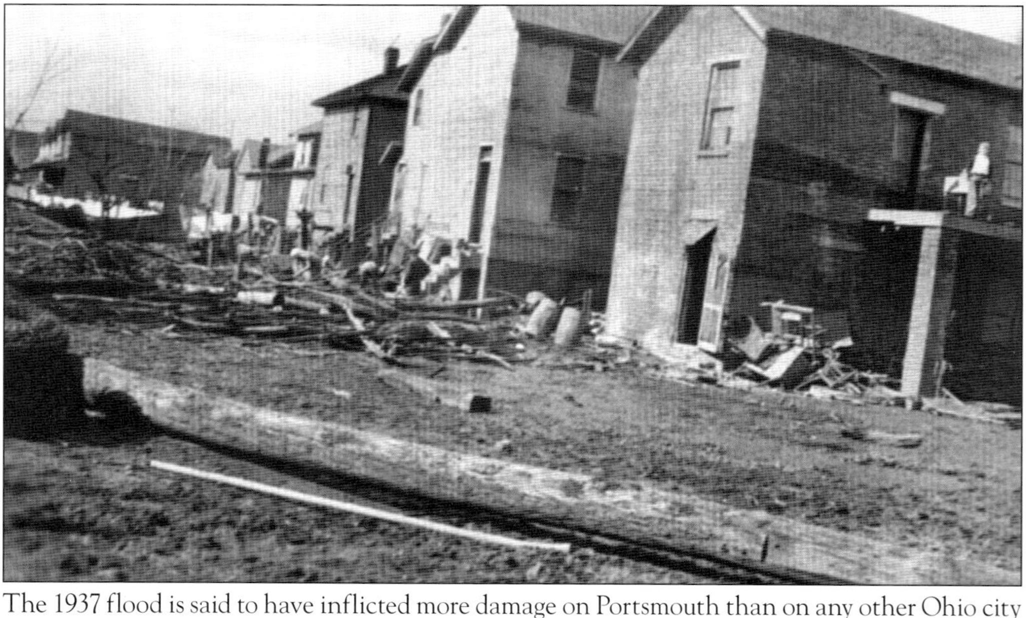
The 1937 flood is said to have inflicted more damage on Portsmouth than on any other Ohio city between Cincinnati and Pittsburgh. Three-fourths of the city was reported under water. All of the many small houses dotting the riverbank were either washed away or ruined beyond repair. Countless other homes were damaged.

The leafless branches of a tall tree in the front yard of a house on Portsmouth's Young Street cast a perfect reflection in the floodwaters that fill the street. Although not ravished like those that stood closer to the Scioto and Ohio Rivers, even these houses did not escape the floodwaters. An early estimate placed the flood damage to the city at $5 million, but ultimately, that figure was increased to more than $17 million.

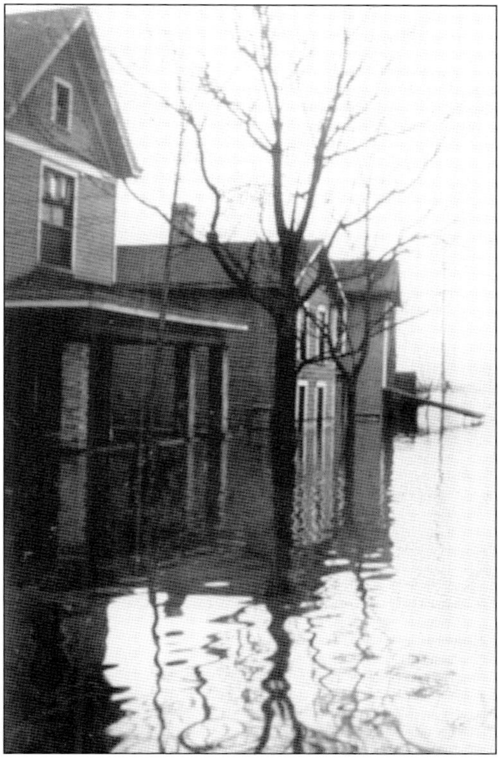

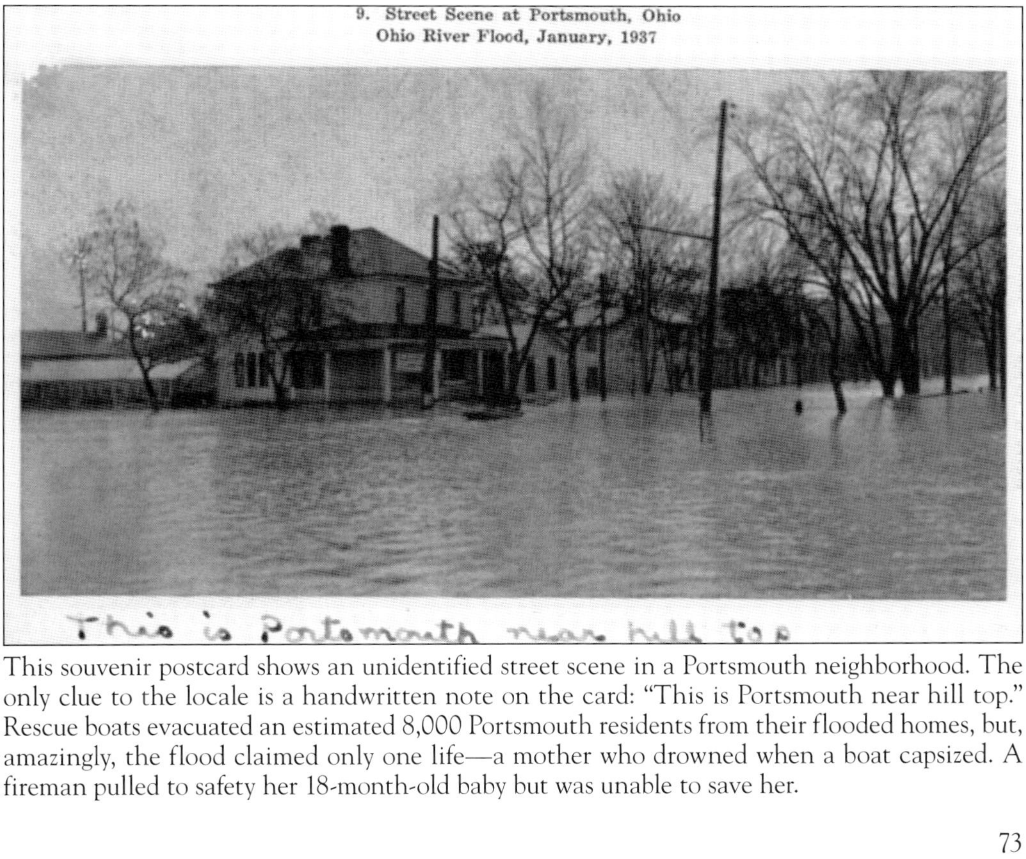

This souvenir postcard shows an unidentified street scene in a Portsmouth neighborhood. The only clue to the locale is a handwritten note on the card: "This is Portsmouth near hill top." Rescue boats evacuated an estimated 8,000 Portsmouth residents from their flooded homes, but, amazingly, the flood claimed only one life—a mother who drowned when a boat capsized. A fireman pulled to safety her 18-month-old baby but was unable to save her.

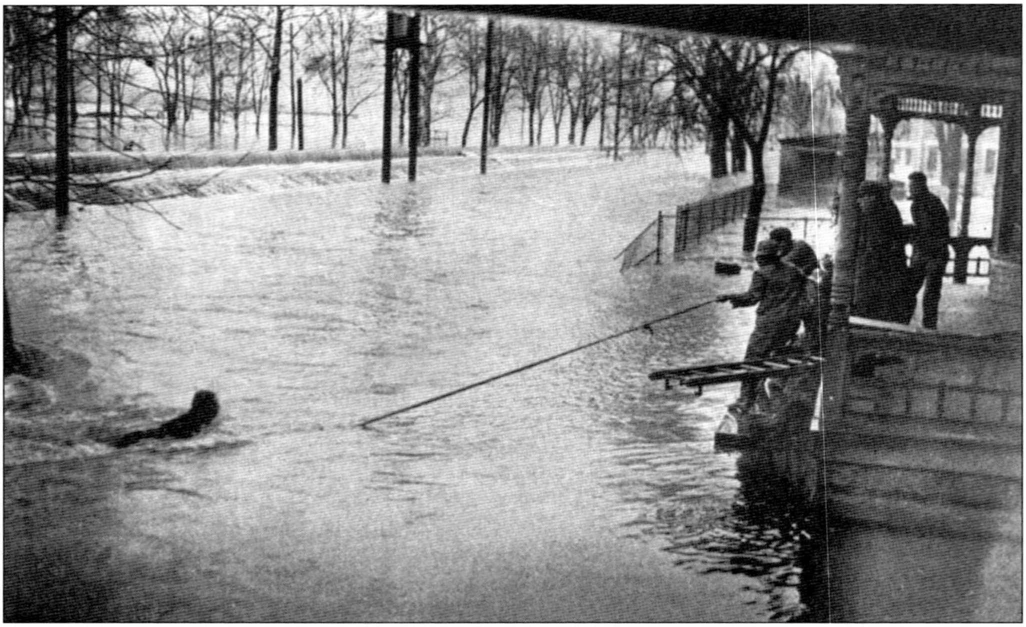

Swept off his feet by the raging floodwaters, this Portsmouth man faced certain death by drowning. Twice he missed the rope thrown to him by would-be rescuers. Finally, on a third attempt, he was able to grasp the rope and be pulled to safety. Note the water in the background rushing over the top of Portsmouth's $1-million floodwall, which proved inadequate to keep the 1937 flood from inundating the town.

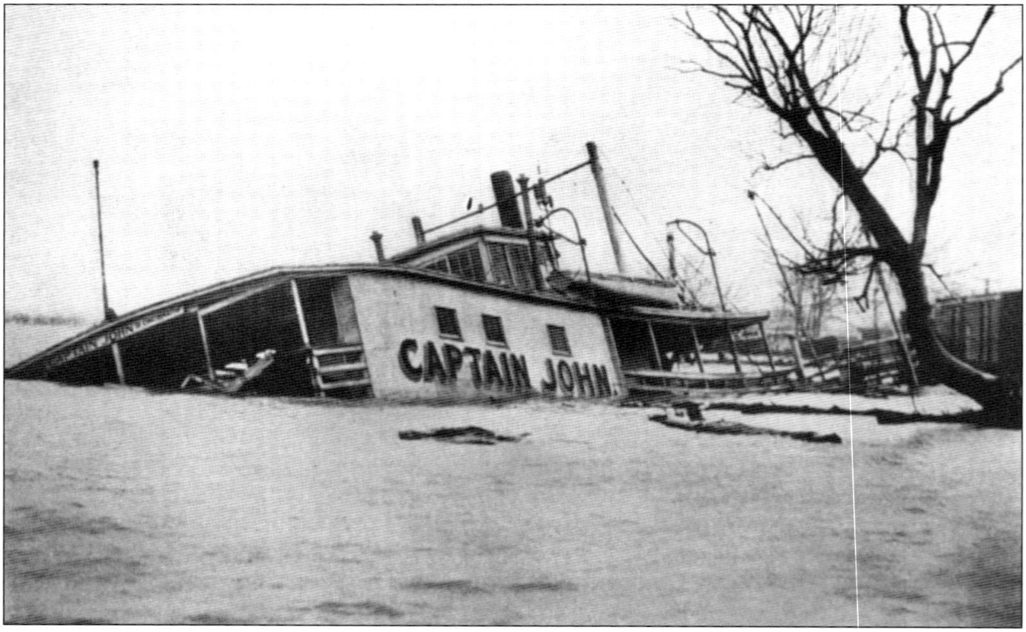

The stern-wheel ferryboat *Captain John* was christened the *Nina Paden* when she was built in 1896 and later was renamed the *City of Ashland* when she began serving passengers there. When Capt. John Davis bought her, he changed her name again. On January 21, 1937, she was ferrying passengers between Portsmouth and West Portsmouth across the flooded Scioto River when she struck a log and sank.

There was no panic in Cincinnati on January 18, 1937, when protracted rain sent the Ohio River past the 52-foot flood stage. But the rain kept falling, and the river kept rising. Ultimately, the flood would crest on Tuesday, January 26, at 79.99 feet, a figure unequaled before or since. Two days before, the city experienced its worst day: Black Sunday, when water faucets went dry, the electricity failed, and fires swept through the city's industrial district.

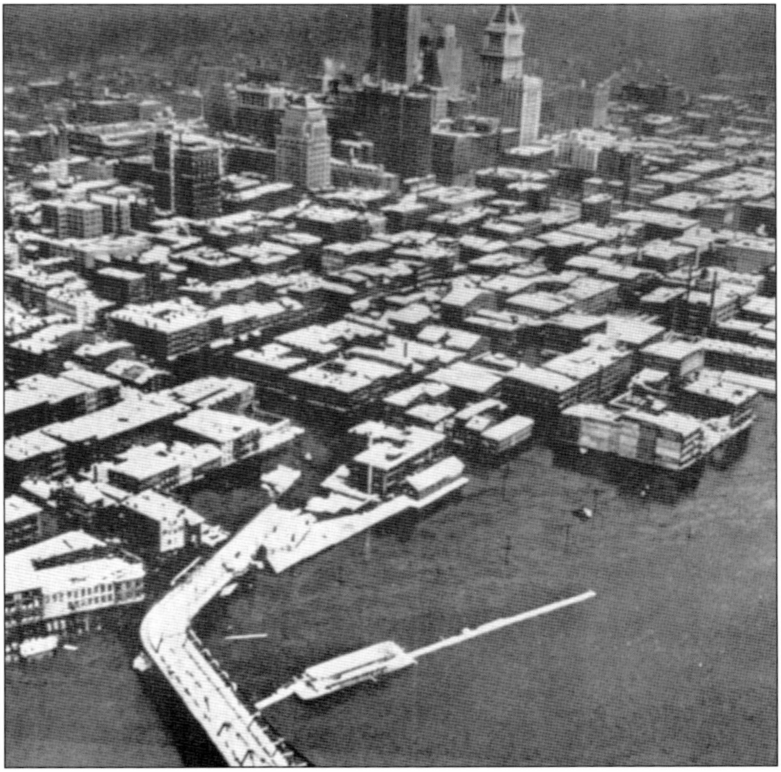

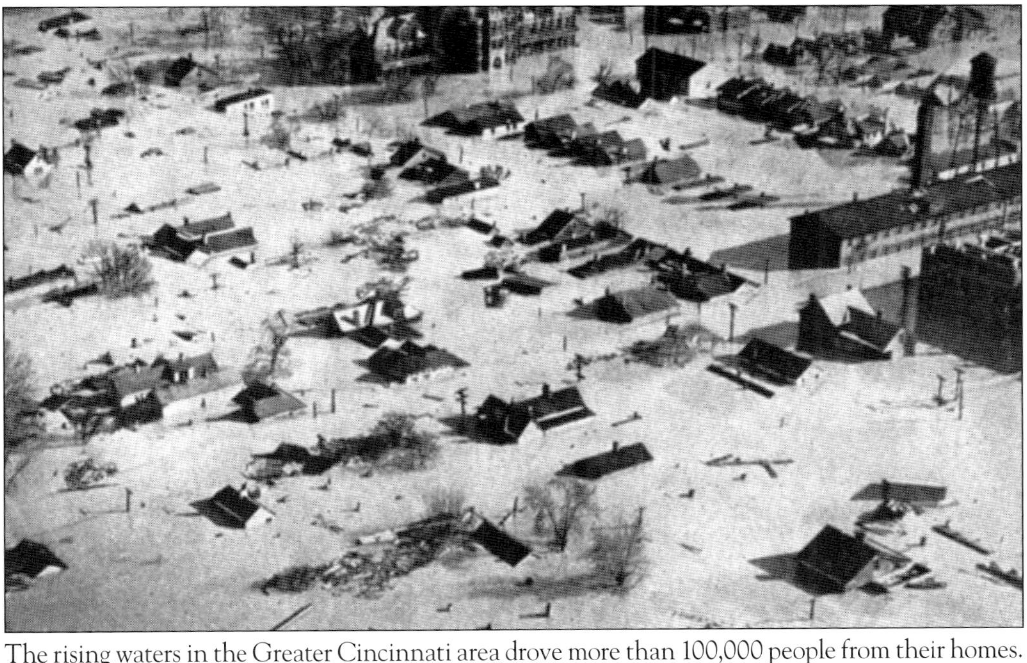

The rising waters in the Greater Cincinnati area drove more than 100,000 people from their homes. The Ohio River would remain above flood stage until February 5. Continuing rain, falling almost steadily day and night, melted the heavy January snow on the ground and rooftops, with the runoff adding to the rising water. It is estimated that one-sixth of Hamilton County was underwater at the flood's peak. Hundreds of homes were washed away or damaged beyond repair.

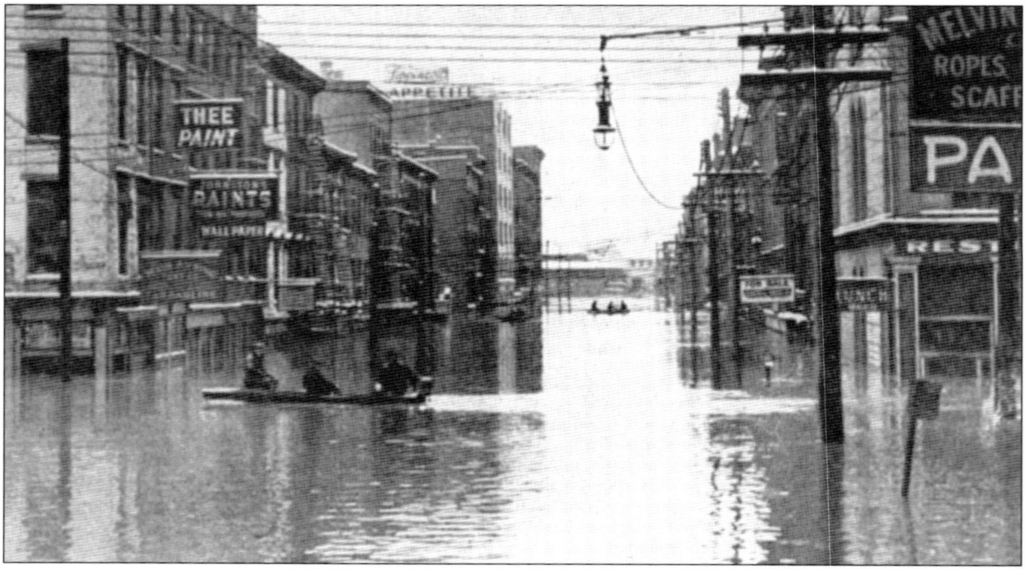

At its peak, the flood turned downtown Cincinnati into a lake, which could be traveled only by boat. All watercraft larger than a rowboat or canoe were requisitioned for rescue or relief work. City officials ordered all businesses and factories closed, an edict that may not have been necessary given that few workers had any way of getting to work. The city was sliced into thirds by water for 19 days.

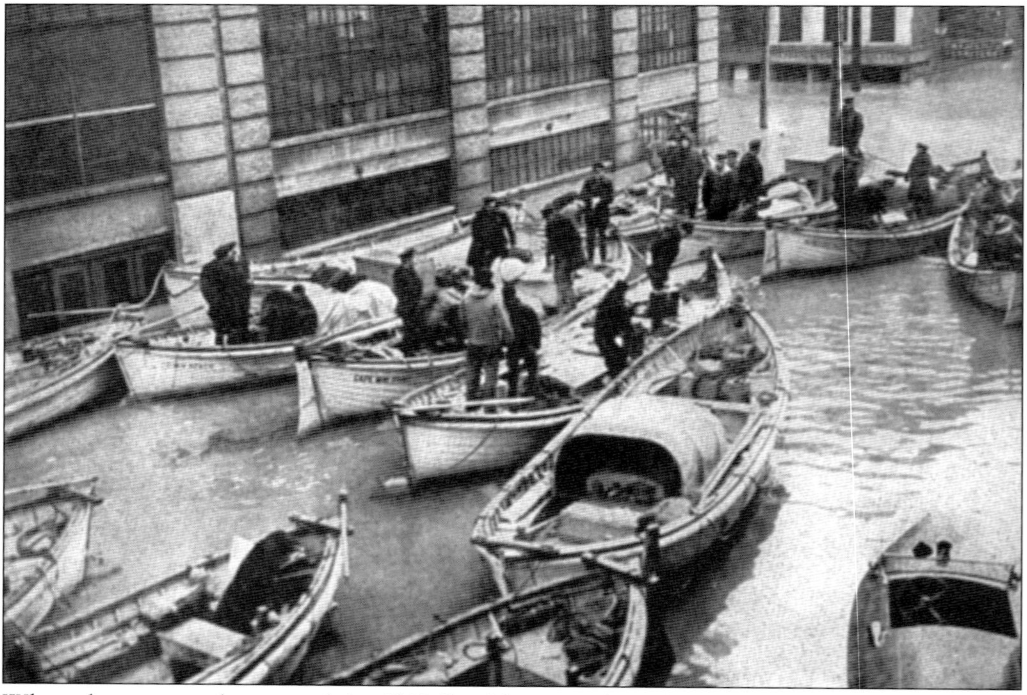

When the mammoth scope of the 1937 flood became clear, the U.S. Coast Guard stripped its Atlantic Coast stations of every boat and able-bodied man that could be spared and rushed them by train to the stricken valley. Here a flotilla of the coast guard craft is assembled at Third and Walnut Streets in Cincinnati. On January 31, the coast guard reported it had 380 boats on duty in the flood zone and 25 others on the way.

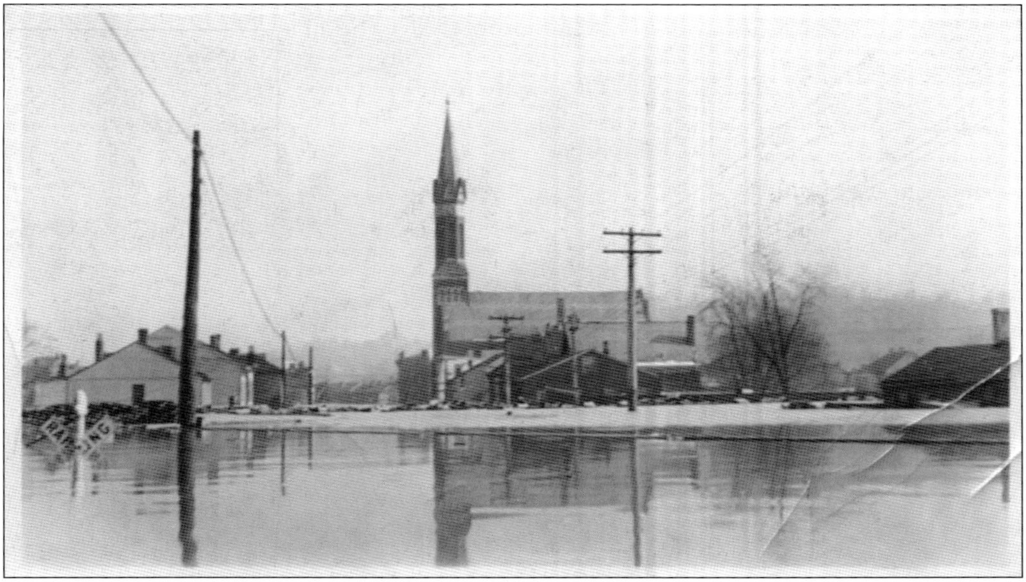

From its headwaters in Butler County, 28-mile-long Mill Creek meanders through the heart of Greater Cincinnati before it empties into the Ohio River. Much of the 1937 flood damage in the city came not from the Ohio River itself, but from a swollen Mill Creek that overflowed its banks. Typical was this flood scene at Cherry and Hoffner Streets looking toward Knowlton's Corner in the city's Northside neighborhood.

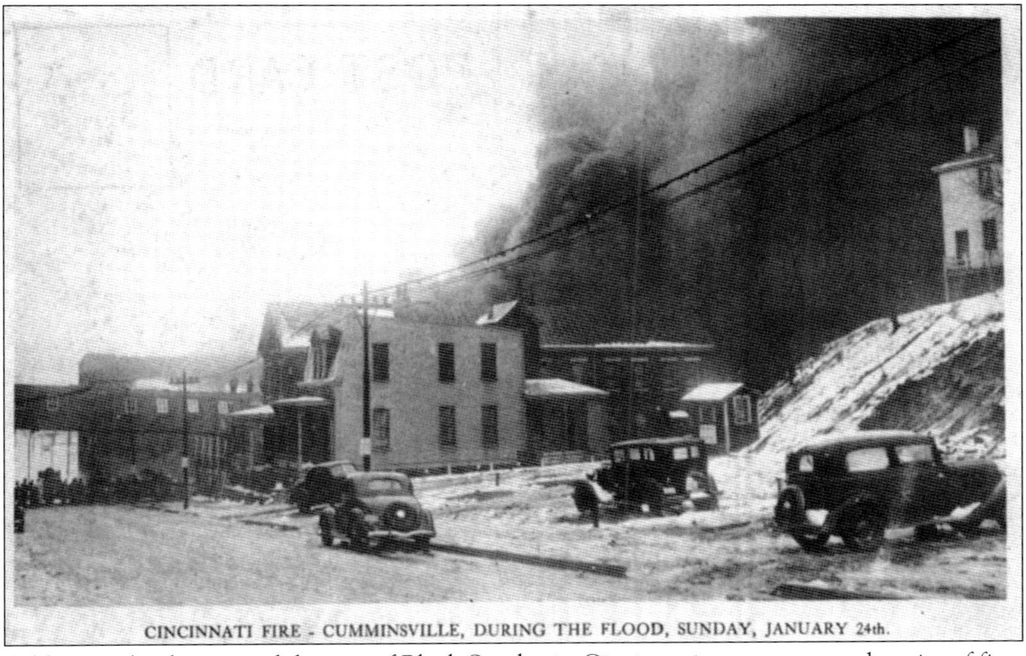

Adding to the danger and disaster of Black Sunday in Cincinnati was a mammoth series of fires that erupted in the Cumminsville industrial district when giant gasoline storage tanks overturned, sending thousands of gallons of fuel into Mill Creek. A stray spark ignited the floating gasoline. The resulting fires, one of which is shown here, took more than 12 hours to put out and burned more than 3.5 square miles. Damage was estimated at $1.5 million.

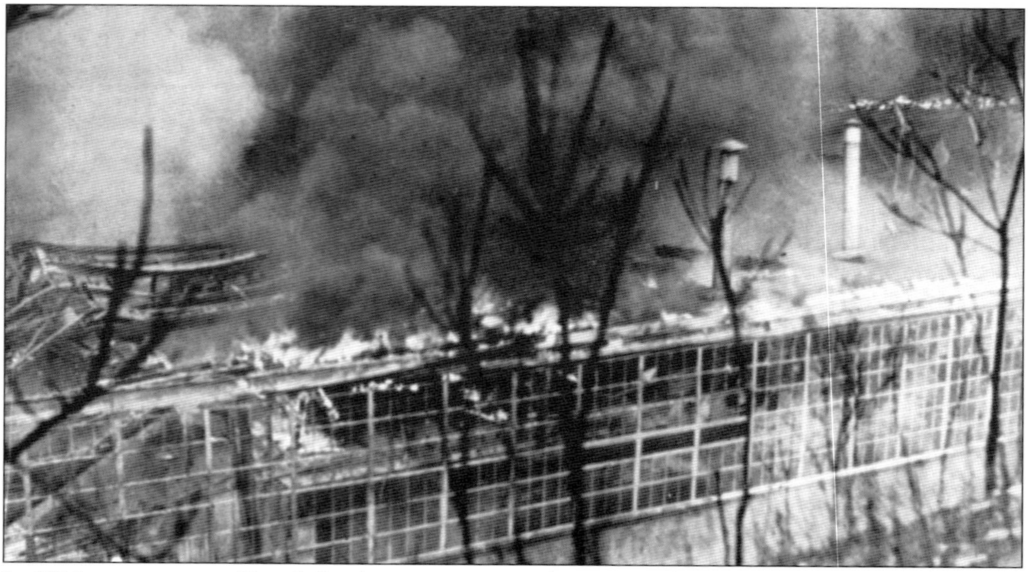

In 1920, entrepreneur Powel Crosley set out to purchase a simple radio set. Shocked by the high prices he found, he decided to build one himself. He did so, and before long he was producing inexpensive radios by the thousands at his Cincinnati plant. A fire broke out in the plant during the 1937 flood and destroyed most of it. Undeterred, Crosley rebuilt and resumed production.

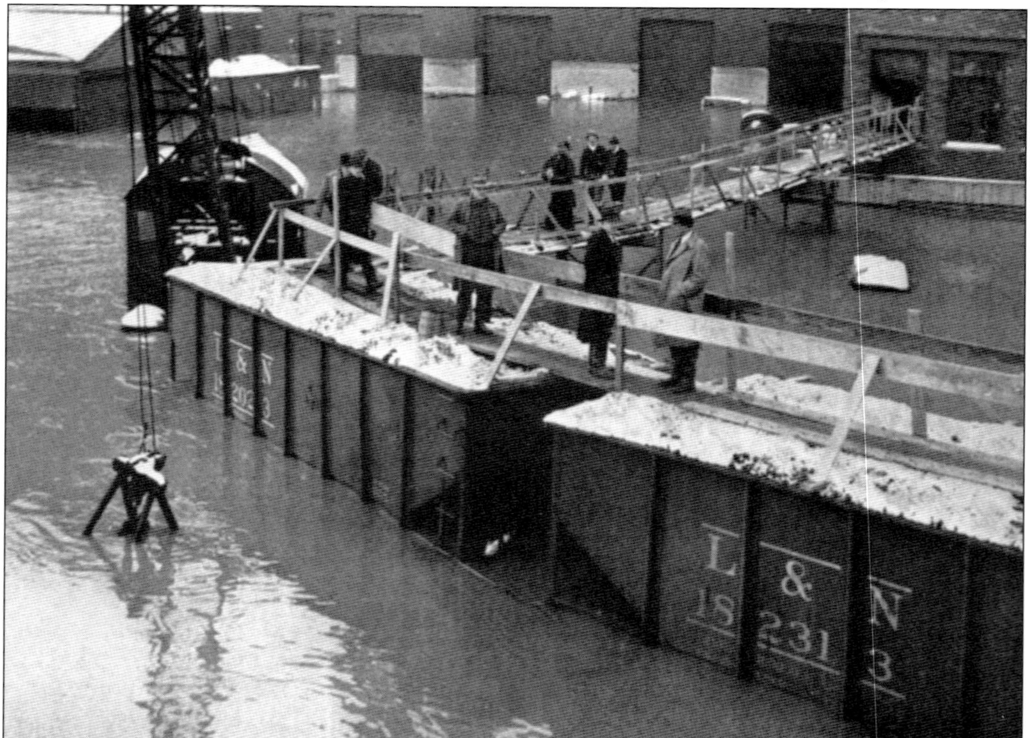

Workers at Cincinnati's power plant are shown leaving work after a long shift. Their only route out of the plant is a temporary bridge built over a string of marooned Louisville and Nashville Railroad coal cars. Workers at the plant labored all day and all night to keep vital electric power flowing to the flood-stricken city. Even so, power had to be rationed.

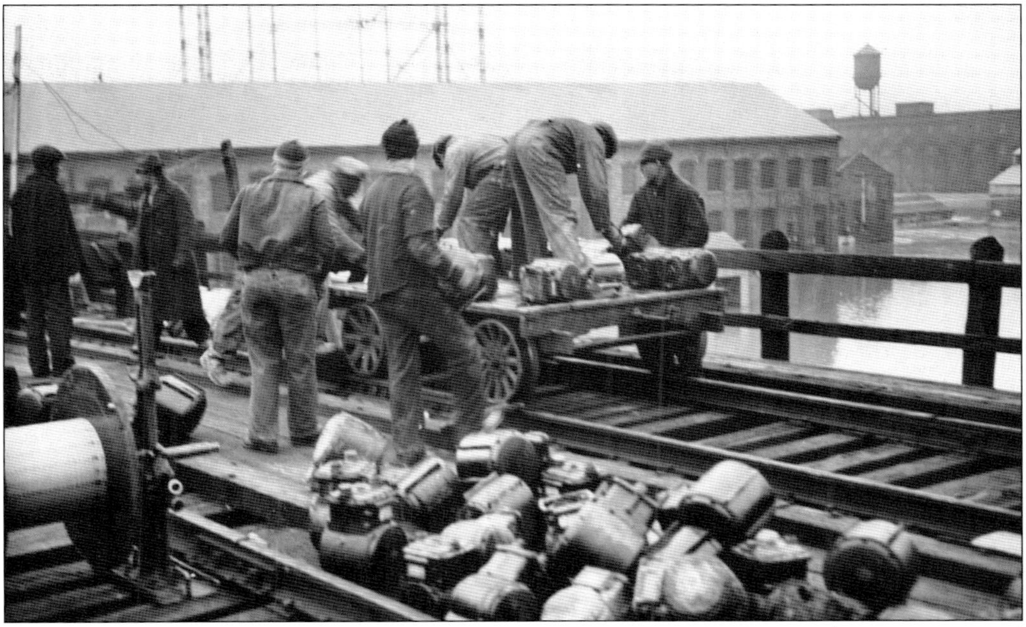

The railroads performed truly remarkable feats during the 1937 flood. Special trains evacuated refugees to higher ground and brought relief supplies to cities cut off by flooded roads. This Chesapeake and Ohio Railway crew in Cincinnati is hard at work loading an unusual cargo—part of 4,000 damaged gas meters being sent off for repair so they will be ready for use when the city's gas service is resumed.

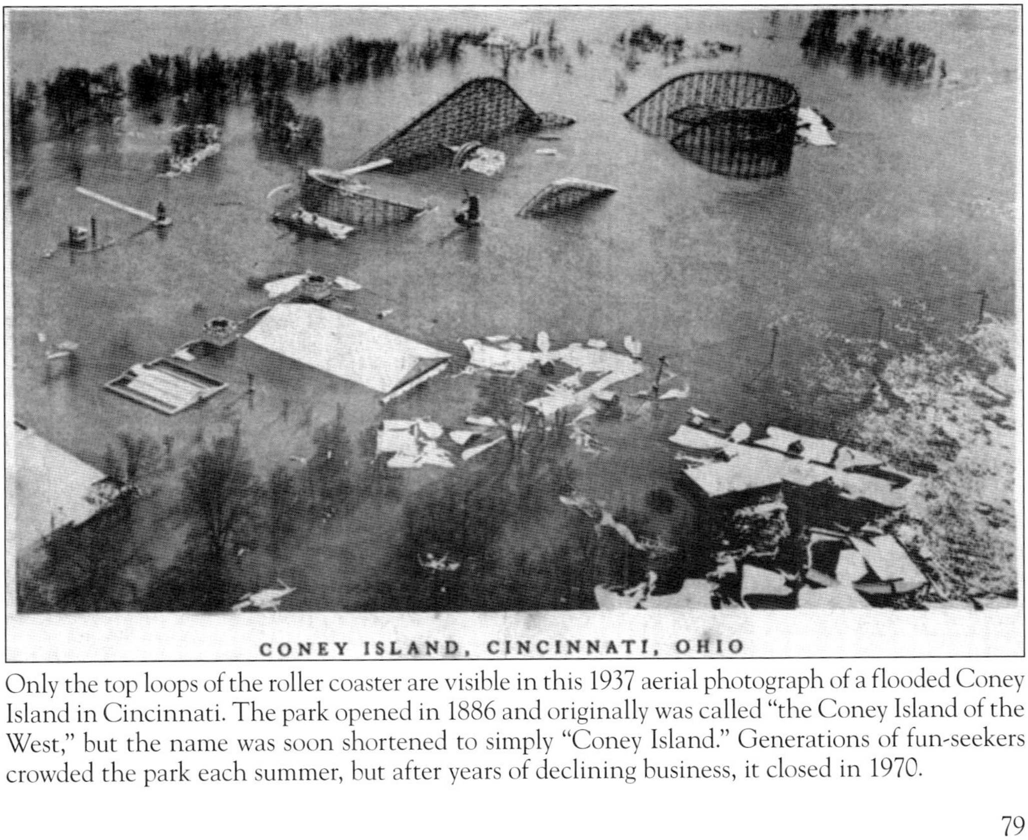

CONEY ISLAND, CINCINNATI, OHIO

Only the top loops of the roller coaster are visible in this 1937 aerial photograph of a flooded Coney Island in Cincinnati. The park opened in 1886 and originally was called "the Coney Island of the West," but the name was soon shortened to simply "Coney Island." Generations of fun-seekers crowded the park each summer, but after years of declining business, it closed in 1970.

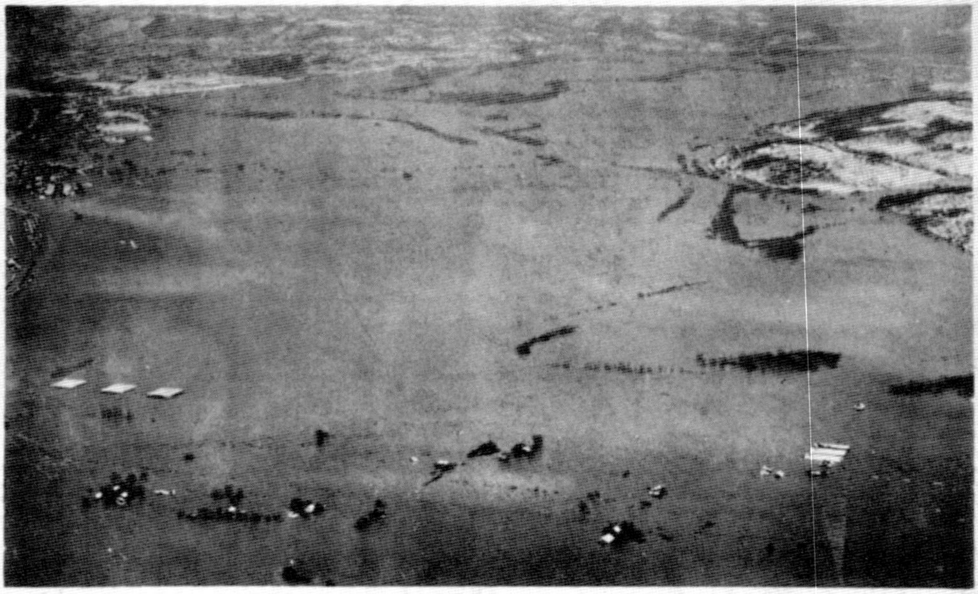

LUNKEN AIRPORT, CINCINNATI, OHIO

Lunken Airport was the center of early aviation in Cincinnati. In 1929, American Airlines had its beginnings there, offering flights to Chicago. The 1937 flood spilled over a nearby levee and inundated the airport, as shown in this aerial view. The airport's location in the flood plain spelled an end to plans for its expansion. In 1946, the airlines pulled out of Lunken and started operations at the Greater Cincinnati Airport in Northern Kentucky.

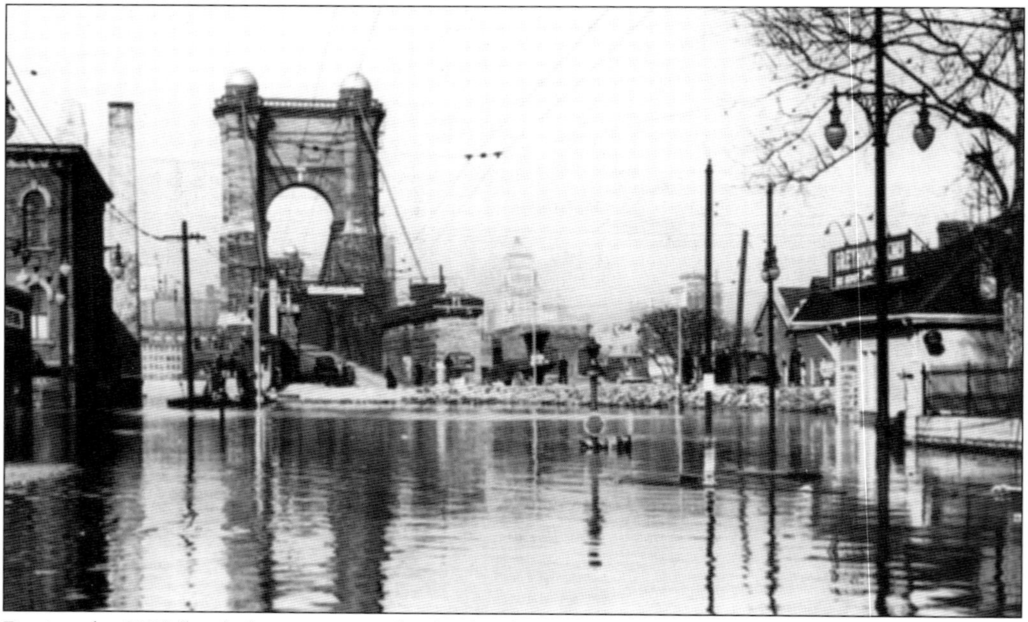

During the 1937 flood, the suspension bridge (at the rear left of this photograph) linking Cincinnati and Covington, Kentucky, was the only river crossing between Stubenville, Ohio, and Cairo, Illinois, that remained open—a distance of more than 800 miles. Designed by famed bridge builder John Roebling, who later designed the Brooklyn Bridge in New York City, the massive bridge first opened to traffic in 1867. Today it has been designated a National Historic Landmark.

Six

KENTUCKY 1937

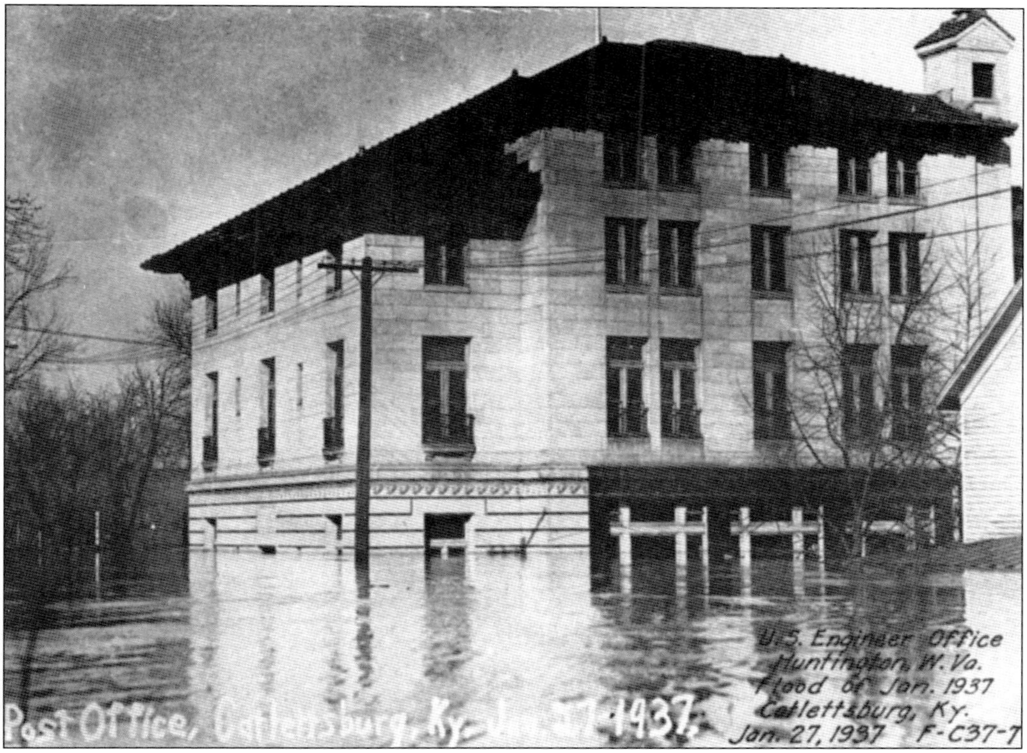

Catlettsburg, the county seat of Boyd County, Kentucky, is located at the confluence of the Ohio and Big Sandy Rivers, just across the Big Sandy from West Virginia. The January 1937 flood inundated 80 percent of the town to an average depth of 17 feet. All normal business activities and utility services were suspended. This view shows the U.S. Post Office in Catlettsburg on January 27, 1937. (Courtesy U.S. Army Corps of Engineers.)

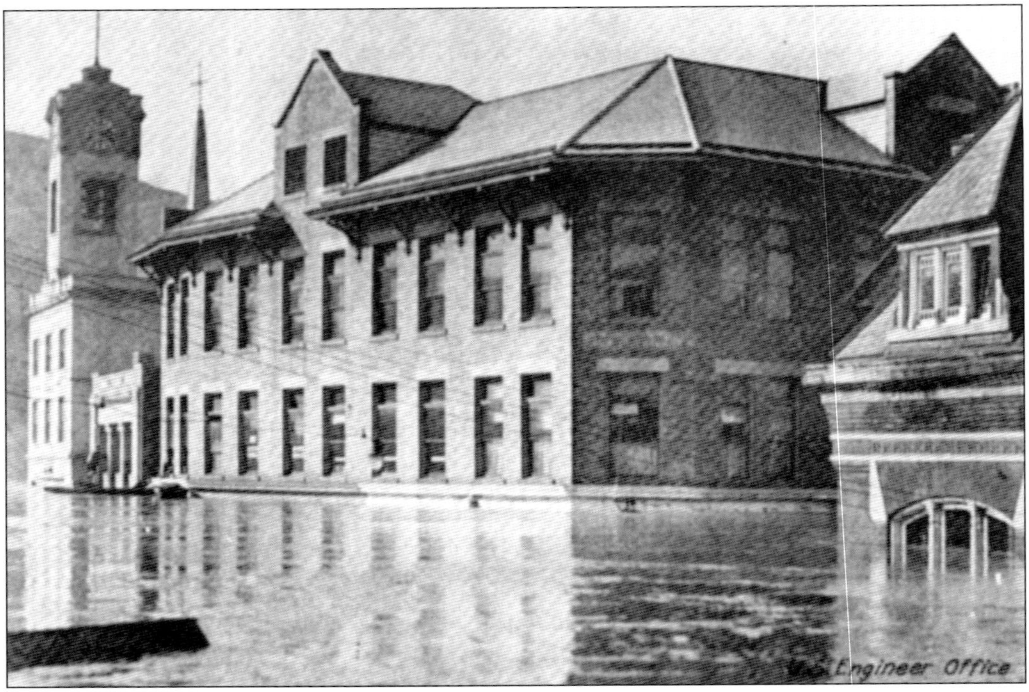

Named for early settlers Alexander Catlett and his son Horatio, early Catlettsburg flourished as a steamboat landing and market city for timber felled on the hillsides and floated down the Big Sandy River to the Ohio River. But by the 1930s, nearby Ashland had long since eclipsed it as the county's largest city and center of commerce. This 1937 photograph shows a flooded Division Street in Catlettsburg. (Courtesy U.S. Army Corps of Engineers.)

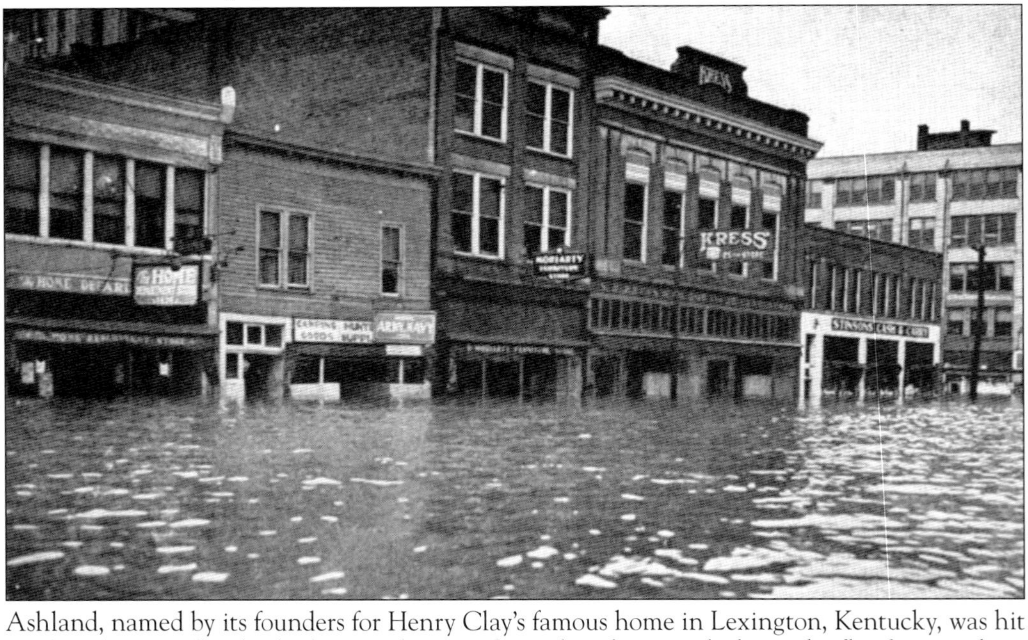

Ashland, named by its founders for Henry Clay's famous home in Lexington, Kentucky, was hit hard by the 1937 flood, which crested at 73.8 feet. This photograph shows the flood scene along Winchester Avenue, one of the major streets in the city's downtown. Old-time residents said they could never remember a previous flood reaching so far into the downtown.

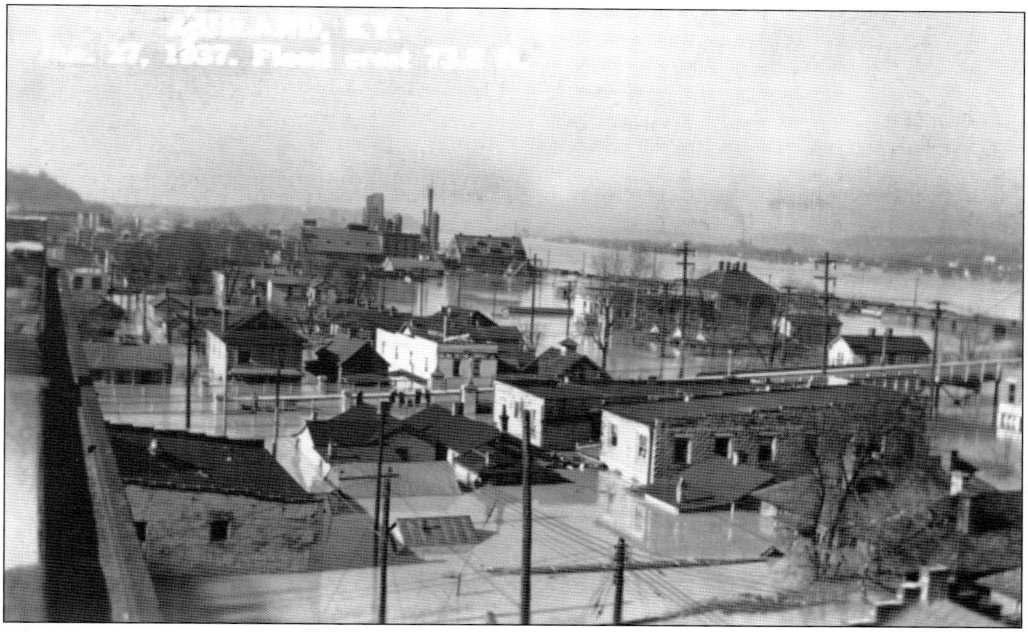

This 1937 view of the flood in Ashland was taken from a downtown rooftop, perhaps that of the now-demolished Ventura Hotel. The edge of the rooftop vantage point can be seen at the left side of the photograph. That is the Ohio River in the distance. At its peak, the flood inundated most of the business district, industrial area, and residential sections of Ashland. (Courtesy Charles R. Nichols.)

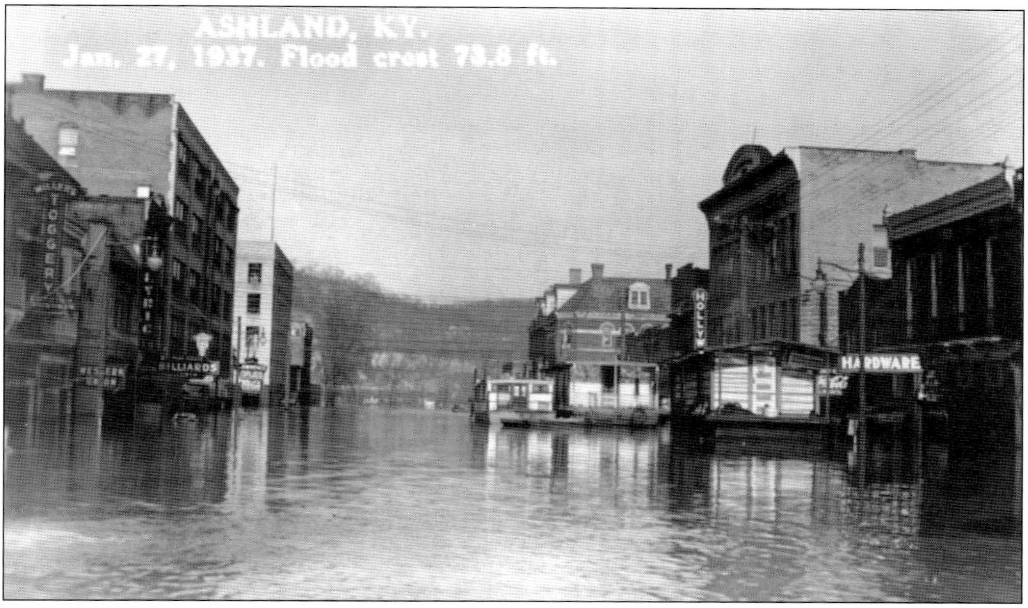

In the hard times of the 1930s, shanty boats along the Ohio River's banks were home to many families, who felt fortunate to have a roof over their heads even if it was not on dry land. The 1937 flood tore several of these makeshift homes from their moorings. They were then swept into downtown Ashland, coming to rest on Sixteenth Street. The photographer who took this picture was facing north, toward the river, with the shanty boats floating at the right. (Courtesy Charles R. Nichols.)

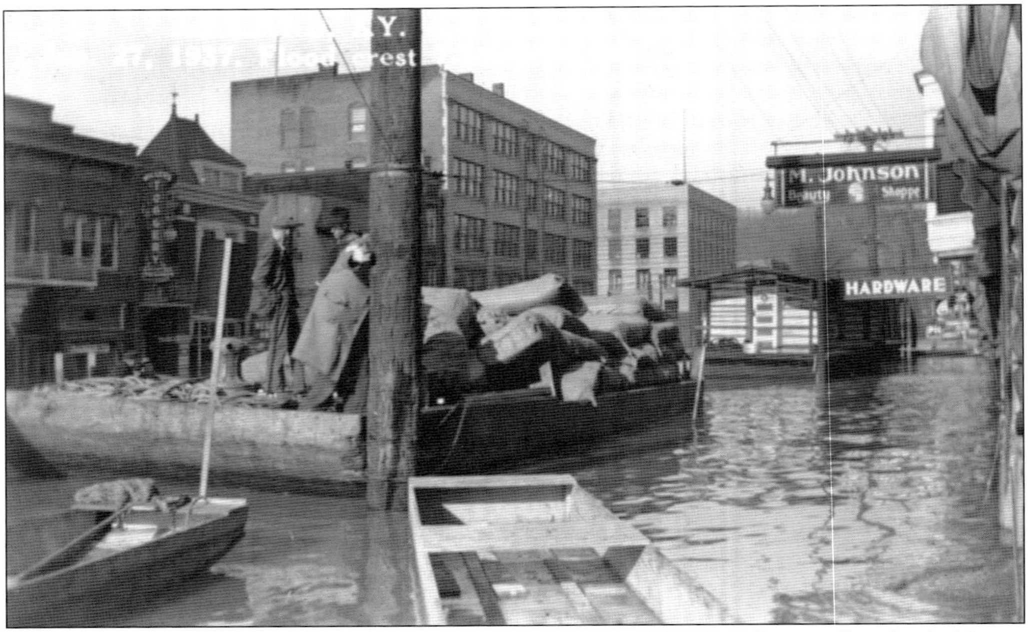

Here is another 1937 view of flooded Sixteenth Street in Ashland, with a sandbag-loaded barge floating in the foreground and a wayward shanty boat in the background, just to the left of the hanging "Hardware" sign. Another hanging sign advertises "M. Johnson Beauty Shoppe." All normal business activities along Sixteenth Street were halted by the high water and then the post-flood cleanup. Significantly, no lives were lost in Ashland because of the flood. (Courtesy Charles R. Nichols.)

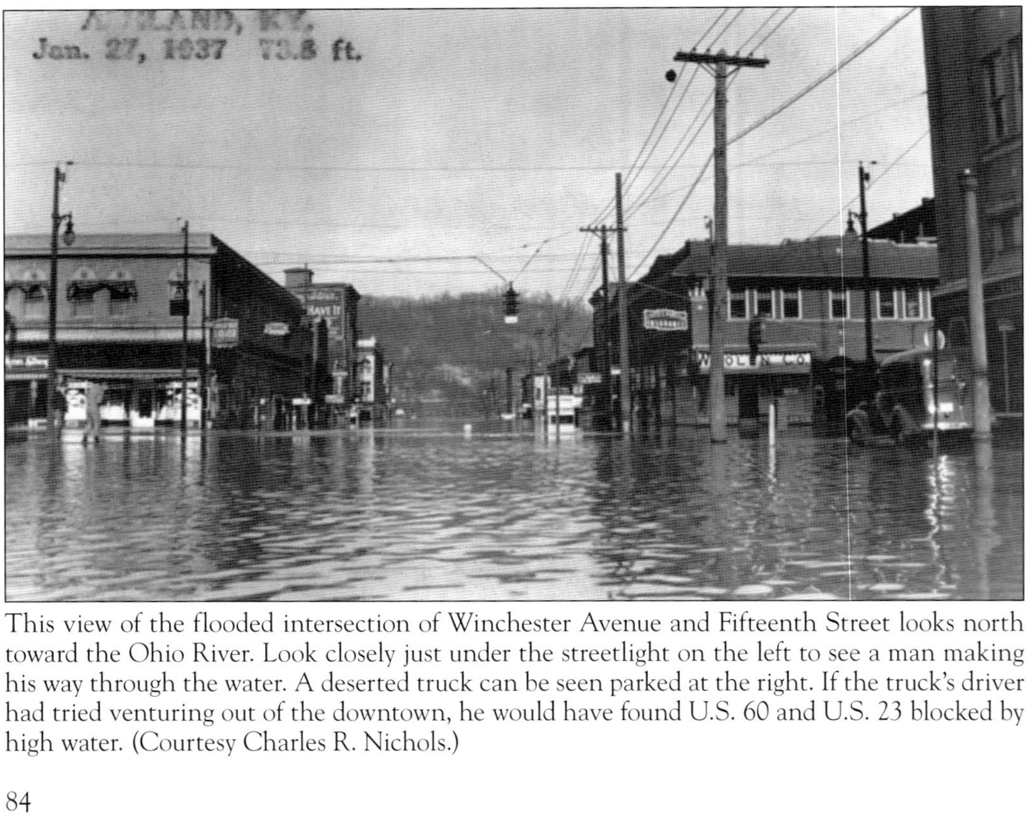

This view of the flooded intersection of Winchester Avenue and Fifteenth Street looks north toward the Ohio River. Look closely just under the streetlight on the left to see a man making his way through the water. A deserted truck can be seen parked at the right. If the truck's driver had tried venturing out of the downtown, he would have found U.S. 60 and U.S. 23 blocked by high water. (Courtesy Charles R. Nichols.)

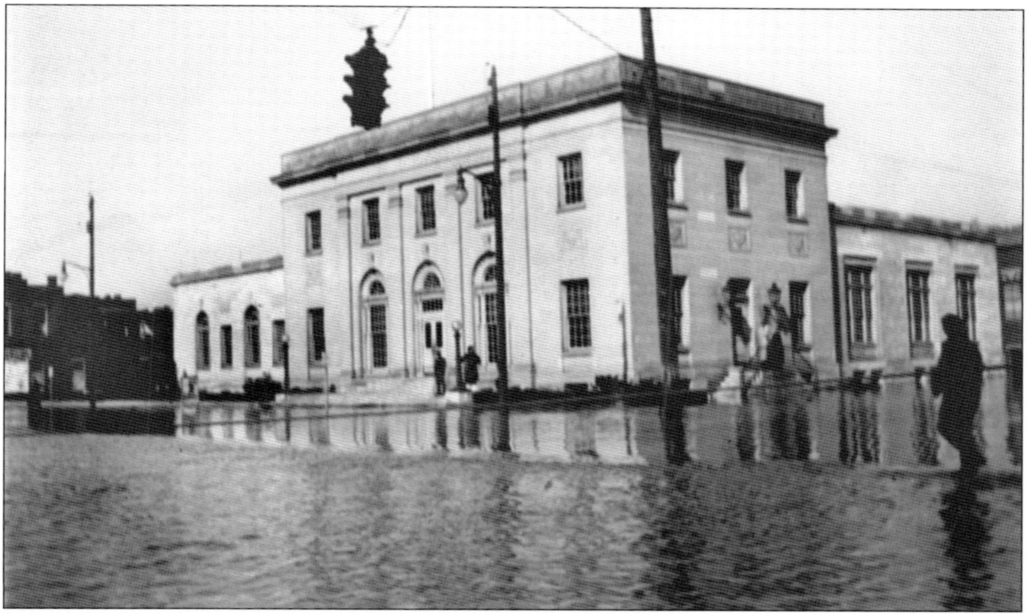

Like the other buildings along Winchester Avenue, the U.S. Post Office on Winchester Avenue was encircled by the 1937 floodwaters. Today the classic old structure is listed on the National Register of Historic Places. Since 2000, it has housed the offices and bookstore of the Jesse Stuart Foundation, "devoted to preserving the human and literary legacy of Jesse Stuart and other Kentucky and Appalachian writers." (Courtesy Charles R. Nichols.)

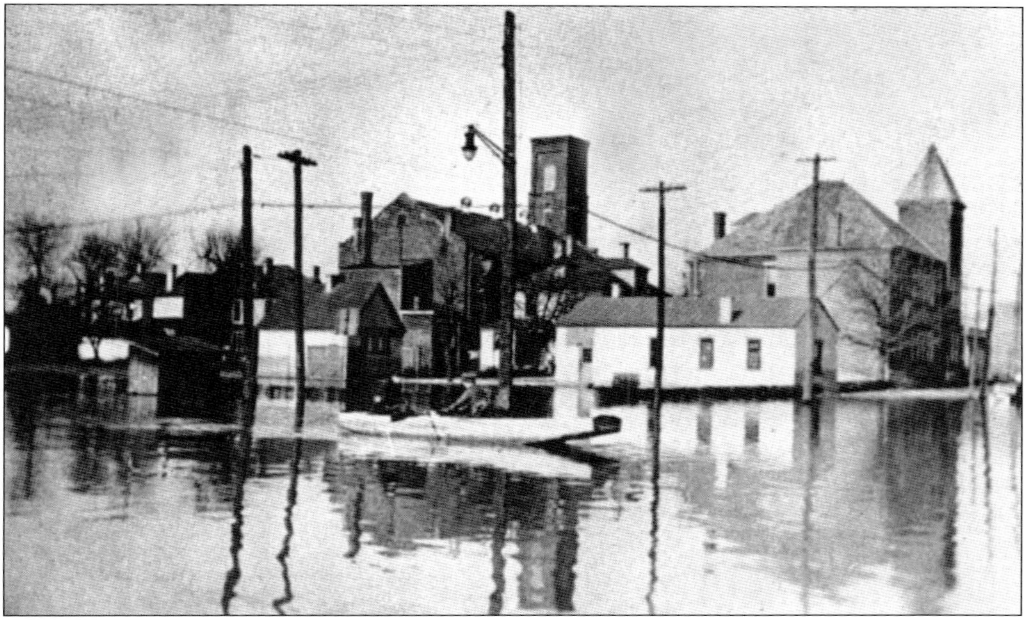

This was the 1937 flood scene looking north from the Chesapeake and Ohio Railway passenger station in Ashland. The station itself escaped flooding, as did the C&O's Sixth Street shops and roundhouse, but the railroad's freight yard and some stretches of its main line were badly flooded. Even so, special C&O trains brought hundreds of flood refuges to Ashland from nearby communities. (Courtesy U.S. Army Corps of Engineers.)

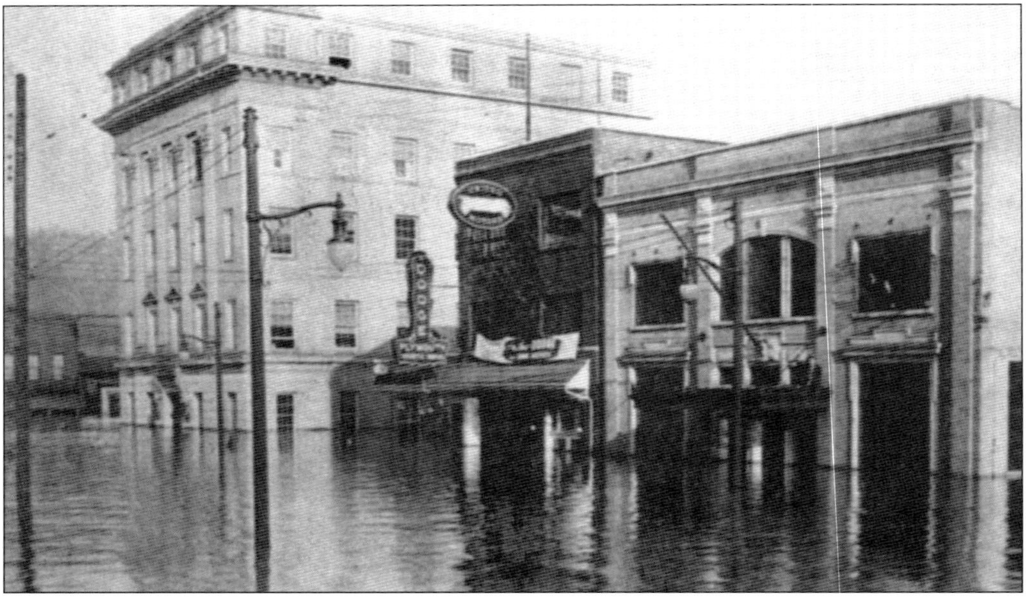

The building at the right in this photograph has housed Ashland's newspaper, the *Independent*, since 1902. It stands just a couple of blocks north of the Ohio River and so was badly flooded in 1937, the only time publication of the paper was suspended. Until local operations could resume, the *Independent* was printed on the presses of the *Big Sandy News* in Louisa, Kentucky. At left is the Ashland City Building. (Courtesy U.S. Army Corps of Engineers.)

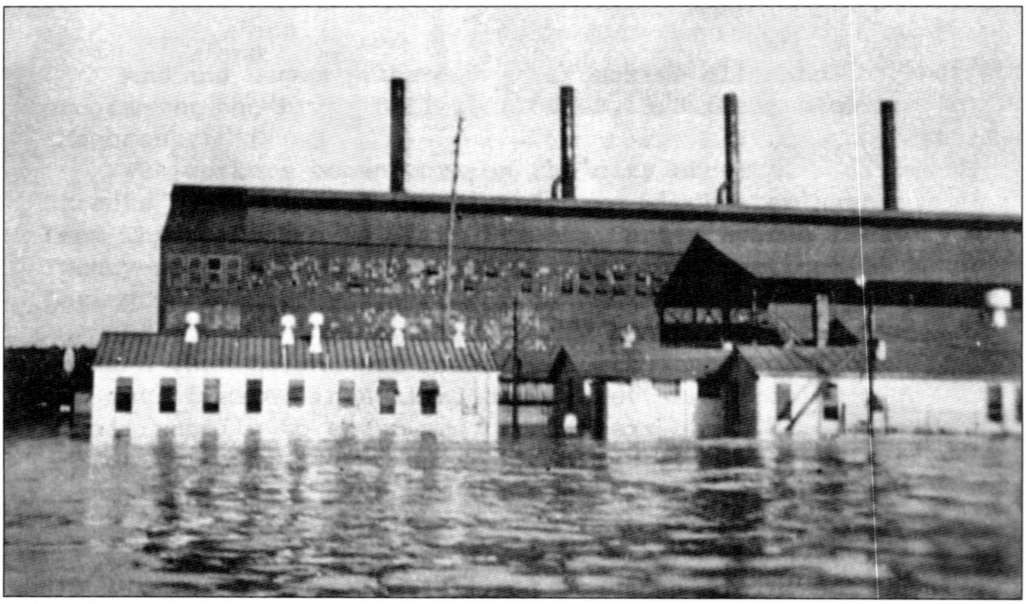

When the 1937 floodwaters reached the American Rolling Mills (ARMCO) plant, the giant steel maker was forced to suspend operations, idling 3,200 workers. Today the company, long a major employer in Ashland, is part of AK Steel. The 1937 flood also disrupted work at the coke plant operated by Allied Chemical and Dye's Semet Solvay Division and the Ashland Oil and Refining Company refinery in Catlettsburg. (Courtesy U.S. Army Corps of Engineers.)

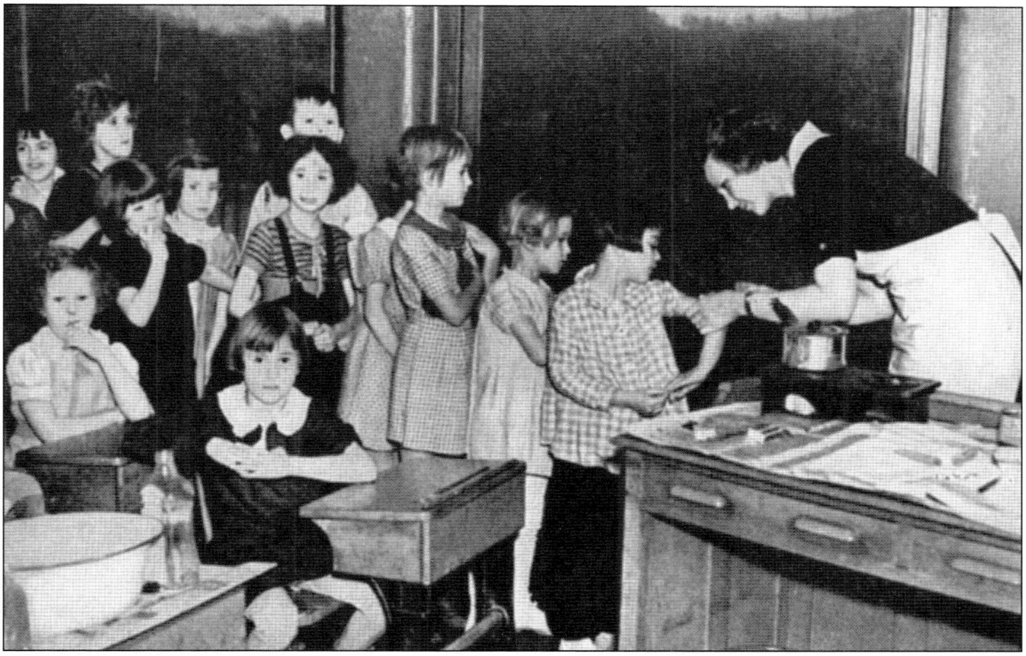

Once the floodwaters receded, Boyd County health officials warned that residents could not return to their flooded homes until the dwellings had been inspected and approved. Officials also urged all citizens to get typhoid inoculations. When their classes resumed, youngsters such as these at this Ashland school were inoculated.

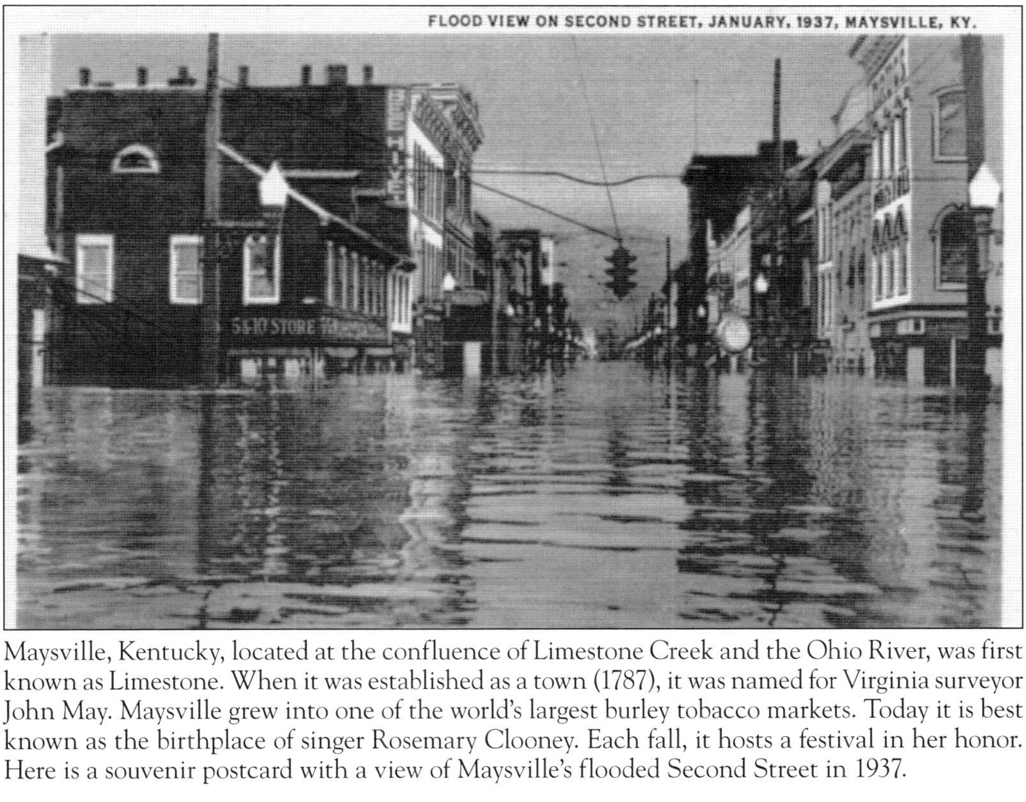

Maysville, Kentucky, located at the confluence of Limestone Creek and the Ohio River, was first known as Limestone. When it was established as a town (1787), it was named for Virginia surveyor John May. Maysville grew into one of the world's largest burley tobacco markets. Today it is best known as the birthplace of singer Rosemary Clooney. Each fall, it hosts a festival in her honor. Here is a souvenir postcard with a view of Maysville's flooded Second Street in 1937.

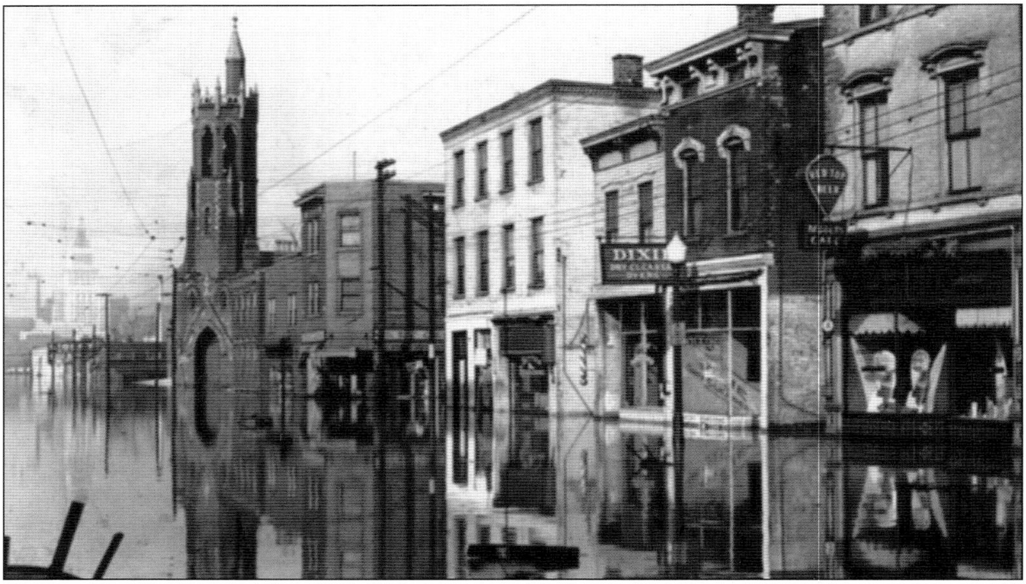

Covington, the largest city in Northern Kentucky, stands just across the Ohio River from Cincinnati and is built primarily on a flat plain. Thus, its streets were quickly flooded when the Ohio left its banks in 1937. Here is a view of flooded Madison Avenue. U.S. Coast Guard crews and boats from New Jersey and northern Illinois reported for rescue duty and then, once the worst crisis was over, moved on down the river to stricken Louisville.

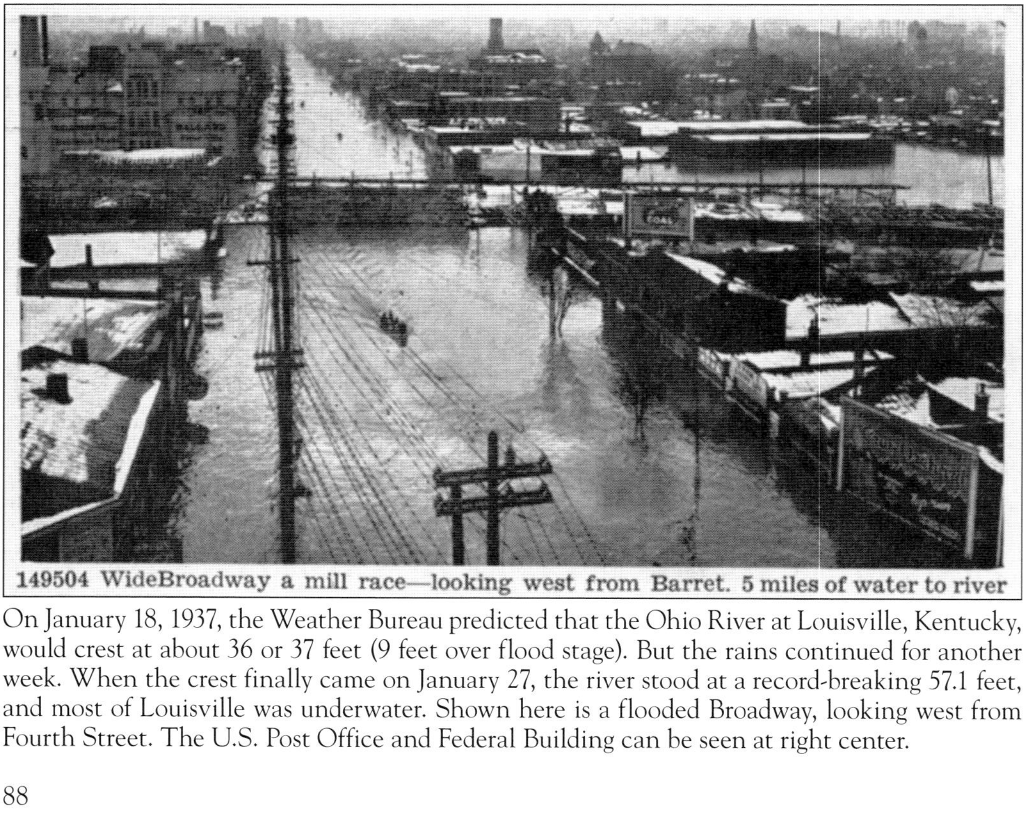

On January 18, 1937, the Weather Bureau predicted that the Ohio River at Louisville, Kentucky, would crest at about 36 or 37 feet (9 feet over flood stage). But the rains continued for another week. When the crest finally came on January 27, the river stood at a record-breaking 57.1 feet, and most of Louisville was underwater. Shown here is a flooded Broadway, looking west from Fourth Street. The U.S. Post Office and Federal Building can be seen at right center.

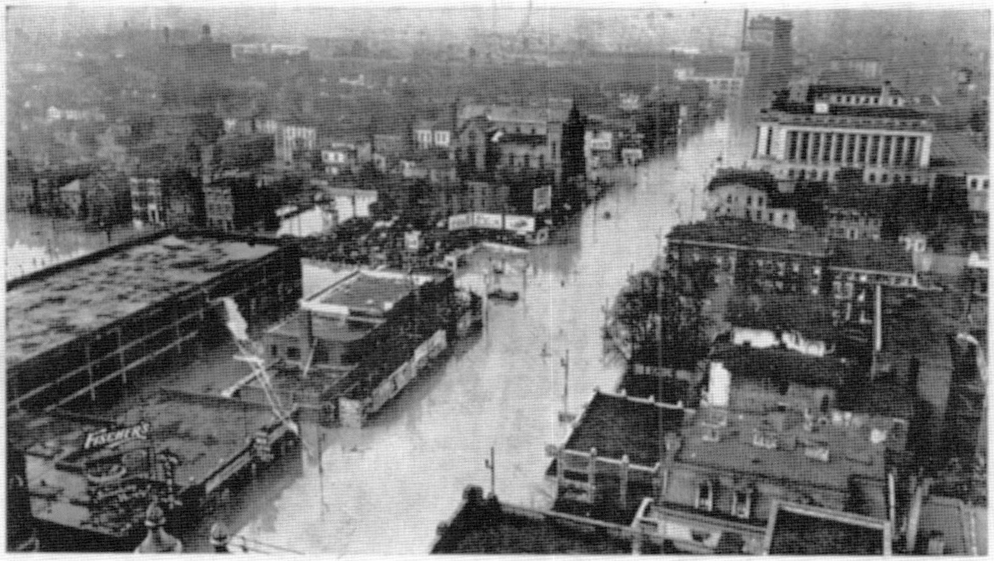

149501 Broadway looking west from Brown Hotel to L. & N. Railroad offices

Originally known as Dunkirk Road and later as Prather Street, Broadway grew longer and wider as the city of Louisville expanded south from the Ohio River. Over the years, it became the southern terminus of the business district, which stretched along Fourth Street. This 1937 view of a flooded Broadway was taken looking west from Barret Avenue. From here, it was a watery five miles to the river.

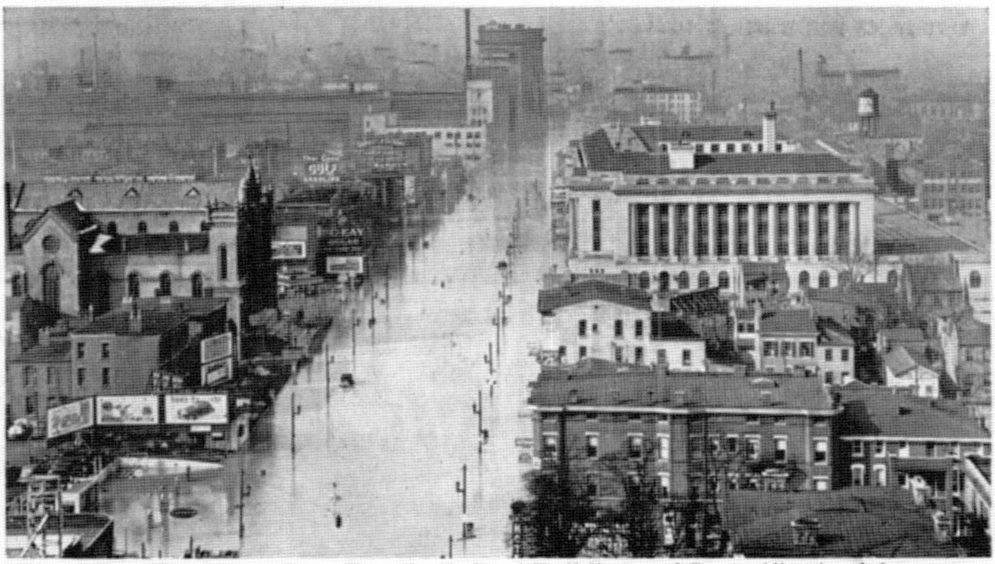

149685 Broadway west from Fourth, Federal Building and Post office in right center

This view of the flooded Broadway was taken looking west from Louisville's historic Brown Hotel on the northeast corner of Fourth Street and Broadway. In the distance is the mammoth building that housed the offices of the Louisville and Nashville Railroad Company (L&N). In the 1930s, more than 2,000 L&N employees worked there. As the floodwaters rose, special L&N trains shuttled refugees from the flooded downtown to the city's dry neighborhoods.

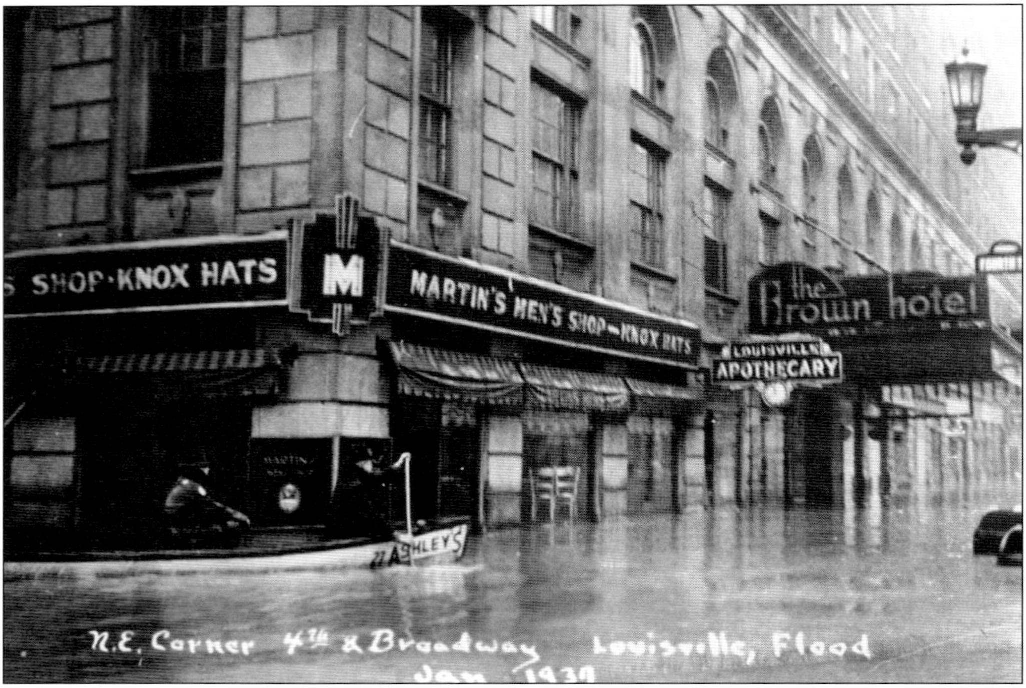

Louisville's rising floodwaters trapped 300 guests and 50 employees at the Brown Hotel. It would be more than a week before they could safely leave. One of the bellboys caught a fish in the hotel lobby while sitting on the stairs. Owner J. Graham Brown had the fish mounted and hung on the wall of the hotel grill.

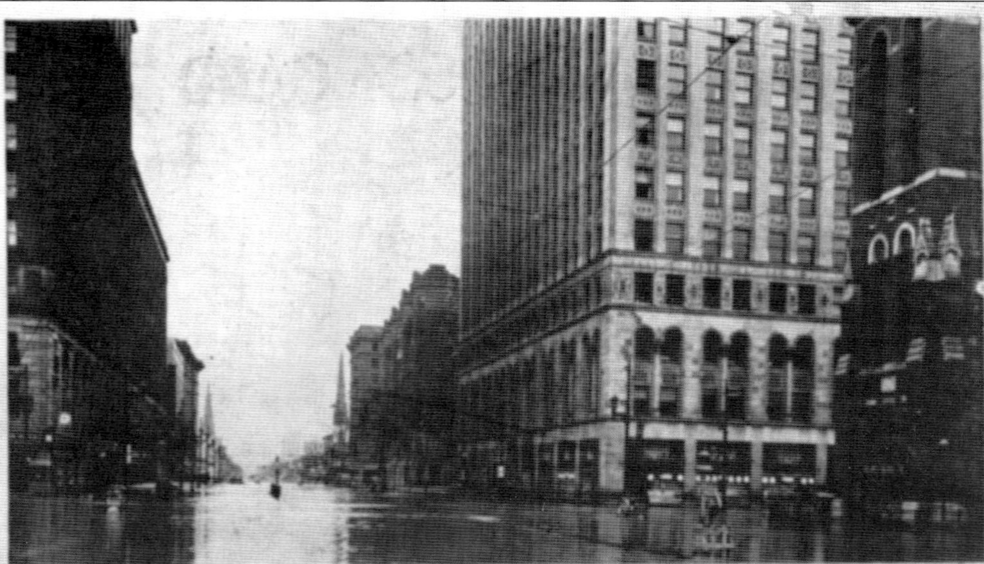

149512 Broadway looking east from Fourth Avenue. Heyburn Building in foreground

This is a view of the flooded Broadway looking east from Fourth Street, one of downtown Louisville's busiest thoroughfares. The large building at right is the Heyburn Building. Completed in 1928, the 17-story classic revival–style structure was built by William R. Heyburn, president of the Belknap Hardware and Manufacturing Company. (For a view of the flooded Belknap warehouse, see page 95.)

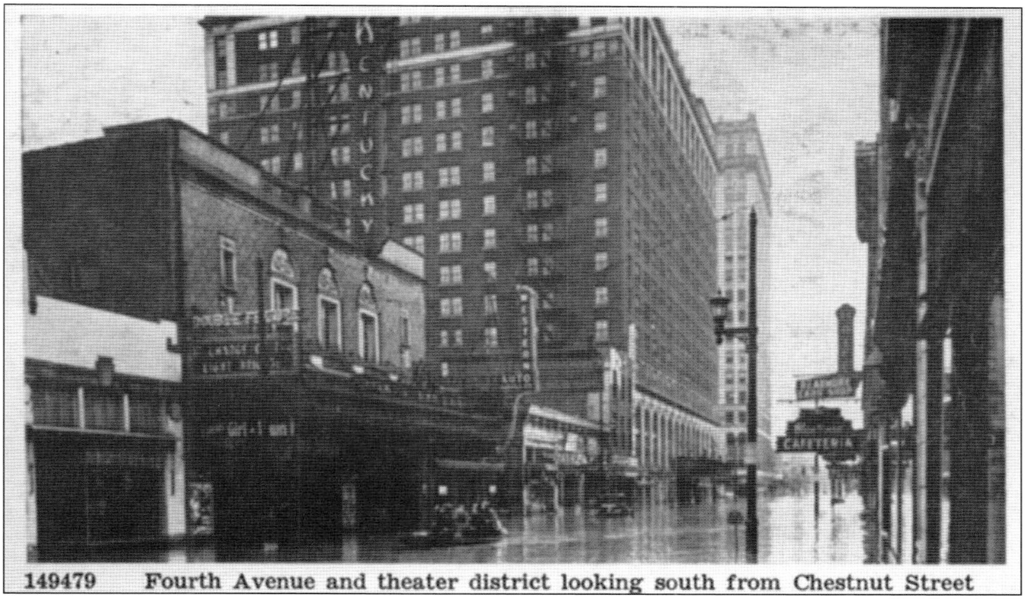

In this photograph, a loaded boat can be seen making its way past the Kentucky Theater, one of many movie palaces that once lined Louisville's Fourth Street. Built in 1921 in the ornate classic revival style, the theater had a lobby with a large chandelier and two perfumed fountains, and an auditorium with a stained-glass skylight. By the 1970s, the once-grand theater had fallen on hard times and was showing mostly horror movies and "kick flicks." It closed in 1981.

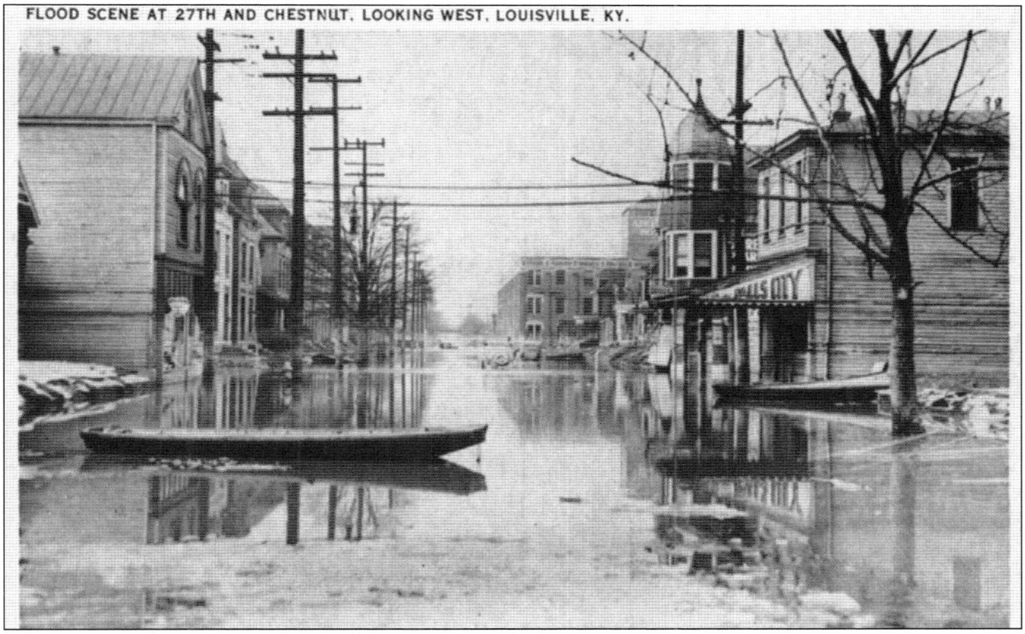

An unattended skiff floats in the flooded intersection of Twenty-seventh and Chestnut Streets. A sign on the building at right, presumably a saloon, advertises Falls City beer. Beer was brewed in Louisville from the city's earliest days, and it once was home to a dozen or more breweries. Falls City, founded in 1905, grew to become Kentucky's largest brand, but, like other small brewers across the country, it could not compete with the big national brands and was forced to close in 1978.

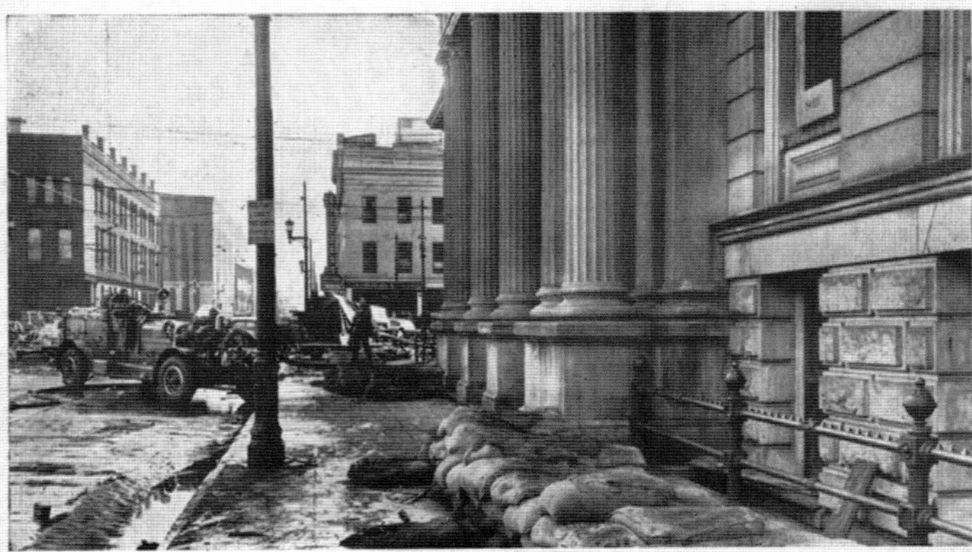

149475 City Hall sand-bagged to protect fire, police and telephone lines for rescue work

At Louisville City Hall, the headquarters of all rescue and relief activities during the flood, a sandbag barrier had to be erected to protect it from rising floodwaters. Note the vintage fire truck at the left of this picture. Louisville mayor Neville Miller was widely praised for his efforts in preparing the city for the flood and then skillfully managing the relief work.

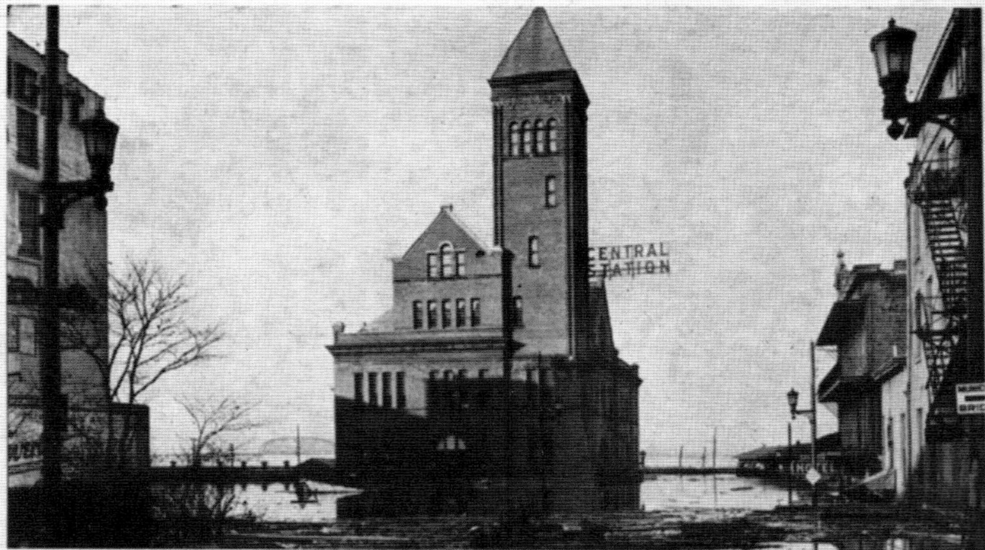

149476 Central Railroad Station isolated, train sheds under water

From the mid-1880s until the 1960s, Louisville was served by two large railroad stations—Union Station at Tenth Street and Broadway and Central Station at Seventh Street and River Road. In its peak years, Central Station (shown here surrounded by high water) handled as many as 40 trains a day. By 1961, the Chesapeake and Ohio Railway (C&O) operated the only two trains still serving the station. In 1963, the C&O shifted those to Union Station. Central Station was demolished in 1968.

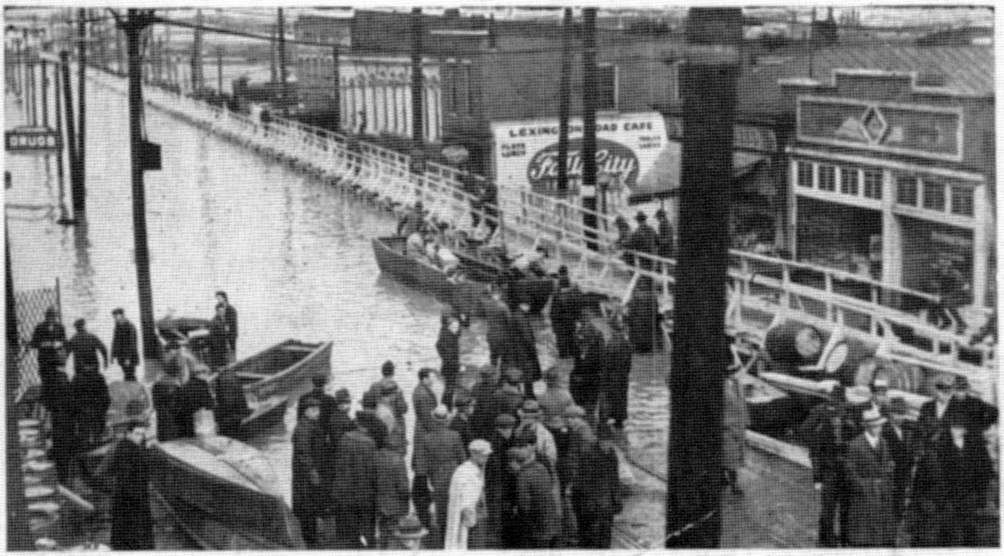

149543½ Pontoon Bridge over Beargrass Creek at Baxter Avenue

As the Louisville floodwaters rose, an improvised pontoon bridge was constructed across Beargrass Creek. Built by a small army of volunteers under the direction of William S. Arrasmith, a local architect and captain in the U.S. Army Reserves, the makeshift bridge was fashioned from planks laid on top of whiskey barrels taken from one of the local distilleries. The 2,000-foot-long span enabled hundreds of refugees to climb out of the busy rescue boats and walk to nearby dry land.

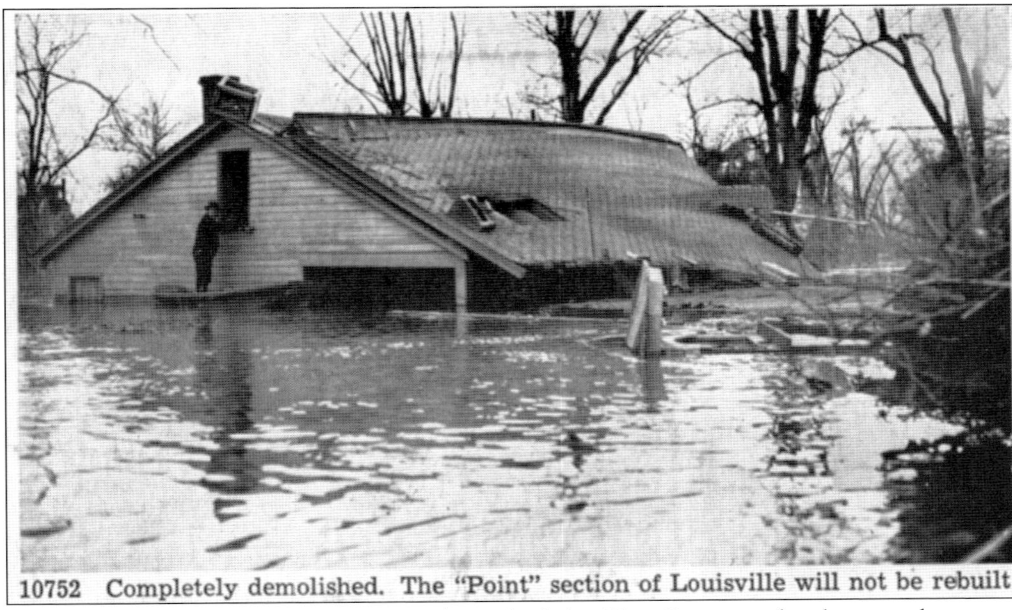

10752 Completely demolished. The "Point" section of Louisville will not be rebuilt

Originally, the mouth of Beargrass Creek reached the Ohio River in what became downtown Louisville, with the creek and the river forming a narrow peninsula. After the creek was cut off, the lower creek bed was filled in, while the upper part became known as "the Point." Beset by recurrent flooding, the area was mostly one of small cottages, such as this one, wrecked by the 1937 flood. Ultimately, the city ruled the area unsafe for residential use and turned a portion of it into a park.

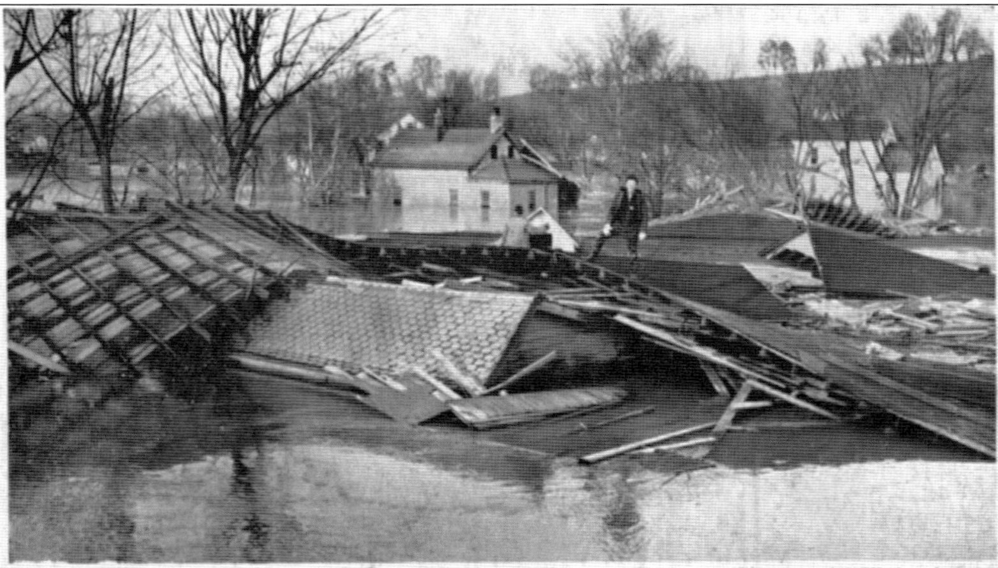

10763 Shippingport wreckage. This part of Louisville will be "parked" in future

In 1820, Shippingport, located on a peninsula of land at the Lower Falls of the Ohio River just downstream from Louisville, boasted 500 residents. But the digging of the Louisville and Portland Canal (1828) turned the town into an island regularly flooded by the Ohio River. Only a few hardy residents remained when the 1937 flood hit, demolishing this house and others. Finally, in the 1950s, expansion at the McAlpine Locks and Dam erased the last sign of the little town.

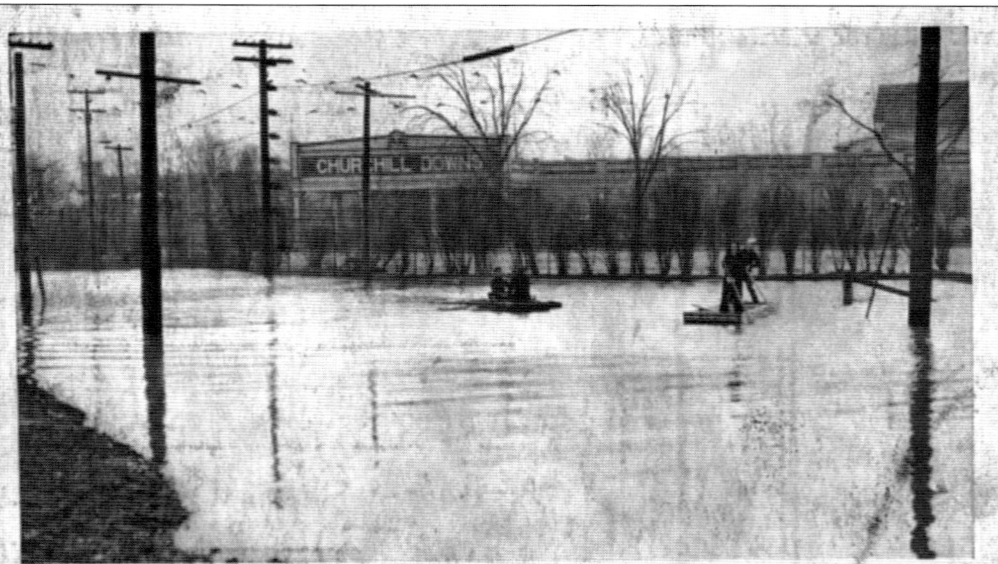

10796 Central Avenue and famous Churchill Downs, offices and track, submerged

Two rafts are paddled along Louisville's water-filled Central Avenue. In the background, behind the trees, is famed Churchill Downs. The 1937 flooding submerged both the Churchill Downs offices and the track, since 1875 the home of the country's best-known horse racing event, the Kentucky Derby. Local legend has it that some venturesome types staged boat races on the flooded track. Despite the flood damage, come May, the track was ready for that year's derby.

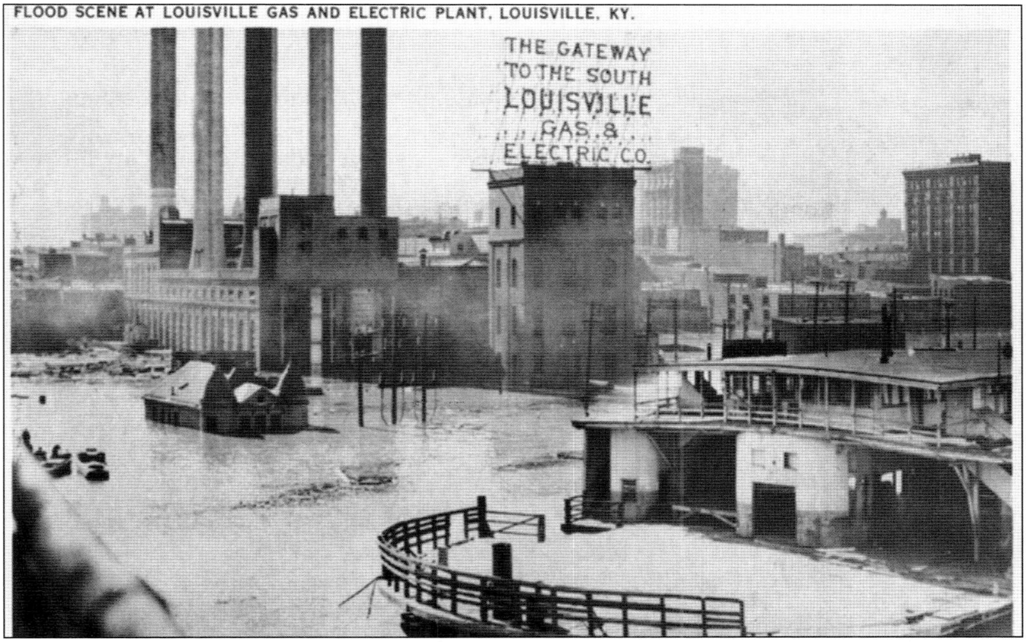

FLOOD SCENE AT LOUISVILLE GAS AND ELECTRIC PLANT, LOUISVILLE, KY.

Both Louisville Gas and Electric Company generating plants were knocked out of service by the rising water. But once the floodwaters began falling, the company's employees worked around the clock, many of them sleeping in the crippled plants, and in less than six weeks had both generators back on-line. Though vastly reduced, some gas service was maintained during the flood.

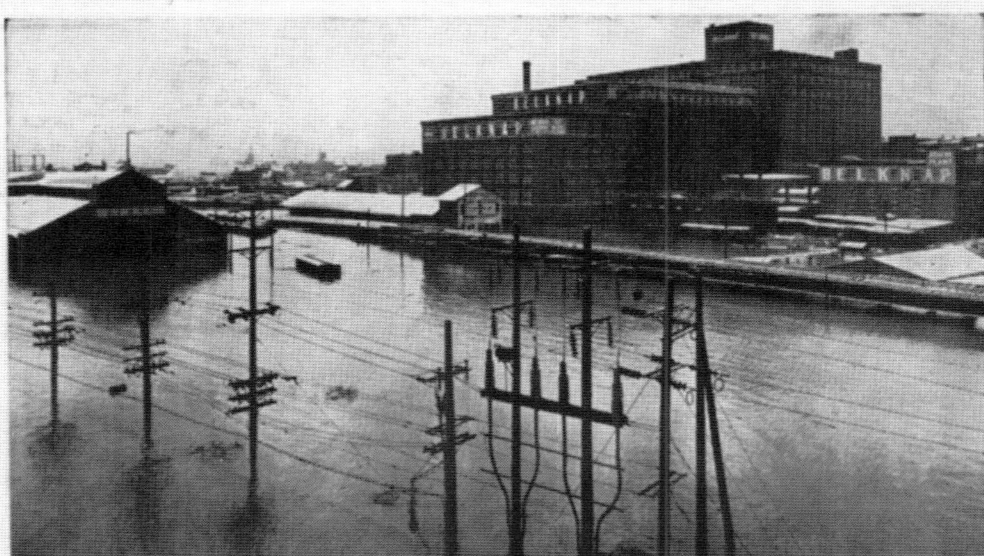

149509 One block from Ohio river. Power cables, tension wires submerged in foreground

The Louisville and Nashville Railroad's Campbell Street Warehouse, at left, stood just one block from the Ohio River and so was quickly submerged by the flooding. In the background is the multi-building warehouse complex operated by the Belknap Hardware and Manufacturing Company. Its lower floors were also flooded. Founded in 1840, Belknap was once the largest hardware wholesaler in the world, but years of financial troubles forced it to close its doors in 1986.

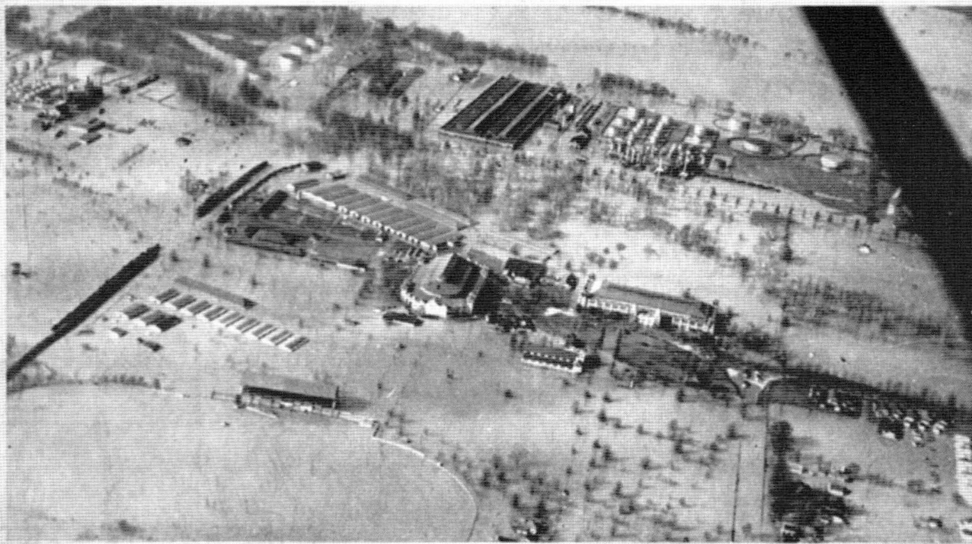

149533 State Fair Grounds, Refining Company, Ford plant in top center

This aerial view of the flooding in the southwestern corner of Louisville shows the old Kentucky State Fairgrounds and, at top center, the Ford Motor Company auto plant at 1400 South Western Parkway. Designed to produce 400 vehicles a day, the Ford plant employed more than 1,000 workers. Nine feet of water flooded the plant, forcing it to close for 60 days while crews repaired the damage.

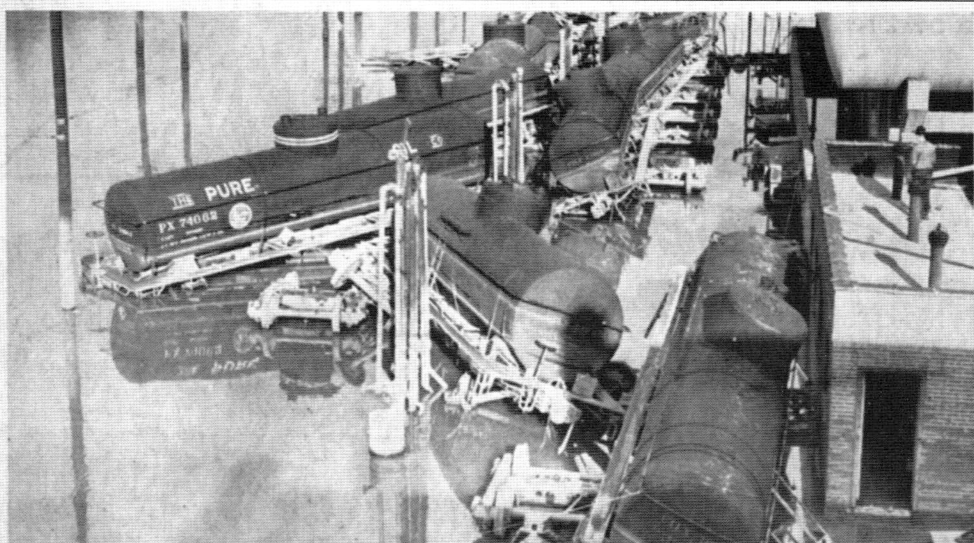

10792 Flood power illustrated. Tank cars floated and piled like kindling

At the height of the flood, all train service in and out Louisville was cancelled. Special L&N trains shuttling refugees from the flooded downtown to dry neighborhoods sometimes had to inch their careful way along tracks covered by 4 feet of water. Other stretches of track were under as much as 20 feet of water. As shown in this photograph, the raging flood tossed around rail cars like they were pieces of kindling wood.

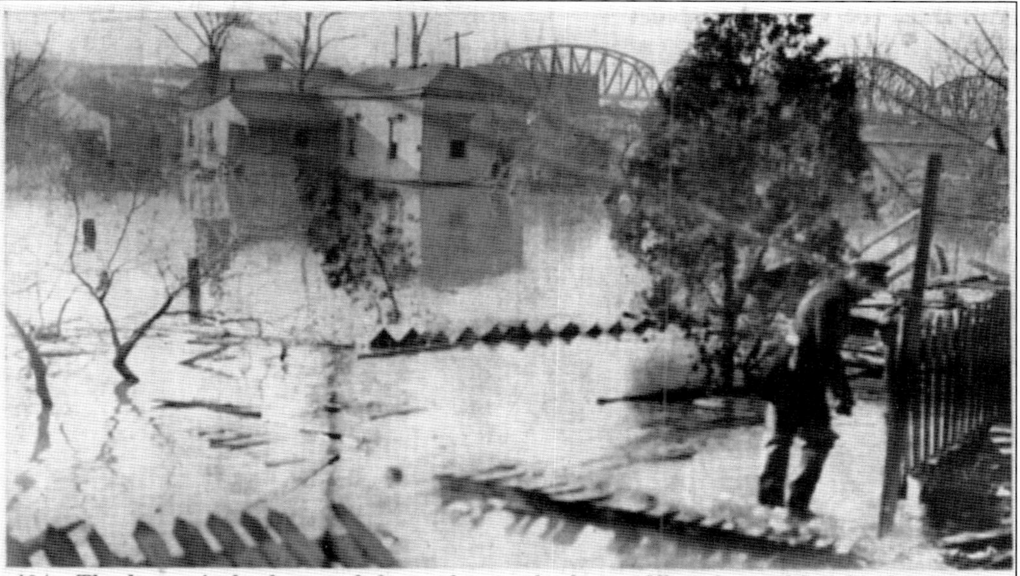

404 The house in background formerly stood where officer is washing his boots.

According to the caption on this souvenir postcard, the house in the background was ripped from its foundation by the flood. It had stood where the police officer is trying to wash some of the mud off his boots. After working around the clock for days, Louisville's exhausted police and firefighters got some welcome help when firefighters from New York, Boston, and other cities and state troopers from more than a half dozen states were flown into the isolated city.

FLOOD SCENE SHOWING ABRAHAM LINCOLN STATUE, 4TH AND YORK, LOUISVILLE, KY.

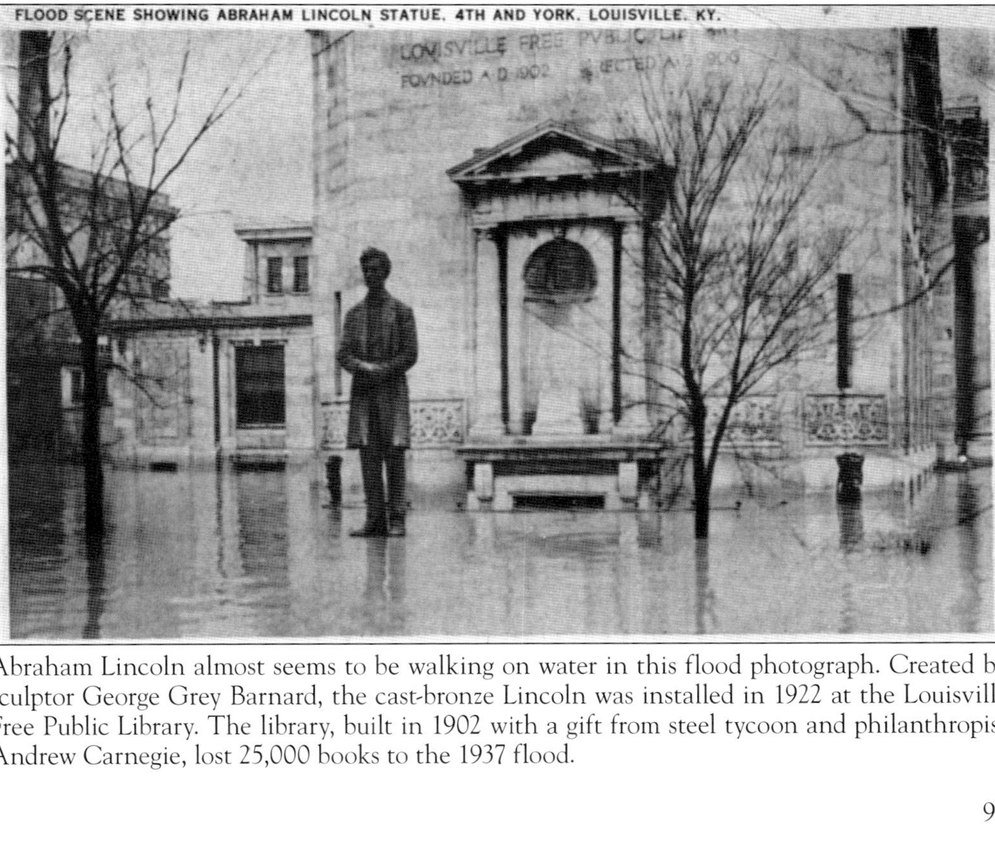

Abraham Lincoln almost seems to be walking on water in this flood photograph. Created by sculptor George Grey Barnard, the cast-bronze Lincoln was installed in 1922 at the Louisville Free Public Library. The library, built in 1902 with a gift from steel tycoon and philanthropist Andrew Carnegie, lost 25,000 books to the 1937 flood.

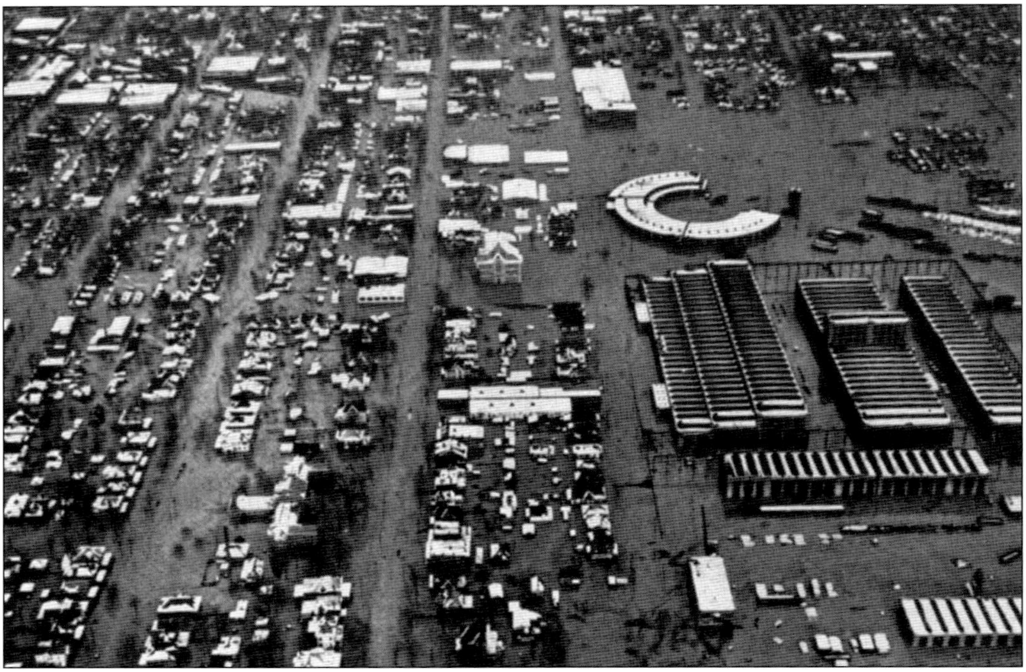

Paducah, Kentucky, was founded by William Clark, of Lewis and Clark fame, who named it after Paduke, a Chickasaw chief said to have befriended the region's first white settlers. The new town's location at the confluence of the Ohio and Tennessee Rivers helped it thrive as a river port but also made it prone to flooding. Still, nothing Paducah had experienced before prepared its residents for the 1937 flood, which all but swept the town off the map.

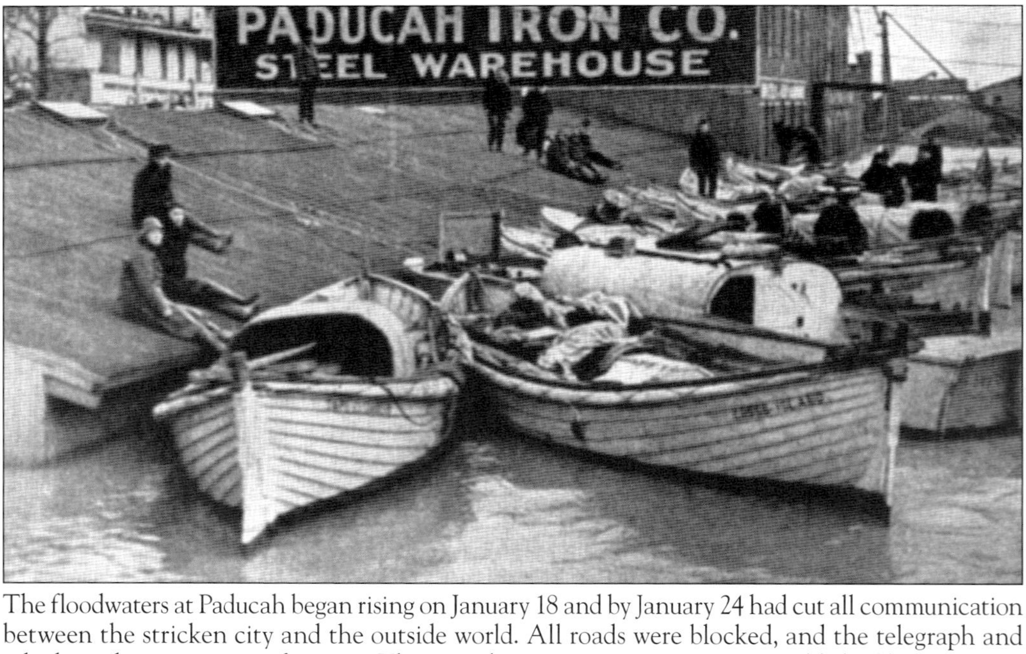

The floodwaters at Paducah began rising on January 18 and by January 24 had cut all communication between the stricken city and the outside world. All roads were blocked, and the telegraph and telephone lines were out of service. The next day communication was reestablished by boat, and, with the water still rising and the situation perilous, authorities undertook the herculean task of evacuating the city via a ragtag flotilla of boats.

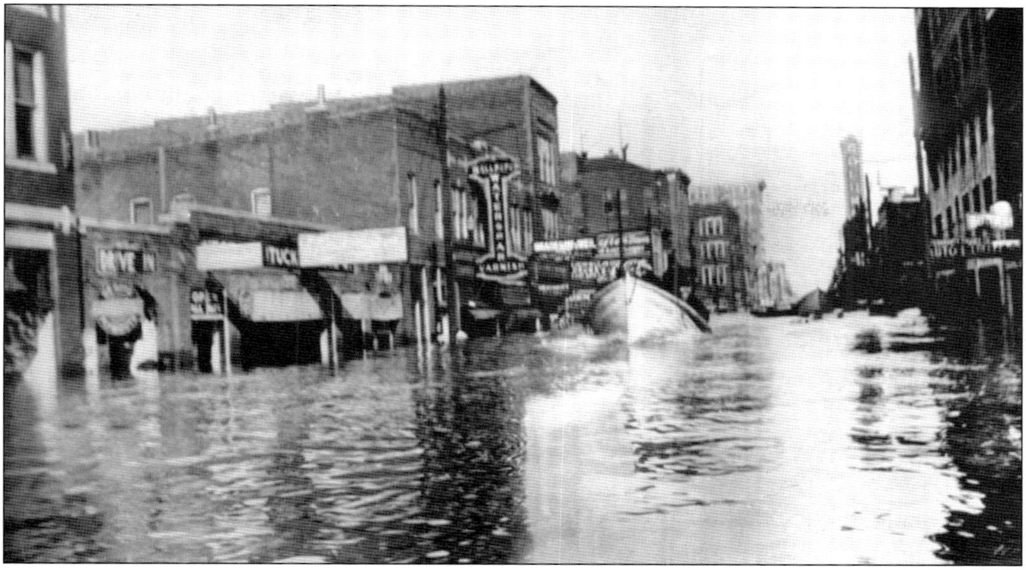

More than 27,000 of Paducah's 33,000 men, women, and children were carried to safety on boats provided by the U.S. Coast Guard, the U.S. Navy, and the Tennessee Valley Authority, along with private craft manned by volunteers from the Red Cross, the American Legion, and other organizations. Unfortunately, a water spot has damaged this souvenir postcard, but it nonetheless provides a dramatic view of a rescue boat cruising along a flooded Broadway. Those evacuated were housed in hastily established refugee camps.

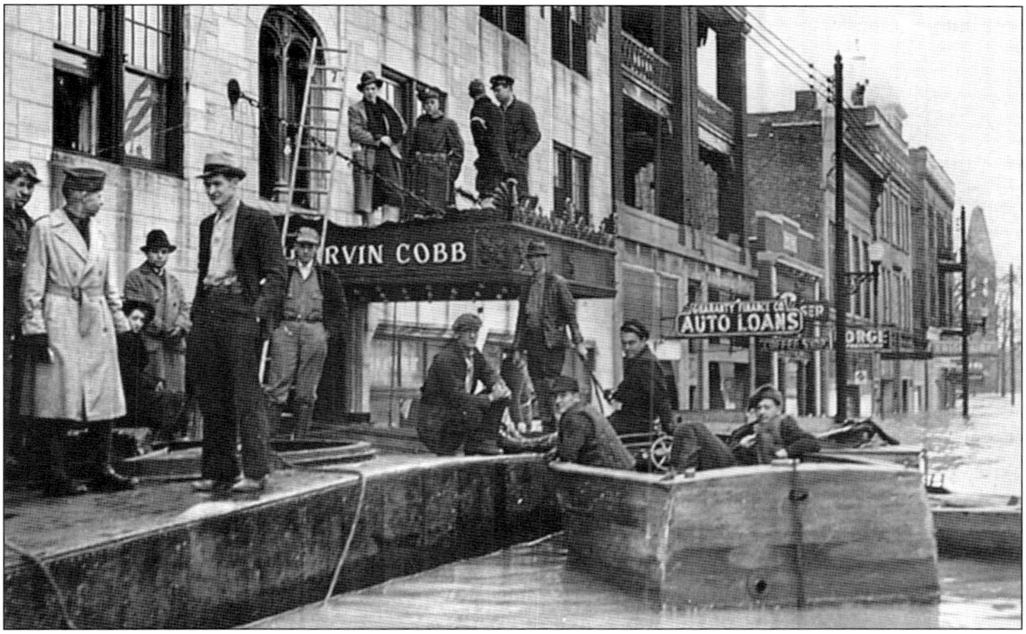

Although mostly forgotten today, author and newspaper humorist Irvin S. Cobb (1876–1944) was one of the best-known men in America in the 1930s and was the namesake of one of the finest hotels in his hometown of Paducah. When the 1937 flood hit, the U.S. Army Corps of Engineers established an emergency headquarters at the Irvin Cobb Hotel. As the floodwaters rose, the ladder perched against the hotel marquee would come in handy. (Courtesy U.S. Army Corps of Engineers.)

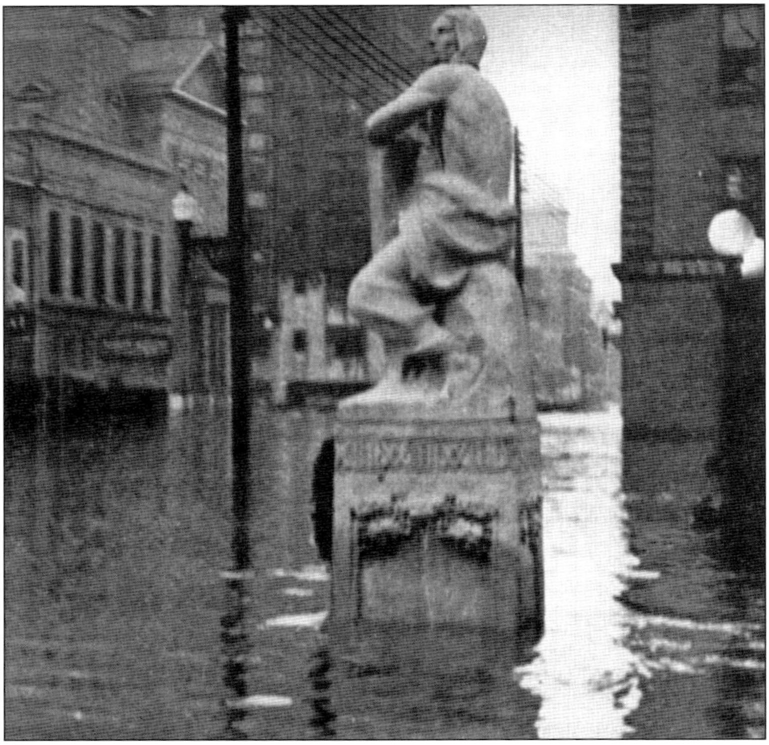

Chief Paduke looks mournfully over his submerged city from his stone seat in front of the U.S. Post Office in Paducah. Only the town's tiny Avondale Heights neighborhood—just a fraction of Paducah's total area—stood high enough to escape the flooding. In most of the residential areas, nothing was visible above the top of the floodwaters except the roofs and upper stories of houses and utility poles. In the downtown, virtually every building was flooded.

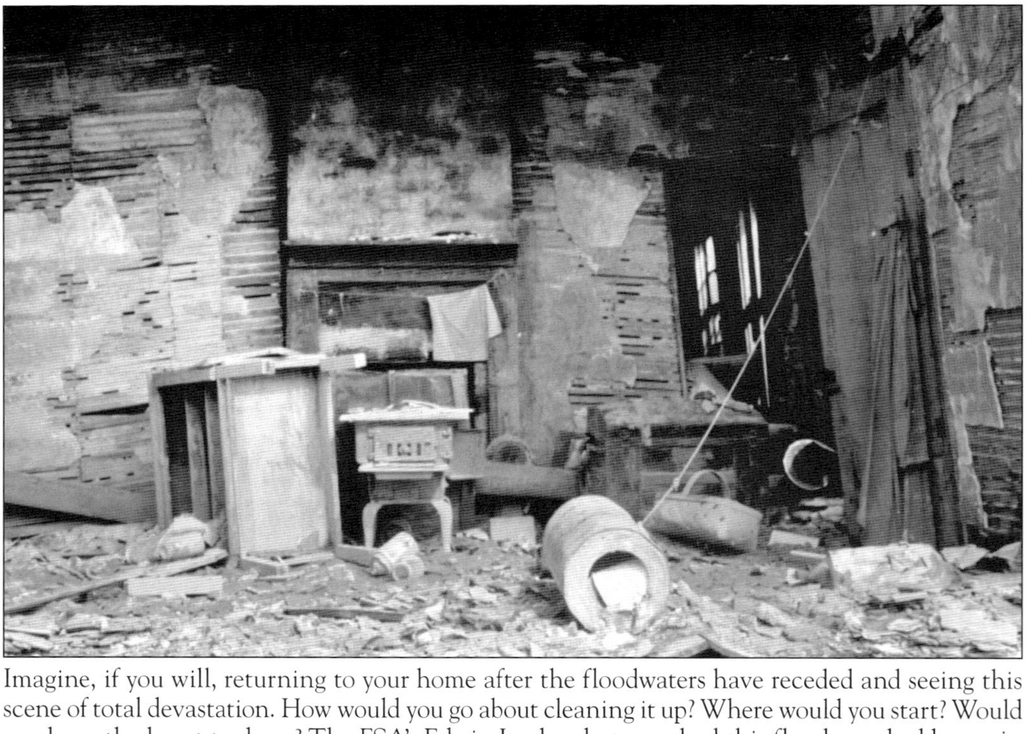

Imagine, if you will, returning to your home after the floodwaters have receded and seeing this scene of total devastation. How would you go about cleaning it up? Where would you start? Would you have the heart to do so? The FSA's Edwin Locke photographed this flood-wrecked house in Smithland, Kentucky. The county seat of Livingston County, Smthland is located at the confluence of the Ohio and Cumberland Rivers. (Courtesy the Library of Congress.)

Seven

INDIANA 1937

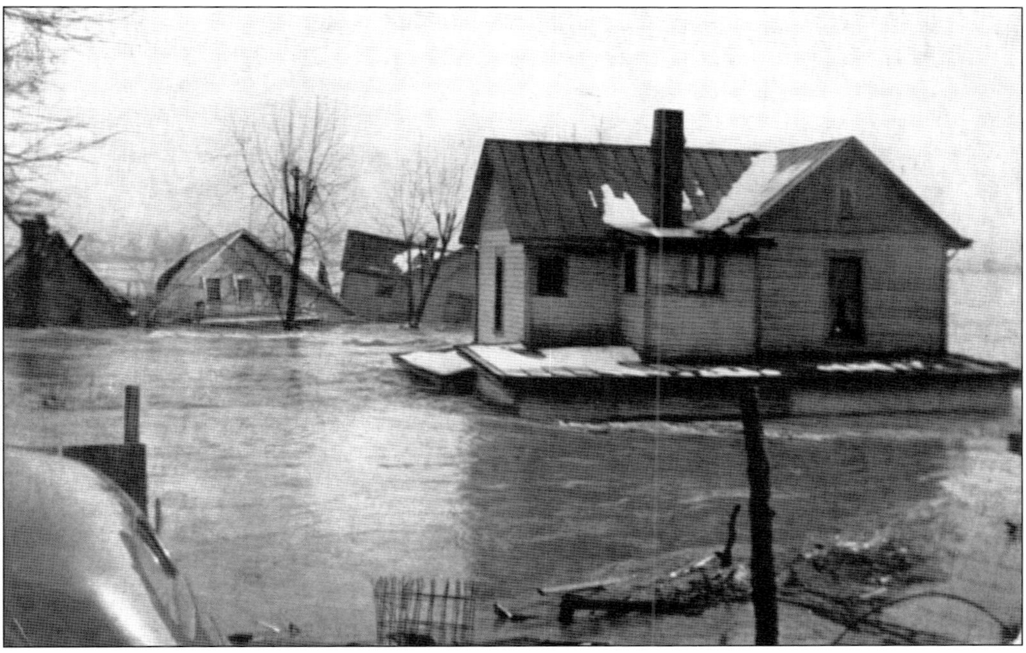

Aurora, Indiana, is a historic river town situated roughly 35 miles west of Cincinnati. This photograph from Aurora is typical of the devastation the 1937 flood inflicted on Indiana's Ohio River communities. The raging water collapsed many houses, ripped others from their foundations, and often reached the second floor of those sturdy dwellings that survived. The damage from the 1937 flood in six Indiana counties was estimated at nearly $13 million.

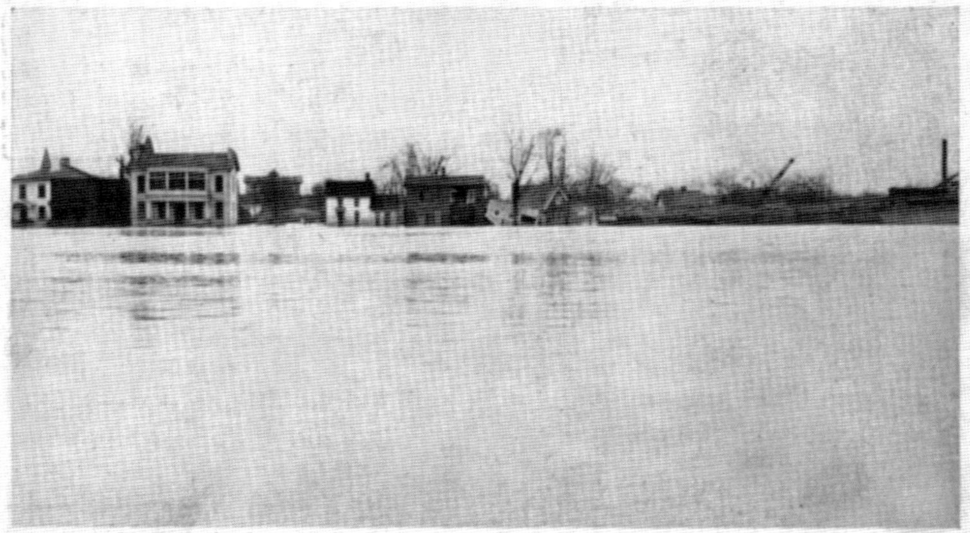

308 They could have delivered coal right to the door in Jeffersonville.

Jeffersonville, Indiana, located across the Ohio from Louisville, Kentucky, was laid out in 1802 after a plan for an "ideal city" drawn by Thomas Jefferson, hence its name. The town's strategic location on the Ohio River quickly made it a center for trade and for boat construction during the steamboat era. But the same river that helped Jeffersonville grow and thrive could be a destructive force as well, as demonstrated in this 1937 photograph of the swollen river.

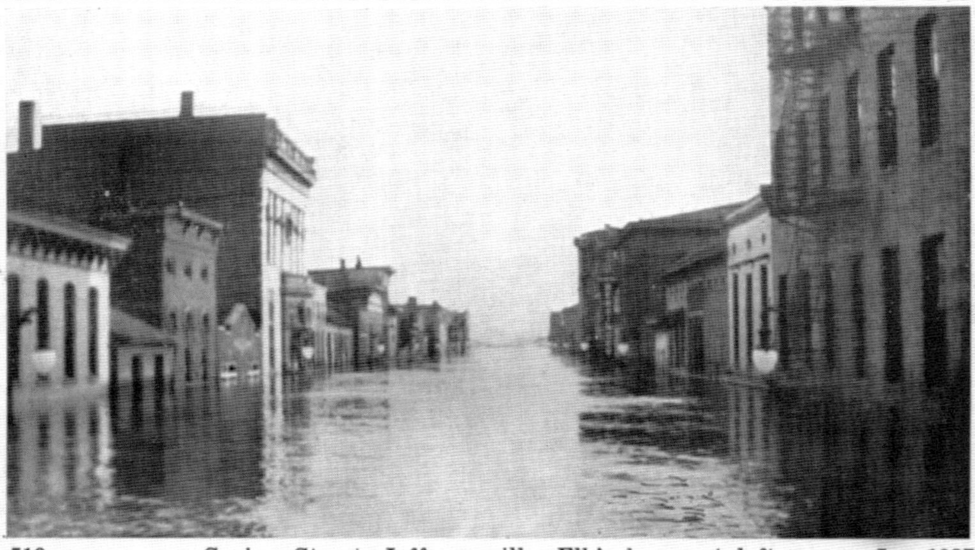

519 Spring Street, Jeffersonville, Elk's home at left Jan. 1937

In the wake of the damaging flood of 1884, the federal government built a levee to protect Jeffersonville. And the levee did its job when the floodwaters came in 1907 and again in 1913. But it proved to be no match for the rampaging 1937 floodwaters, which easily topped it. Soon water stood 22 feet deep along Spring Street, as shown here. The flooded buildings on the left include the Jeffersonville Elks Lodge.

The lower floors of these Jeffersonville buildings at Maple and Spring Streets were totally submerged by the 1937 floodwaters, which crested January 27 at 57.1 feet. That was 40 feet higher than normal and nearly 10 feet higher than the 1884 crest of 47.4 feet. At the right can be seen a flooded grocery store operated by the Great Atlantic and Pacific Tea Company. Merchants along Spring Street and elsewhere downtown lost virtually their entire stocks of merchandise.

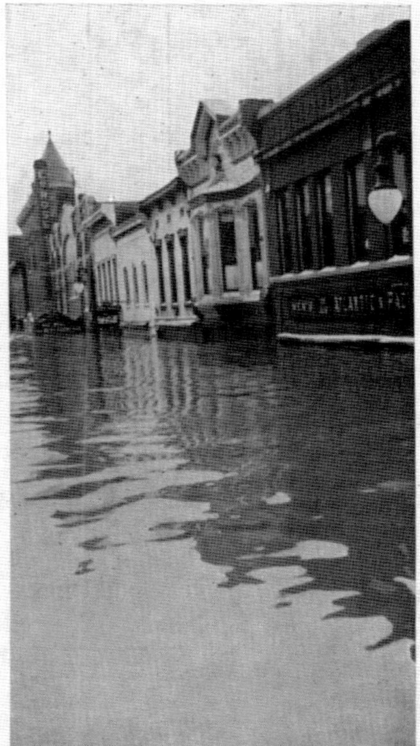

514 Maple and Spring, Jeffersonville, Jan. 1937

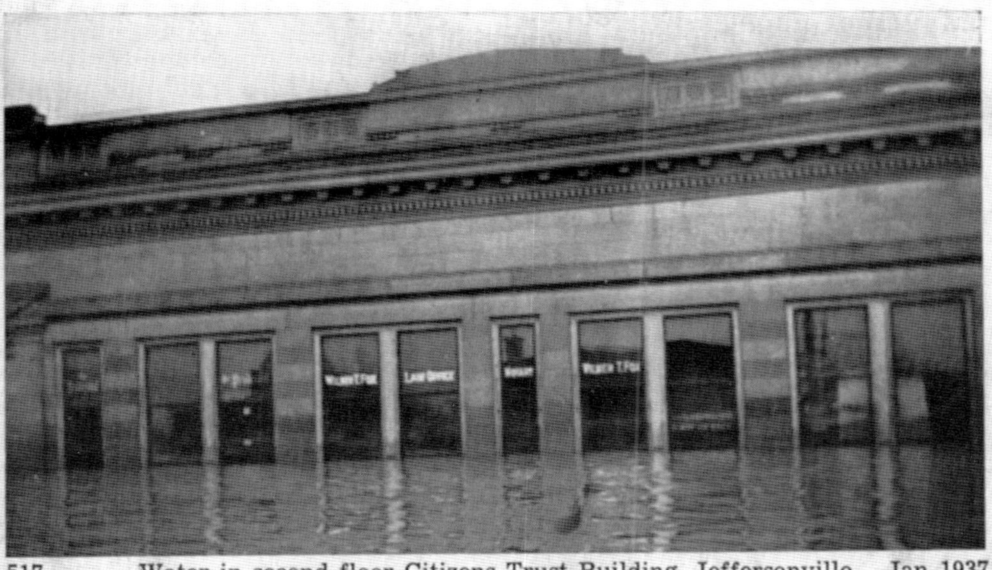

517 Water in second floor Citizens Trust Building, Jeffersonville Jan. 1937

The 1937 floodwaters reached the second floor of the Citizens Bank and Trust Company building at 460 Spring Street. Designed by Louisville architect Arthur Loomis, the bank was built in 1908. Today the historic building is owned and occupied by LifeSpring, Inc., a nonprofit organization that offers a variety of mental health services. LifeSpring has converted the old bank vault into a museum made up of historic artifacts found there.

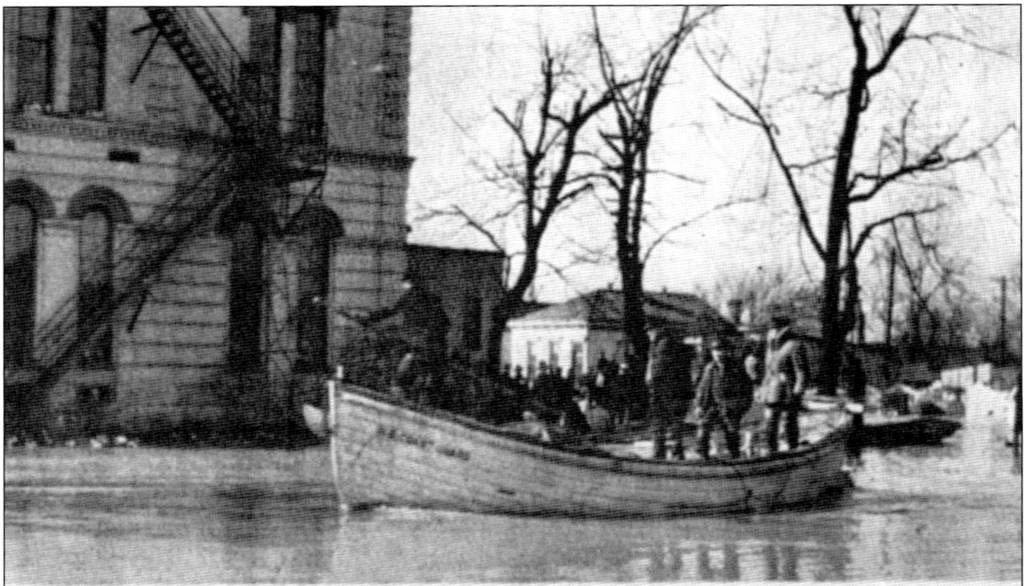

530 Rose Hill School was Central Relief Station for Jeffersonville Jan. 1937

Rose Hill School, a three-story elementary school built atop a small hill at Indiana Avenue and Fourth Street, stood above the floodwaters and so became a place of refugee for desperate Jeffersonville residents forced from their homes by the rising water. Here a U.S. Coast Guard boat can be seen as it makes its slow, careful way to an improvised dock at the old school, seen in the background.

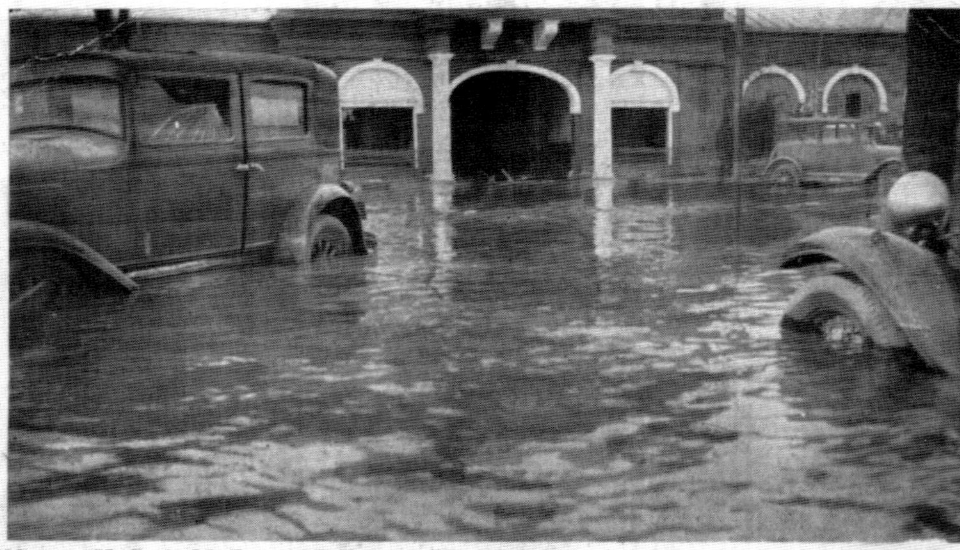

529 U. S. Q. M. Depot, Jeffersonville, thought to be above flood stage Jan. 1937

Jeffersonville's mammoth U.S. Army Quartermaster Depot was thought to be above flood stage. As these 1937 motorists discovered, it was not. The military supply facility was both a local landmark and a major employer in Jeffersonville. The depot had its beginnings in the Civil War. In World War II, its busy buildings extended for more than 10 city blocks. The army deactivated it in 1958. Today only a handful of the buildings remain.

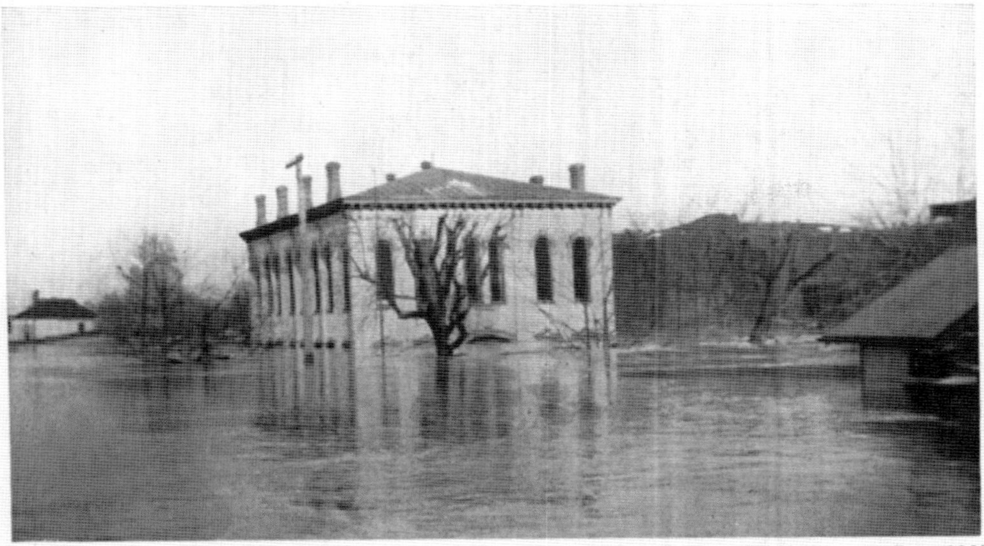

522 One of Jeffersonville's landmarks—Old City Hall Jan. 1937

The old Jeffersonville City Hall, erected on Market Street just west of Spring Street in 1881, housed the town's offices for more than a half century. In 1935, the municipal government moved to a new annex at the Clark County Courthouse. The old building deteriorated badly over the years and finally was demolished in a 1950s urban renewal project. Here it is seen surrounded by the 1937 floodwaters.

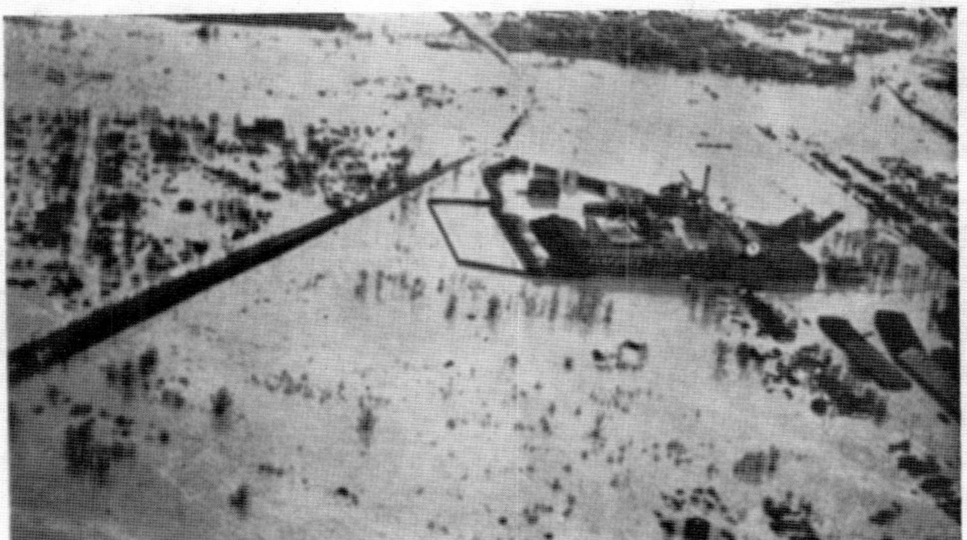

149545 "Across the River"— Colgate plant in Jeffersonville practically submerged

Located at State Street and Woener Avenue, the Indiana Reformatory for Men was a Romanesque structure constructed in the late 19th century. The state of Indiana closed the facility, and in 1923, it was sold to the Colgate-Palmolive-Peet Company, which reopened it the following year as a soap factory. In this aerial view, the 1937 floodwaters can be seen all but submerging the plant.

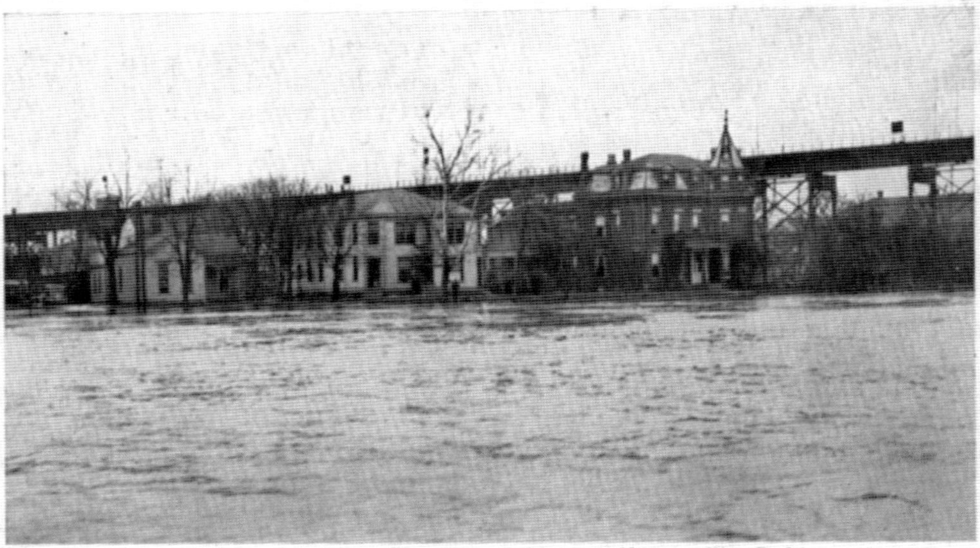

307 River front and Big Four Bridge, Jeffersonville, Ind.

This view shows the flooded Ohio River at the doorsteps of some of Jeffersonville's old riverfront homes, with the Big Four Railroad Bridge in the background. The bridge was built in the 1890s for the Cleveland, Cincinnati, Chicago, and St. Louis Railway, nicknamed the "Big Four Railroad." No longer needed in today's era of rail mergers, the bridge was abandoned and its ramps removed in 1969. Today it is often called the "Bridge to Nowhere."

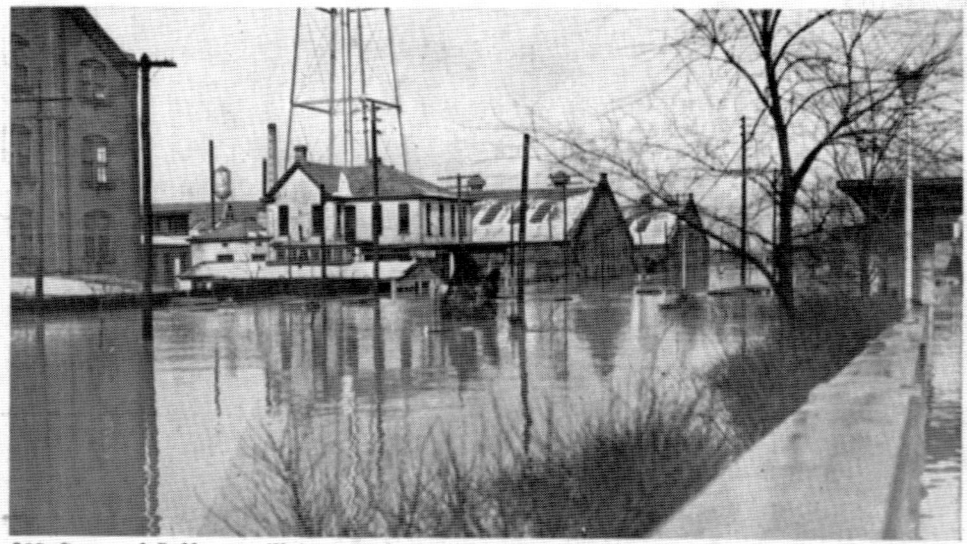

309 Some of Jeffersonville's manufacturing district. Amrican Car & Fdry Co. in center.

As was typical in river towns, many of Jeffersonville's earliest industries were located along the river. One such was the Ohio Falls Car and Foundry Company, founded by a group of local businessmen near the end of the Civil War; it would become a major producer of railroad rolling stock. It was absorbed into the American Car and Foundry Company in 1899. Here the town's flooded manufacturing district can be seen, with the ACF plant in the center.

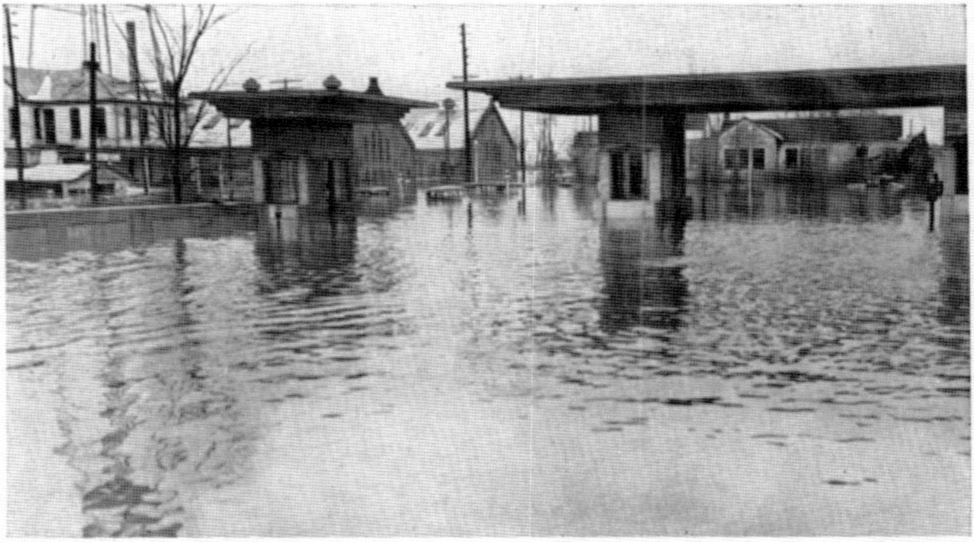

515 Jeffersonville Gate House to Municipal Bridge Jan. 1937

The 1937 flood closed the Municipal Bridge spanning the Ohio River between Louisville, Kentucky, and southern Indiana. Shown here is the flooded gatehouse at the Indiana end of the span. Opened in 1929, the span operated as a toll bridge until 1946. Three years later, the span was renamed the George Rogers Clark Memorial Bridge in honor of the founder of Louisville and Clarksville. Today the Clark-Floyd Counties Convention and Tourism Bureau's administrative offices are located in the toll collection headquarters.

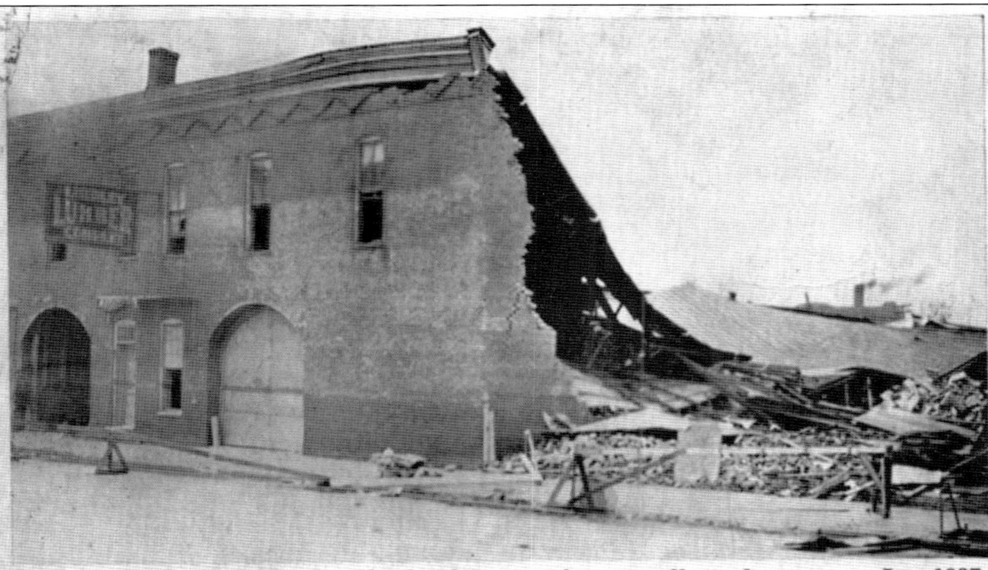

524 Jeffersonville lumber warehouse collapsed Jan. 1937

Dangerously weakened by the force of the raging floodwaters, many buildings such as this Jeffersonville lumber warehouse collapsed. Acting Jeffersonville mayor Edward M. "Tuck" Coots estimated the damage from the flood at more than $10 million. (Coots, the county coroner and a funeral home owner, took over in the absence of Mayor A. W. Jacobs, who was in Florida recuperating from an illness.)

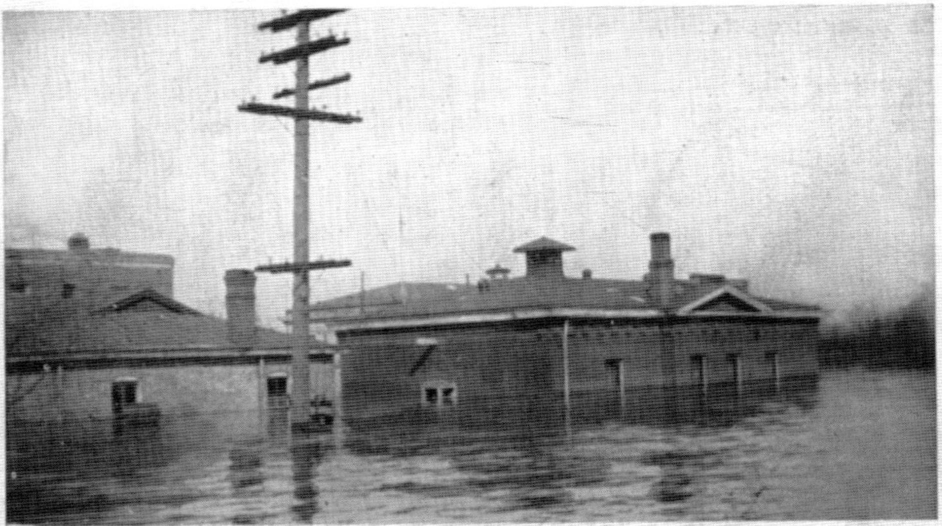

518 Jeffersonville Fire Headquarters completely flooded Jan. 1937

The Jeffersonville Fire Department's headquarters stand completely surrounded by the floodwaters. Fire was a constant concern during the flood because the raging floodwaters would lift houses off their foundations, snapping their gas lines and spewing gas in the air, where it could easily be ignited by a careless smoker or a simple spark.

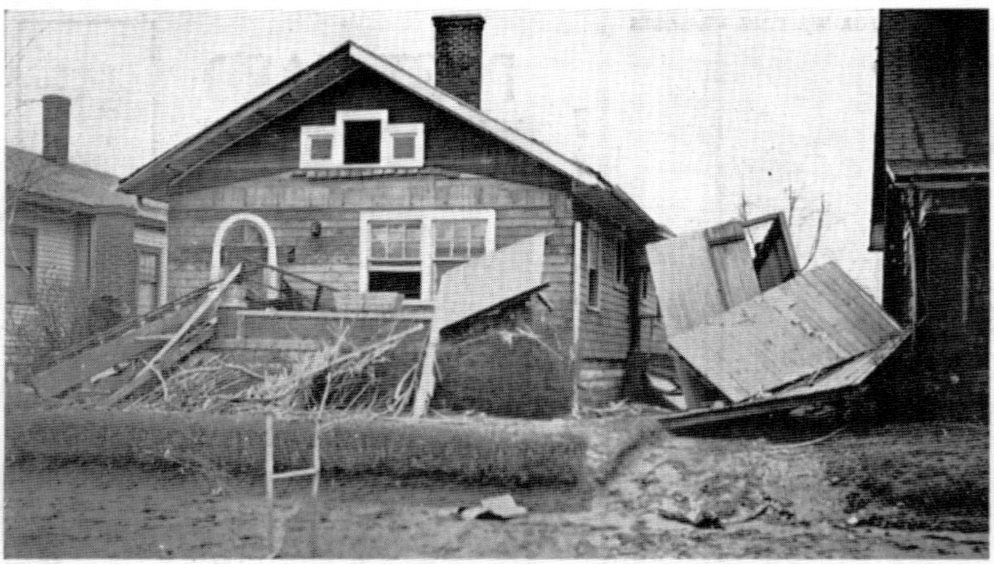

304 Chestnut Street, Jeffersonville, Ind., as it was left.

By the time the full force of the flood fell upon Jeffersonville, most of the citizens had been evacuated. Many of those who were bundled aboard relief trains bound for Indianapolis were penniless, with little more than the clothes on their backs. When the railroad's passenger coaches were filled, unheated boxcars were pressed into service. When the evacuees returned, they were greeted by scenes such as this, a wrecked house on Chestnut Street.

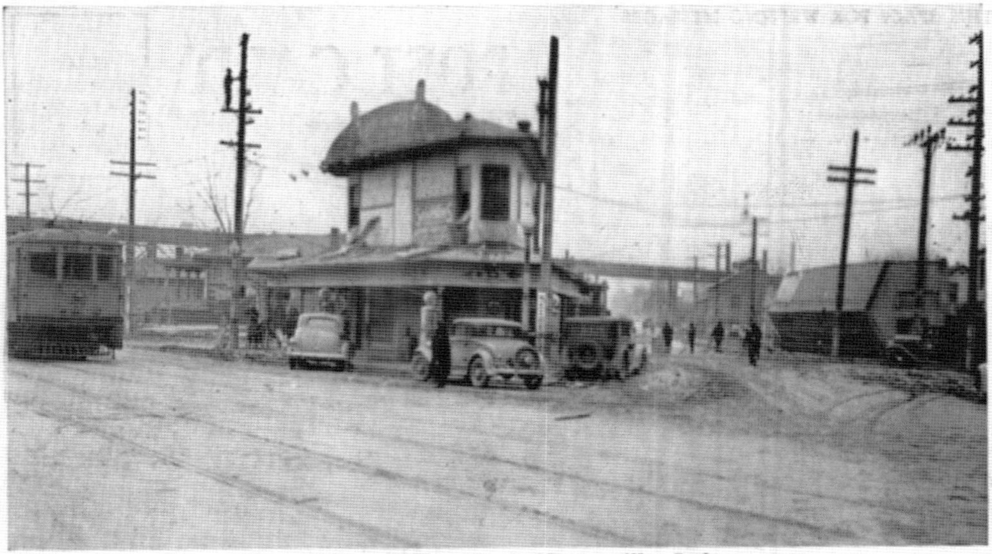

302 Main and Fourth, Jeffersonville, Ind.

With the floodwaters gone, Jeffersonville began returning to normal. In this scene at Main and Fourth Streets, the streetcar is running again, and motorists have converged on a gas station, hoping the pumps are back in service. You might never know the flood had visited—except for that little house at the right of the photograph that has been turned over on its side.

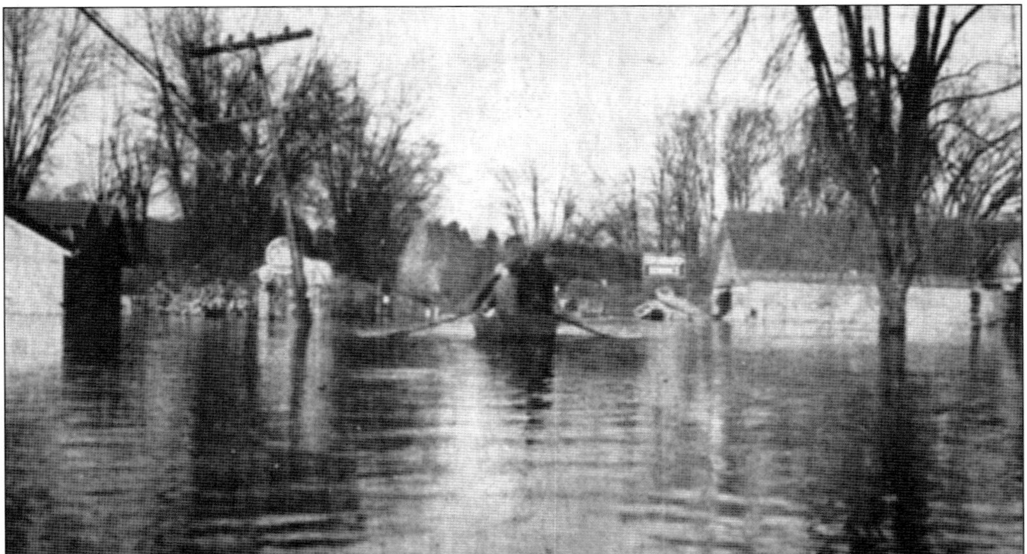

516 Historic village of Utica, Indiana, near Jeffersonville Jan. 1937

In the days before bridges spanned the Ohio River, ferryboats provided the only way to get across. The ferry landing at Utica on the Indiana shore near Jeffersonville became a popular crossing. Trying to cross the river at Jeffersonville was deemed too dangerous thanks to the rocky Falls of the Ohio. Here a lone rowboat makes its way down a flooded street in the historic village.

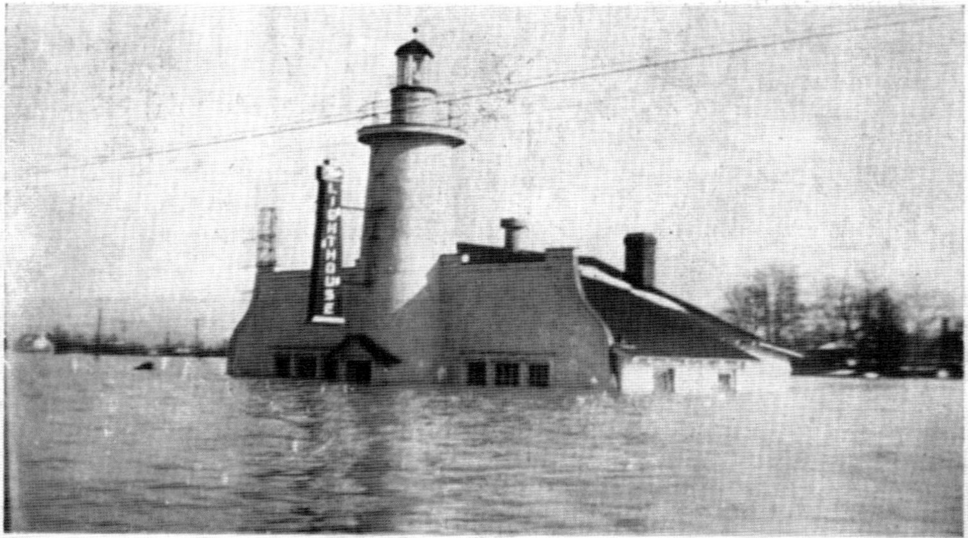

410 One of-the Road Houses between New Albany and Jeffersonville.

The Lighthouse was a popular roadhouse between Jeffersonville and nearby New Albany, Indiana. Ordinarily, its distinctive architecture seemed distinctly out of place so far from the ocean, but it appears right at home in the midst of the floodwaters surrounding it. Obviously, it would be awhile before the Lighthouse would be welcoming any more guests.

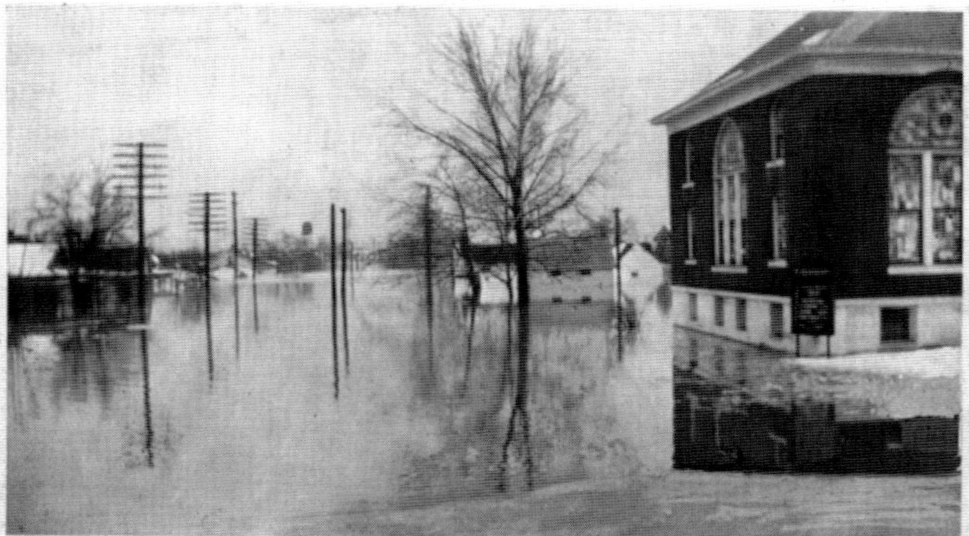

510 United Brethren Church in New Albany Jan. 1937

The 1937 flood caused an estimated $8 million in damage in New Albany. In this view, the floodwaters can be seen inundating several houses and lapping at the foundation of the New Albany United Brethren Church. The flood, the town's worst ever, generated local interest in a floodwall, but work was delayed because of World War II. Construction started in 1949 and was completed in 1953.

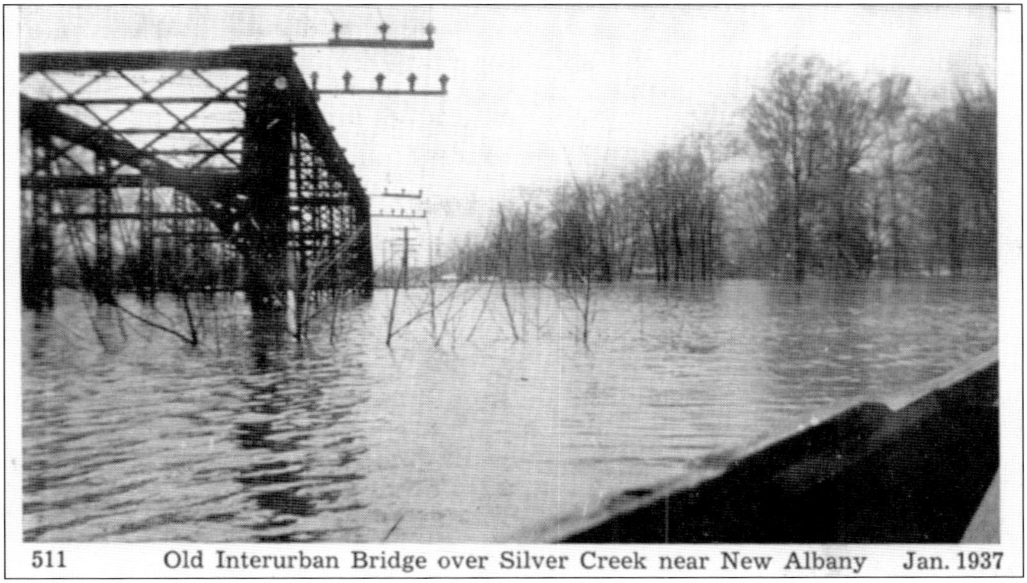

Silver Creek rises in Scott County, Indiana, and flows 34 miles before flowing into the Ohio River. It got its name from a legend that a silver treasure was hidden nearby. In 1937, the creek overflowed its banks and immersed a bridge carrying the tracks of the Louisville and Southern Indiana Traction Company. The company ran an interurban rail line that connected Louisville, Jeffersonville, and New Albany.

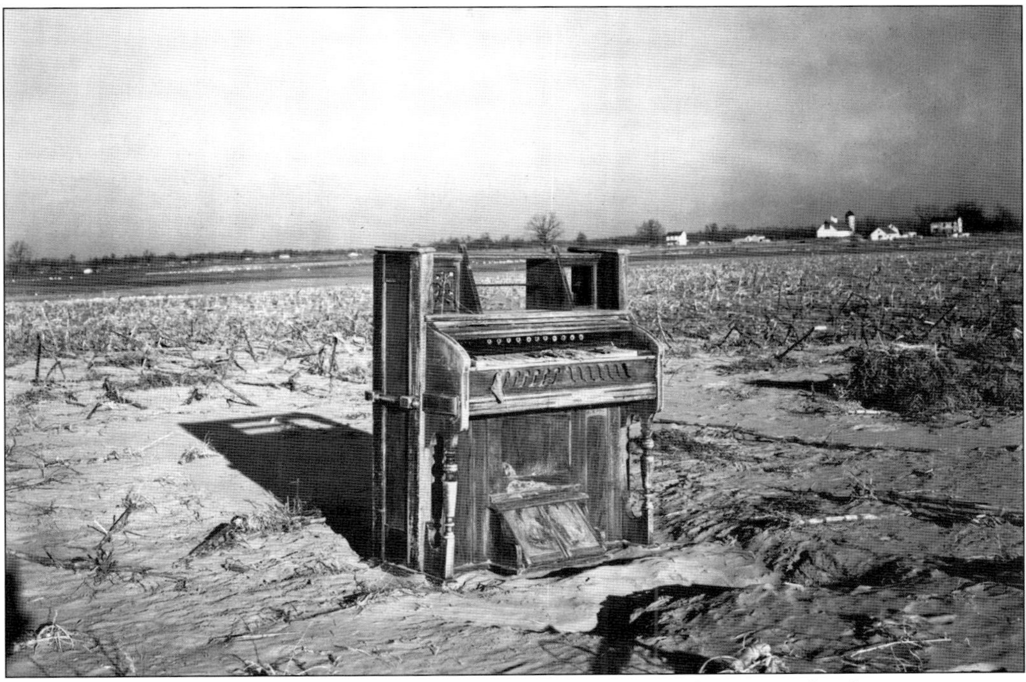

In a graphic example of the enormous power of the 1937 flood, the raging floodwaters swept up this organ from some family's parlor, carried it downstream, perhaps for miles, and then deposited it in this field on a farm near Mount Vernon, Indiana. This dramatic photograph is the work of the Farm Security Administration's Russell Lee, who took many photographs of the flood's aftermath in Indiana and Illinois. (Courtesy the Library of Congress.)

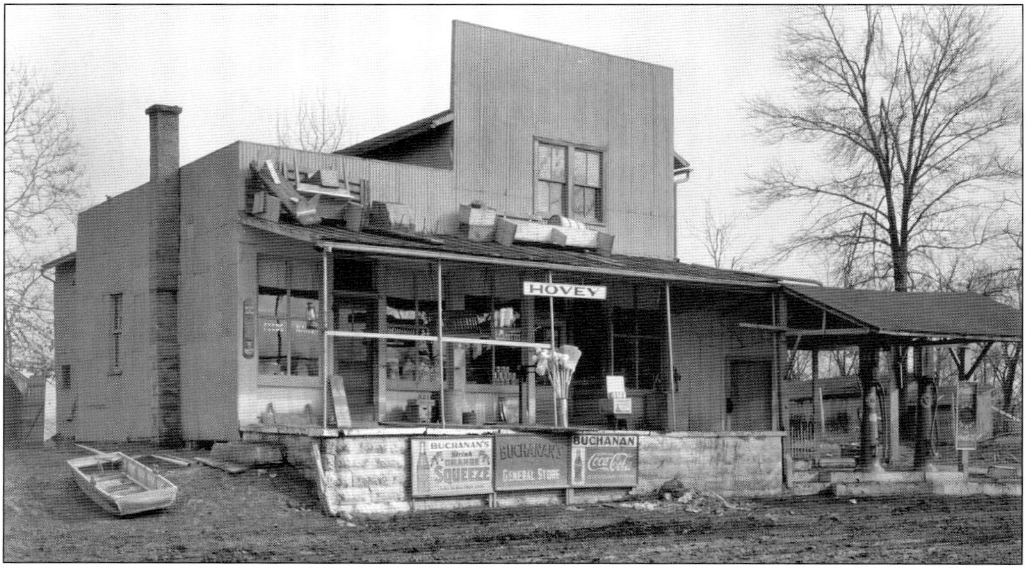

Buchanan's General Store at Hovey in Posey County, Indiana, is open for business again after the flood. Note the furniture on the roof, placed there to protect it from the floodwaters. There is also a small boat on the ground beside the store. No doubt the boat came in handy during the flood. Alvin P. Hovey was a lawyer, Civil War general, diplomat, congressman, and Indiana's governor from 1889 until his death in 1891. (Courtesy the Library of Congress.)

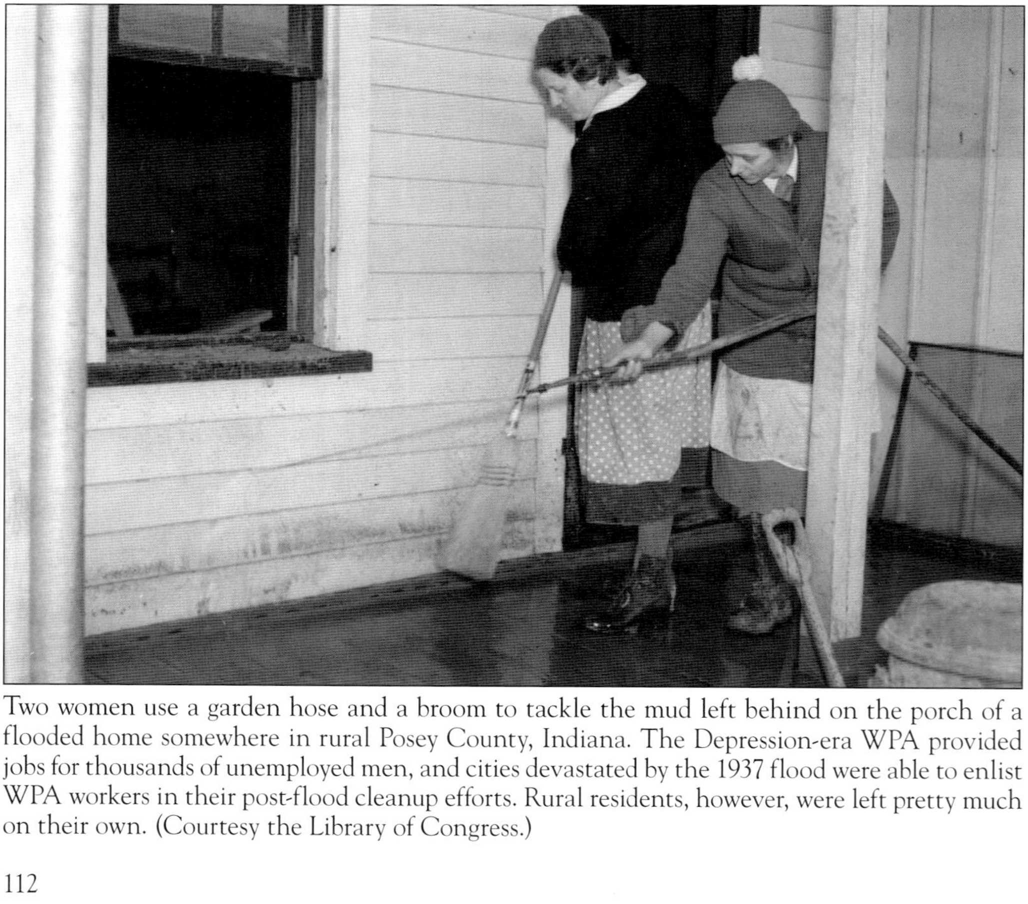

Two women use a garden hose and a broom to tackle the mud left behind on the porch of a flooded home somewhere in rural Posey County, Indiana. The Depression-era WPA provided jobs for thousands of unemployed men, and cities devastated by the 1937 flood were able to enlist WPA workers in their post-flood cleanup efforts. Rural residents, however, were left pretty much on their own. (Courtesy the Library of Congress.)

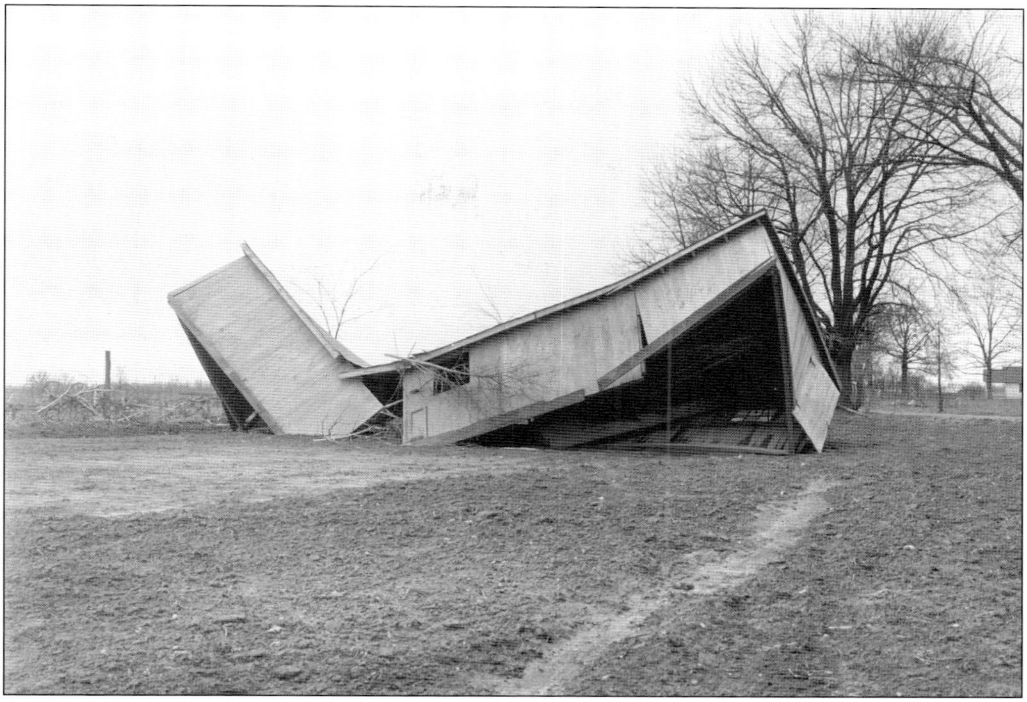

Believe it or not, this was a chicken house before the 1937 flood inundated this farm in Posey County, Indiana. The raging floodwaters not only knocked the frame structure off its foundation, but also left it twisted like a pretzel. One Indiana farmer later told of seeing his house swept away by the flood, which then obligingly brought him another that it deposited on his property. (Courtesy the Library of Congress.)

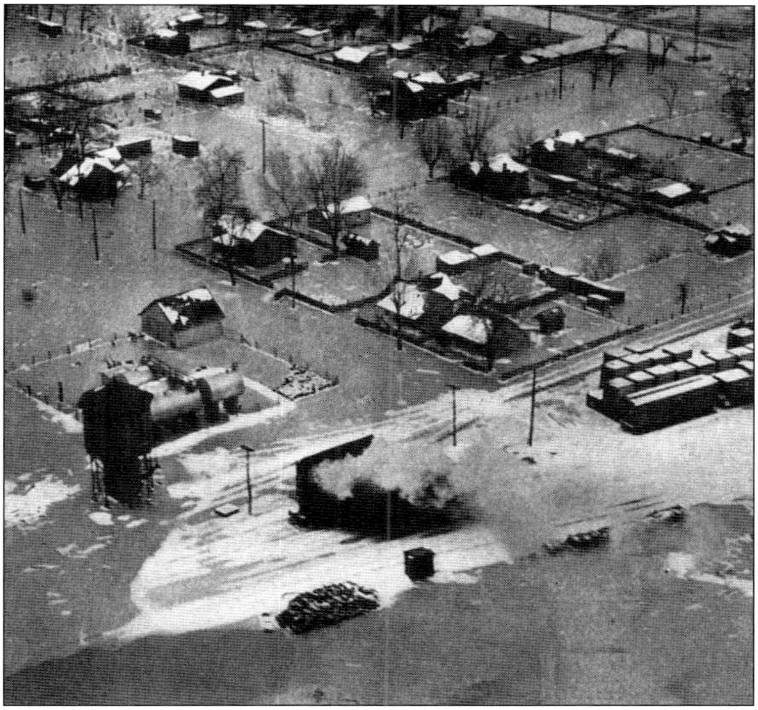

A Chicago newspaper photographer looking down from an airliner took this aerial shot of a flooded Evansville, Indiana. Records show January 1937 was the wettest single month (14.78 inches of rain and snow) in Evansville history, and that added to the torrent of water working its way down the Ohio River. Ten miles of the city's streets were covered with water; the U.S. Coast Guard arrived for rescue duty, and Red Cross shelters overflowed with refugees.

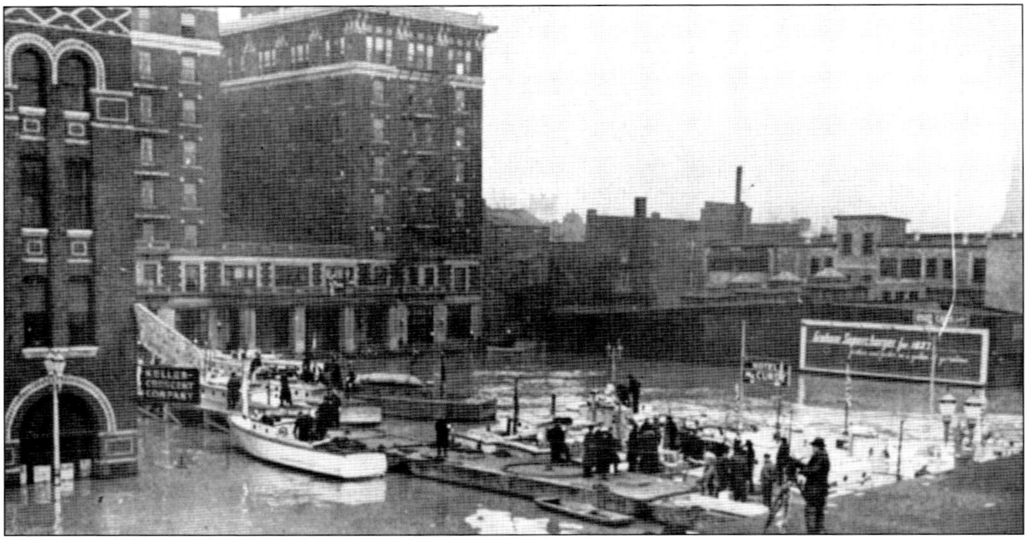

In Evansville, Locust Street and the Hotel McCurdy at the riverside became a handy improvised harbor for U.S. Coast Guard craft and other boats used in the rescue effort. A wooden catwalk was built from the hotel to the nearby Elks Club. Built in 1917, the 300-room hotel was a showplace. Its popular Rose Room ballroom was known for its romantic views of the river. In January 1937, however, the view was anything but romantic.

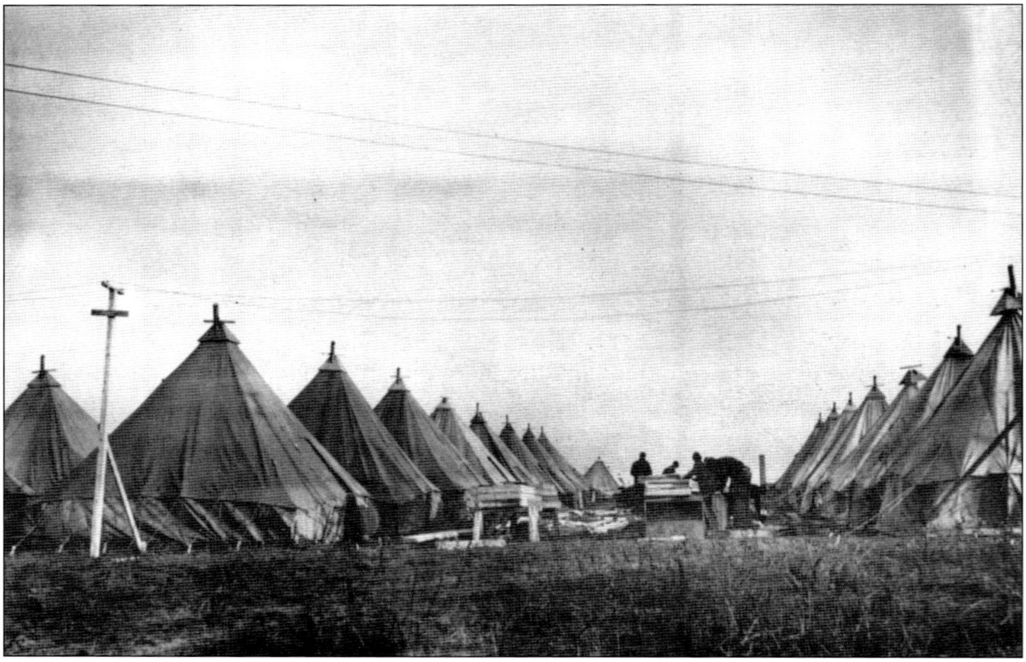

The American Red Cross worked with the National Guard and the U.S. Army to establish tent cities to house refugees driven from their homes by the 1937 flood. The location of this camp is unidentified. It could have been any one of dozens established in various spots throughout the Ohio Valley. Given their military origins, the camps were far from luxurious. Nevertheless, the pyramid-shaped tents were a welcome sight to many refugees who had prayed they would find a safe, dry place to stay.

Eight

ILLINOIS 1937

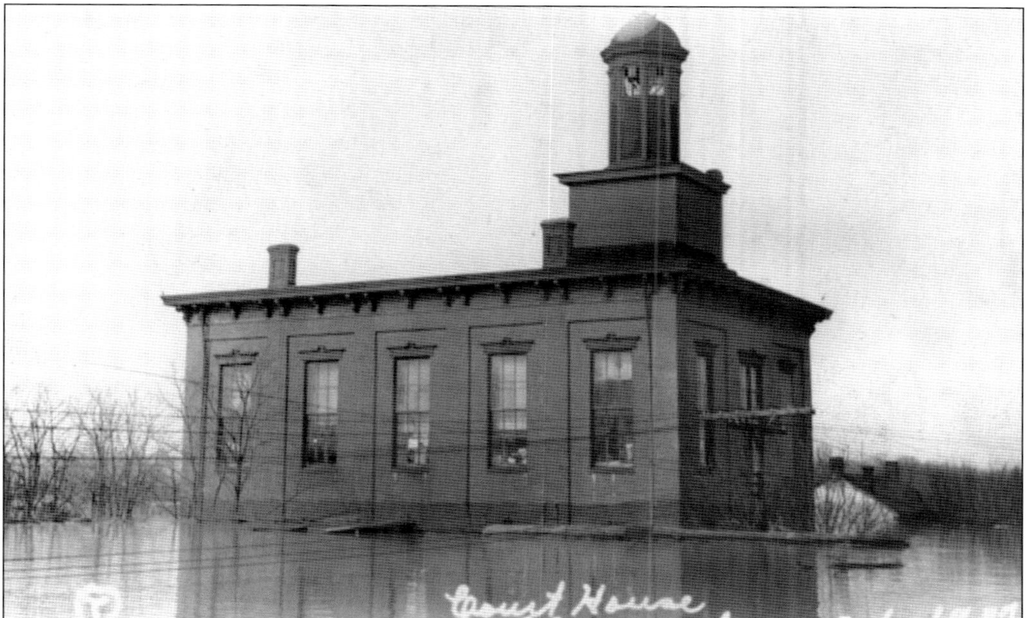

Founded in 1810, Shawneetown was the first town chartered in Illinois and was home to the state's first bank. Regularly victimized by flooding, the thriving river port responded by building a series of higher and higher levees. By the 1930s, the town felt safe behind a 60-foot levee. Then came 1937, when the river poured over the levee and swamped the town, including the Gallatin County Courthouse (shown here). At that point, most of the disgusted townspeople packed up and moved three miles north to build a new Shawneetown. The area they left is now known as Old Shawneetown.

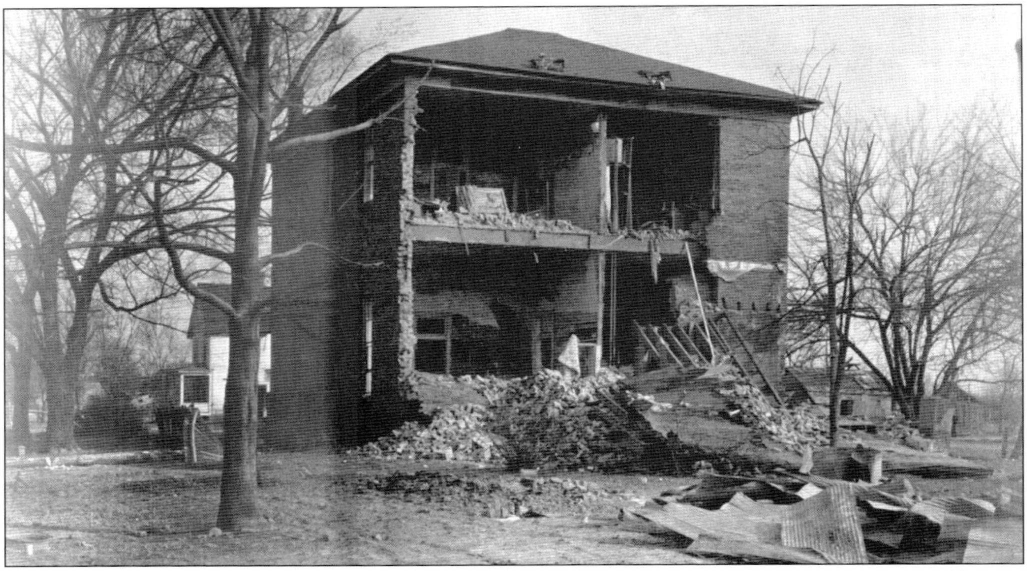

FSA photographer Russell Lee's caption for this photograph, taken at Shawneetown, Illinois, identifies the collapsing brick structure as "the old Catholic seminary after the flood." One entire wall has fallen away. Flooding was by no means a new experience for Shawneetown. Between 1901 and 1937, the town flooded eight times. But the damage from most of those floods was minor. No one was prepared for the devastation brought by 1937's high water. (Courtesy the Library of Congress.)

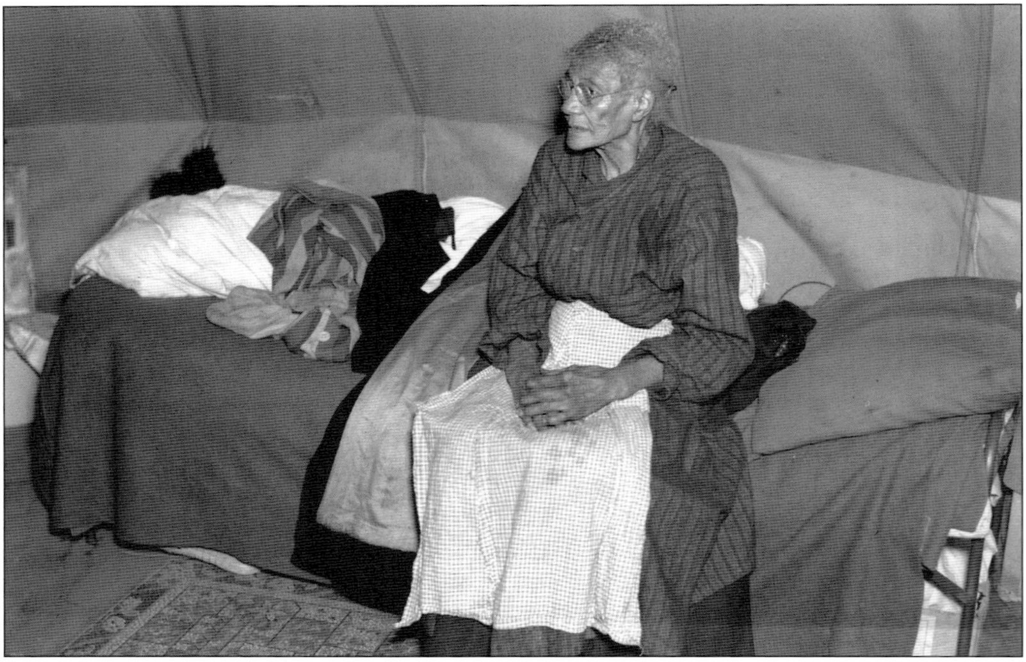

Thousands of men, women, and children who were driven from their homes by the 1937 flood were sheltered in dozens of tent cities the Red Cross established in various locations. Russell Lee photographed 91-year-old Ellen McAllister as she sat on the edge of her bunk at a camp near Shawneetown. She was said to be the camp's oldest resident. (Courtesy the Library of Congress.)

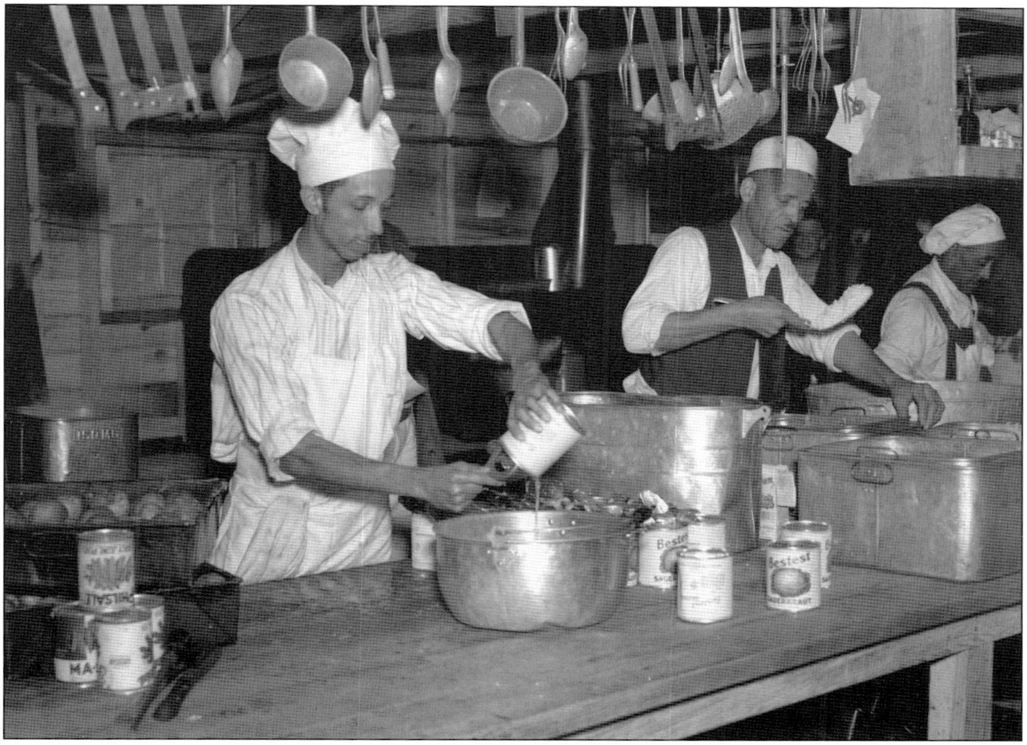

Many of the refugees remained in the tent cities for weeks, fed by Red Cross workers using military kitchen equipment and working from menus prepared by nutritionists at Red Cross headquarters in Washington, D.C. Here a trio of workers can be seen preparing a meal at the Shawneetown tent camp. The Red Cross later estimated it fed nearly 200,000 people, some for a day or two and others for weeks. (Courtesy the Library of Congress.)

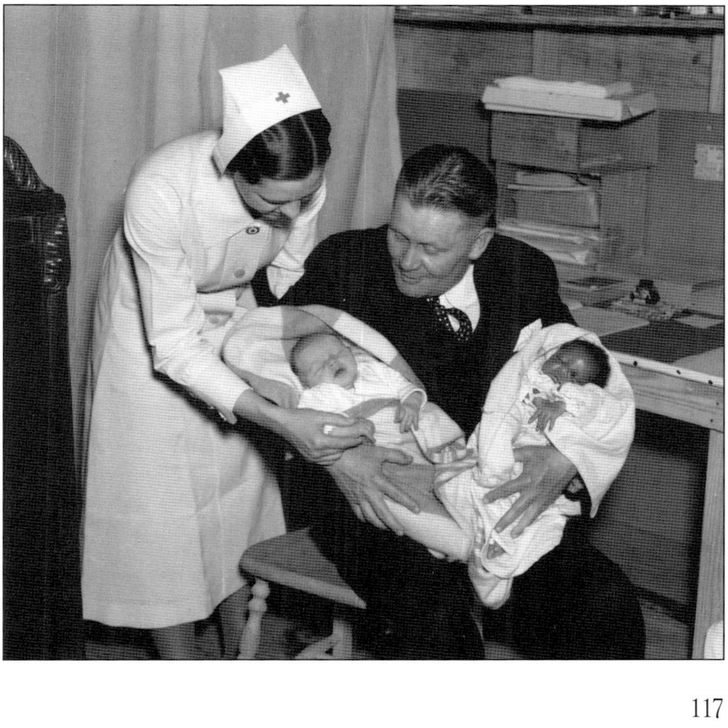

The district manager of the Red Cross flood relief effort is shown holding the first two babies born at the refugee camp near Shawneetown. With many of the region's hospitals flooded, officials had to establish emergency medical facilities at the refugee centers. The flood brought with it a virtual epidemic of pneumonia and a wide range of other illnesses. Doctors and nurses worked around the clock in improvised conditions. (Courtesy the Library of Congress.)

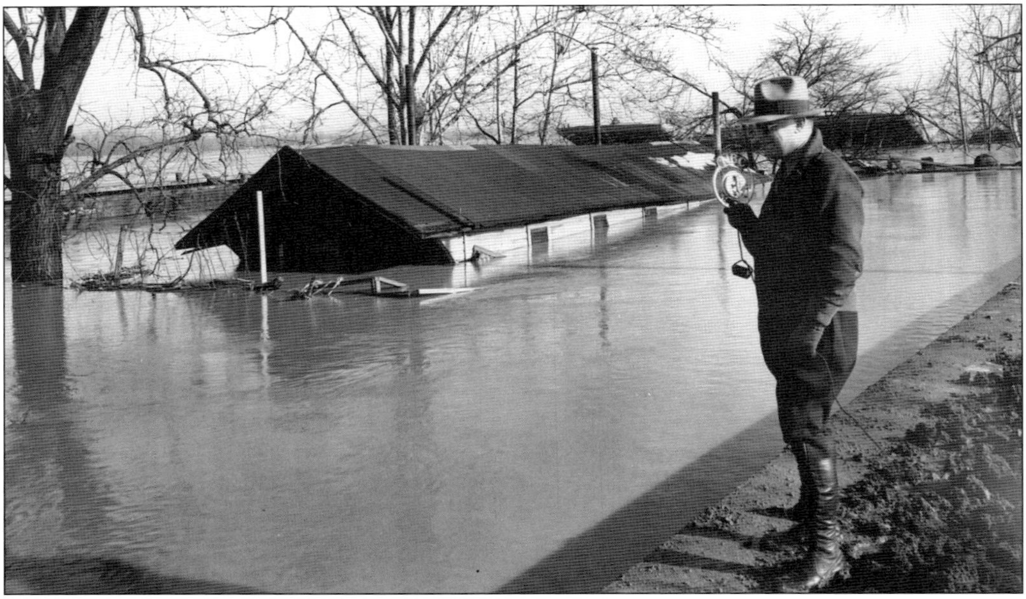

Radio stations throughout the Ohio Valley responded to the 1937 flood with hours of on-the-scene reporting, and a number of big-city stations rushed reporters to the scene. Here Hal Totton of Chicago's WMAQ, microphone in hand, surveys the damage in a southern Illinois neighborhood. Today Totton is remembered for doing the first radio play-by-play airing of a baseball game—a contest between the Chicago Cubs and Pittsburgh Pirates on April 20, 1925.

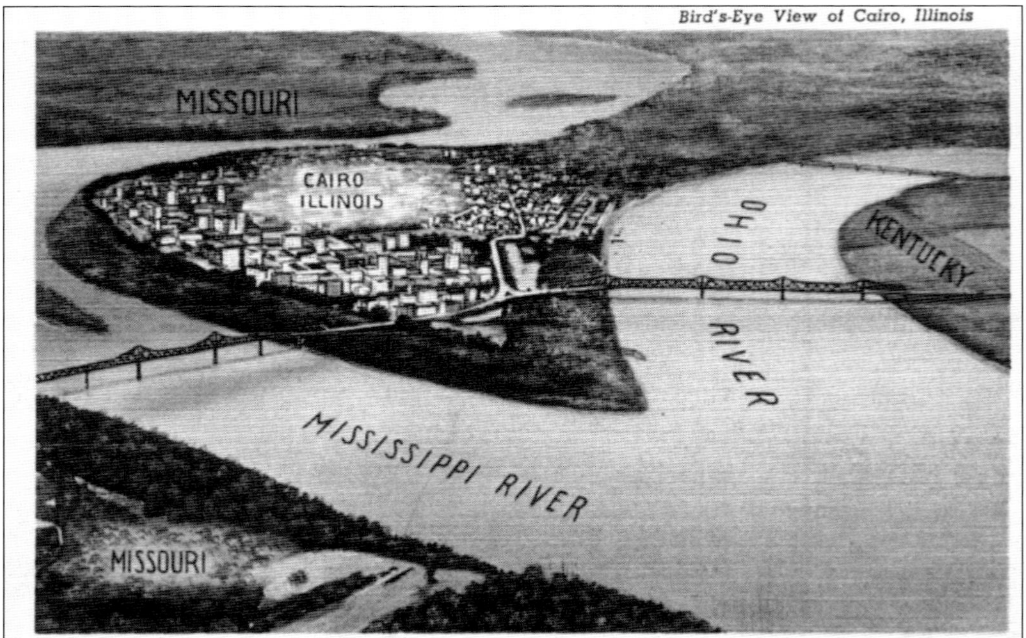

The little town of Cairo in Illinois is named for the city in Egypt, but it is pronounced "KAY-ro," like the syrup. Cairo is located at the southernmost tip of Illinois where the Ohio River meets the Mississippi River. This means, as this picture postcard shows, that the Ohio borders one side of town and the Mississippi the other side. Its strategic location made Cairo a busy river port but also meant it was subjected to frequent floods.

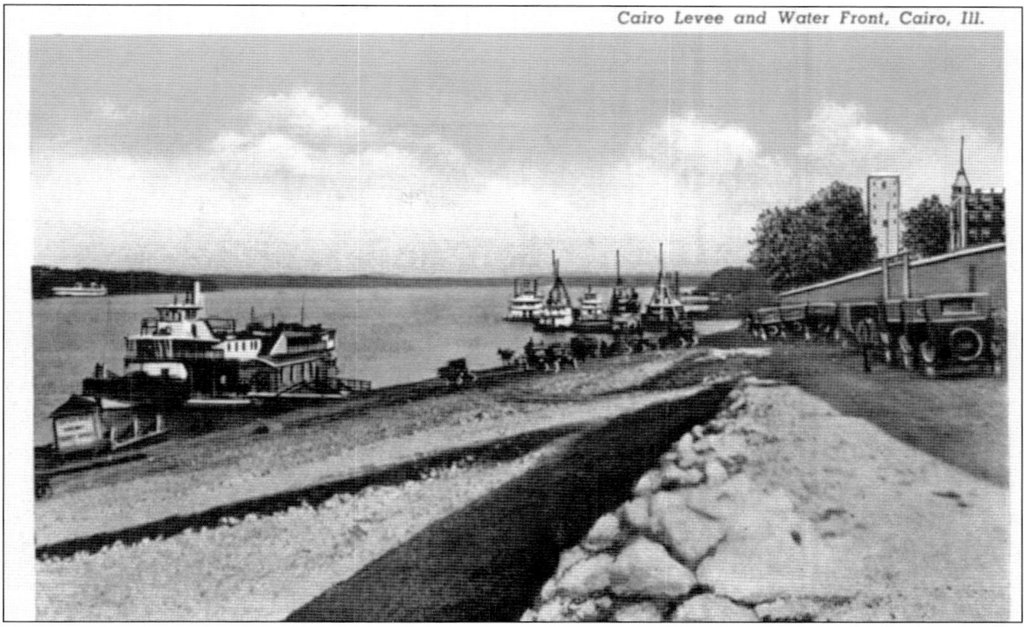

Cairo responded to the flood threat by constructing not one but two levees. One was built around a huge flat area outside of town and another (shown here) to protect Cairo itself. The idea was that if the floodwaters threatened to top the Cairo levee and enter the town, then the other levee could be dynamited and the water would rush through that break, flooding the flat land but relieving the threat on the Cairo levee.

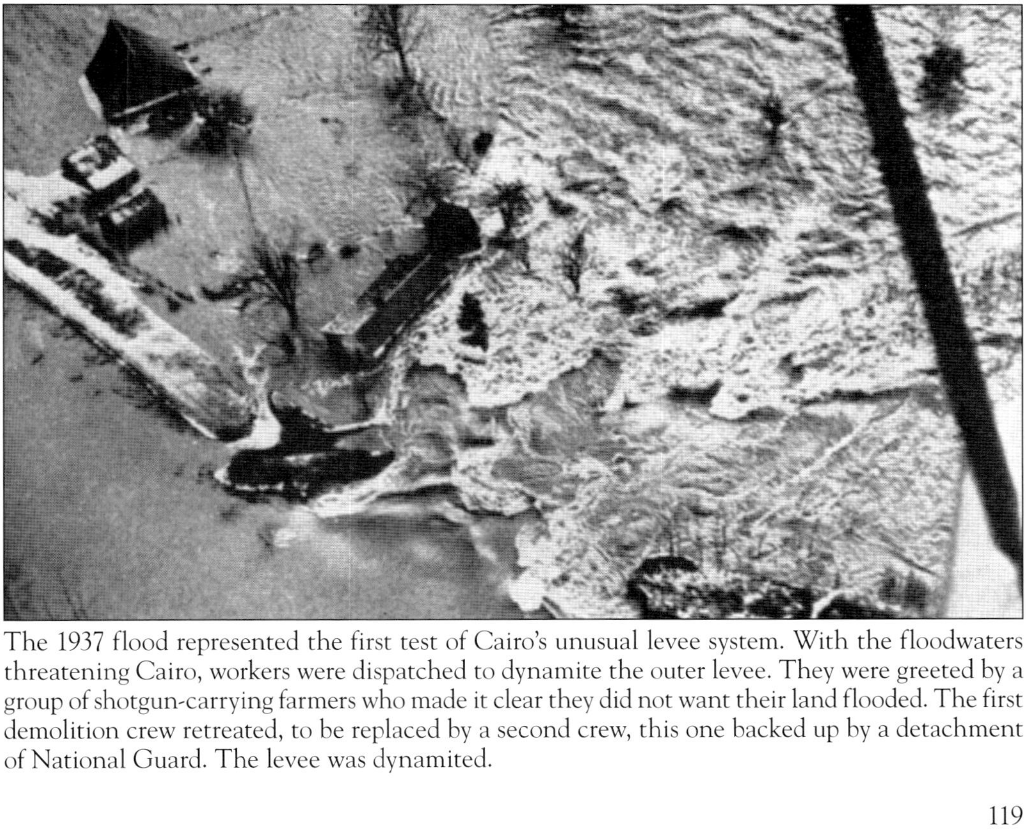

The 1937 flood represented the first test of Cairo's unusual levee system. With the floodwaters threatening Cairo, workers were dispatched to dynamite the outer levee. They were greeted by a group of shotgun-carrying farmers who made it clear they did not want their land flooded. The first demolition crew retreated, to be replaced by a second crew, this one backed up by a detachment of National Guard. The levee was dynamited.

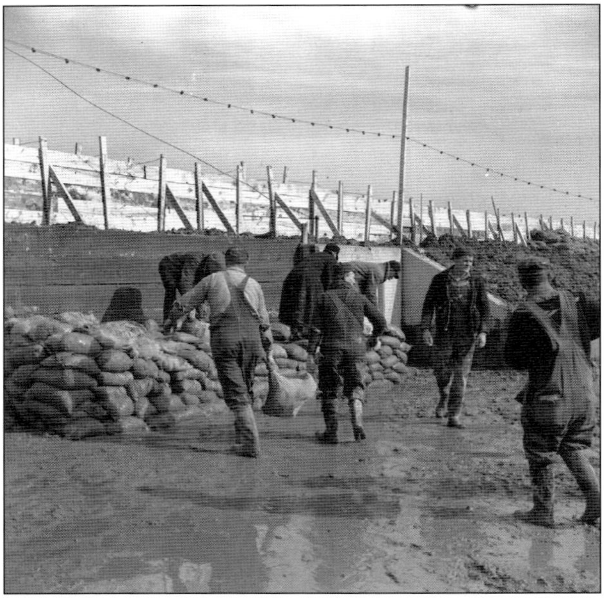

Cairo was safe but only for the moment, for the Weather Bureau warned the river was going still higher. Weary workers added rows of sandbags to the top of the town's levee, then erected a wooden bulwark atop the bags. Cairo was now a sunken island, surrounded by the floodwaters. But when the flood reached its 60-foot crest, the reinforced levee held—and Cairo became the only city on the southern Ohio to escape being inundated by the great flood. (Courtesy the Library of Congress.)

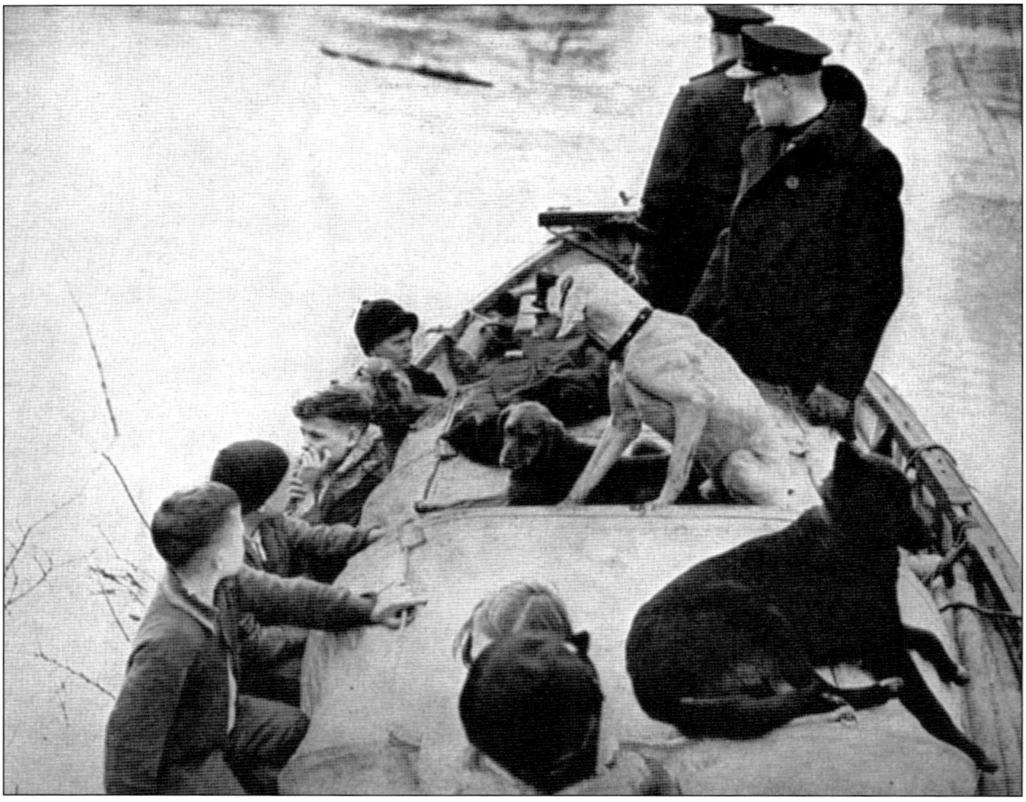

Much of the area inundated when the levee outside Cairo was dynamited was swampland or forest, but some of it was fertile farmland tilled by hundreds of hardworking families. The area's residents were warned to evacuate, but some either did not get the warning or ignored it. Soon rescue boats were busily at work, picking up those marooned by the high water. This boat carries a cargo of children and dogs.

Nine
TAMING THE RIVER

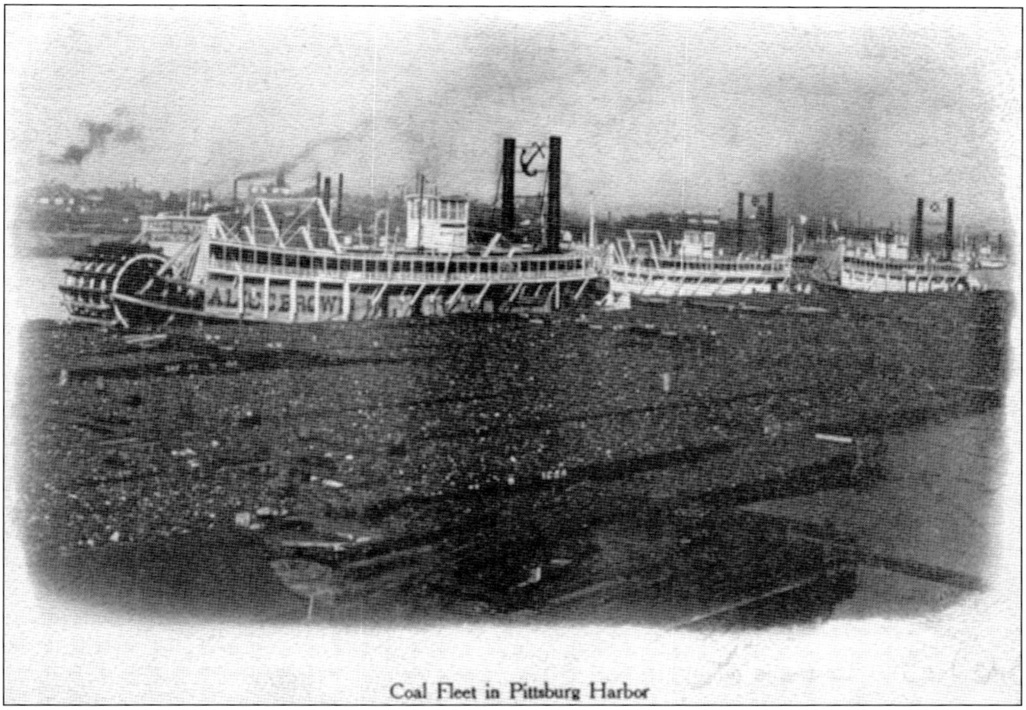

The Ohio River was a watery highway that carried the region's first settlers, their possessions, and livestock downstream. But the Ohio was unpredictable. It frequently flooded, and in dry weather, it sometimes fell so low people could walk across it. When steamboats replaced the river's early flatboats and keelboats, they often had to tie up and wait on a surge of high water before they could travel. Here steamboats and loaded coal barges await high-water stage at Pittsburgh, Pennsylvania.

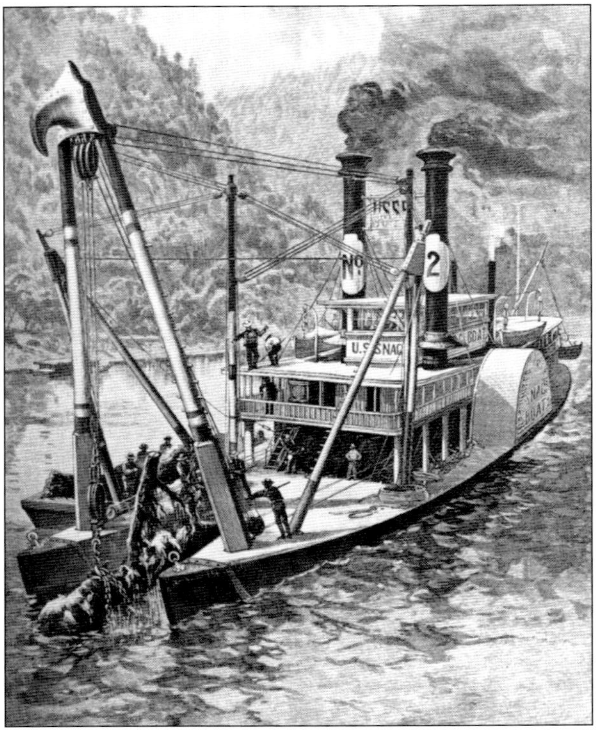

The needs of a growing nation demanded that the Ohio River be harnessed and made a working river. In 1824, Congress directed the U.S. Army Corps of Engineers to begin improving the river for navigation. The corps set to work removing stumps, boulders, and sandbars to better direct the river's flow and deepen the channel. By the 1850s, the corps was using a fleet of especially designed snagboats such as this one.

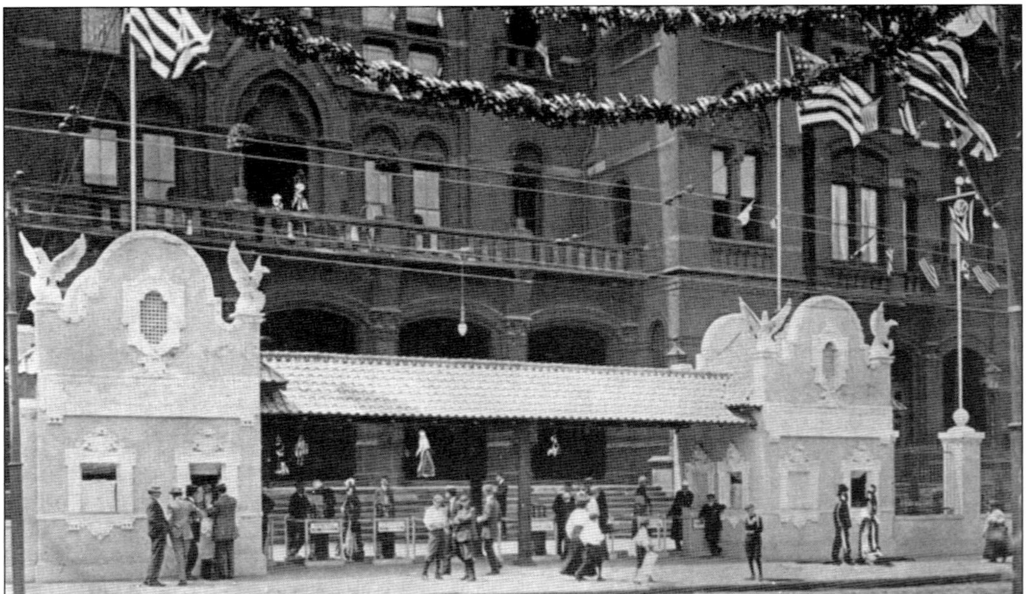

Main Entrance to Ohio Valley Exposition Buildings, Cincinnati, Aug. 29 to Sept. 24, 1910

In 1885, the U.S. Army Corps of Engineers completed the first federally built lock and dam on the Ohio River at Davis Island, six miles below Pittsburgh. Its success led Congress to authorize construction of a system of locks and dams along the Ohio's full length, from Pittsburgh to the Mississippi River, to provide a year-round, 9-foot channel for river traffic. In 1910, the Ohio Valley Exposition was staged in Cincinnati, "Celebrating Progress in the Improvement of Ohio River Navigation."

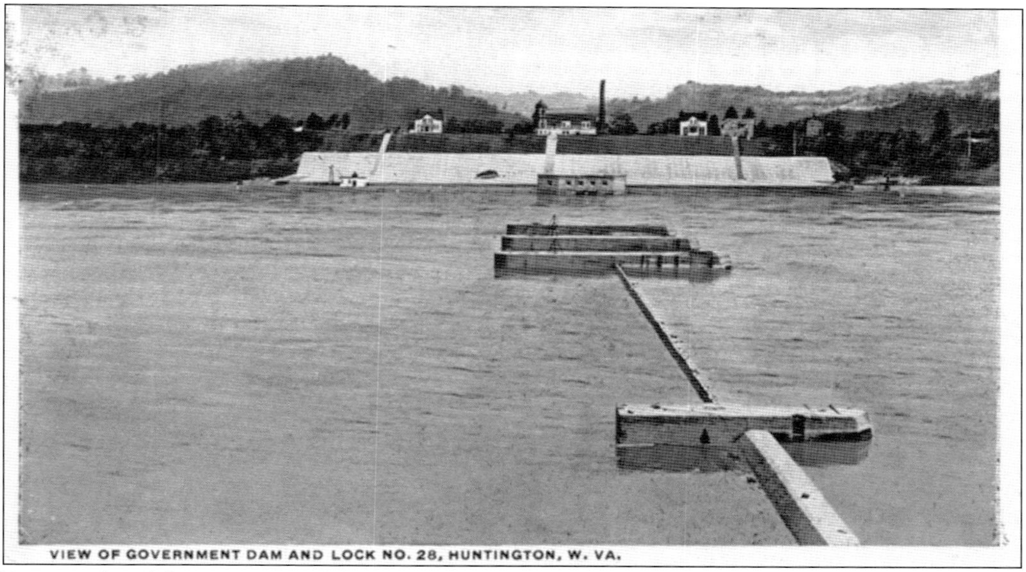

Despite the elaborate 1910 celebration in Cincinnati, it would be 1929 before the entire Ohio River system of locks and dams was completed, the delay resulting in part from the demands of World War I and in part from the frequent failure of Congress to appropriate enough money. When completed, the system consisted of 54 locks and dams such as this one—No. 28 at Huntington, West Virginia.

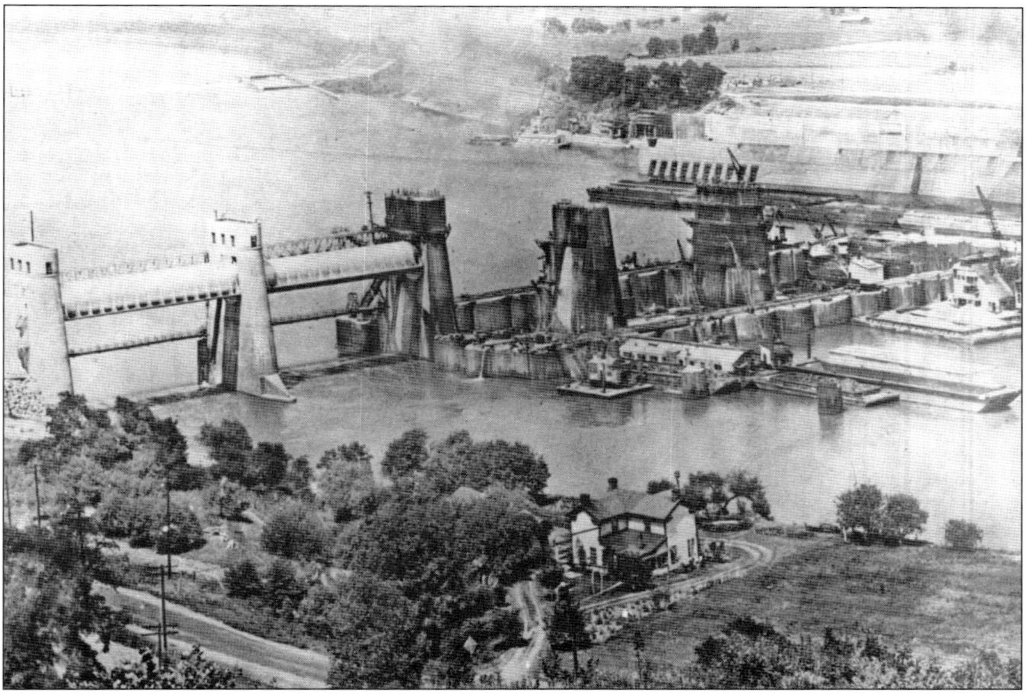

In 1934, the U.S. Army Corps of Engineers began construction of a new type of lock and dam at Gallipolis, Ohio, just below the mouth of the Kanawha River. It is shown here in a c. 1936 construction photograph. When completed in 1938, the new "high-lift" dam replaced six old locks—three on the Ohio and three on the Kanawha. In the decades since, a number of other big dams have been built to replace the river's old locks. (Courtesy U.S. Army Corps of Engineers.)

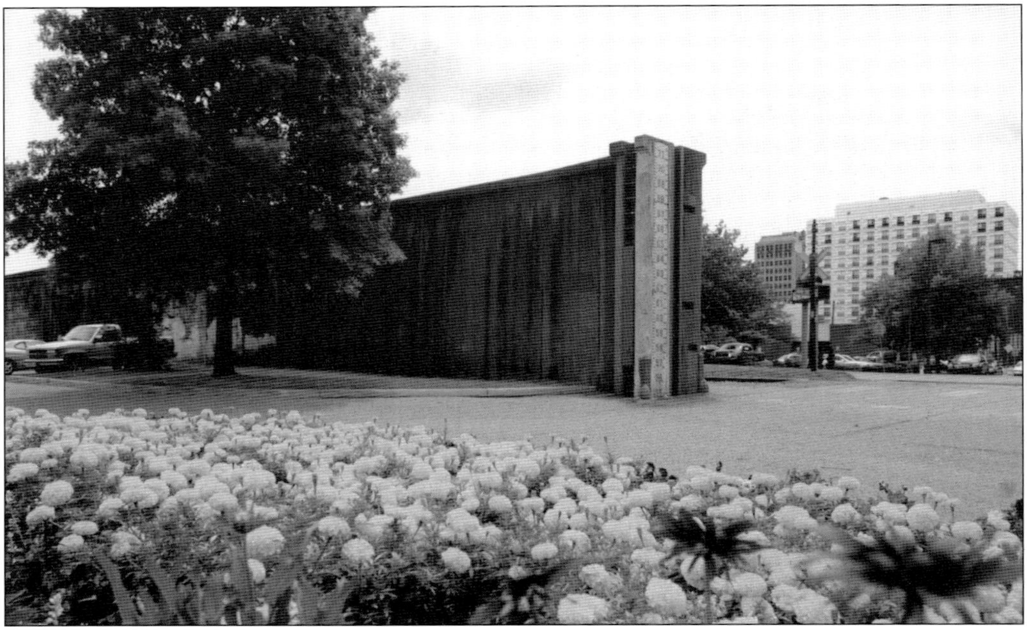

Many people mistakenly believe locks and dams on the Ohio River help control floods such as that of 1937. That is not the case at all. They are critically important but were built solely for navigation purposes. Flood control—or, to be more accurate, flood damage reduction—is achieved by a combination of reservoirs, earth levees, and concrete floodwalls, such as this one in Huntington, West Virginia. (Courtesy the *Herald-Dispatch*.)

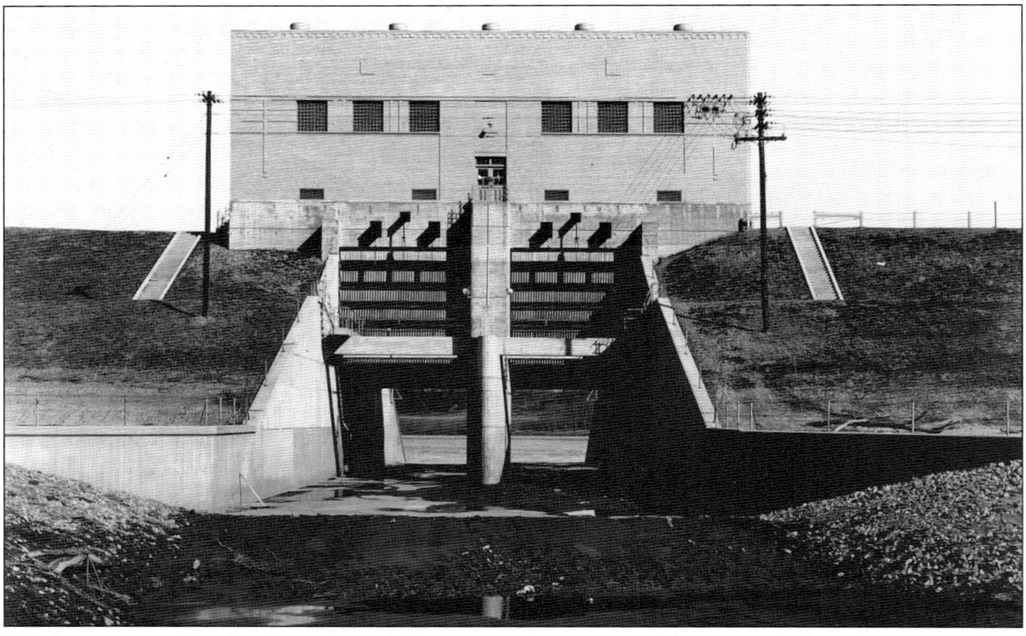

While concrete floodwalls and earth levees are the most visible parts of what the corps calls a "local protection project," those systems also include powerful pumping stations located directly over, or adjacent to, trunk sewers and creek beds. Here is a view of the Fourpole Creek Pumping Station in Huntington, West Virginia. Note the concrete superstructure of art deco design. (Courtesy U.S. Army Corps of Engineers.)

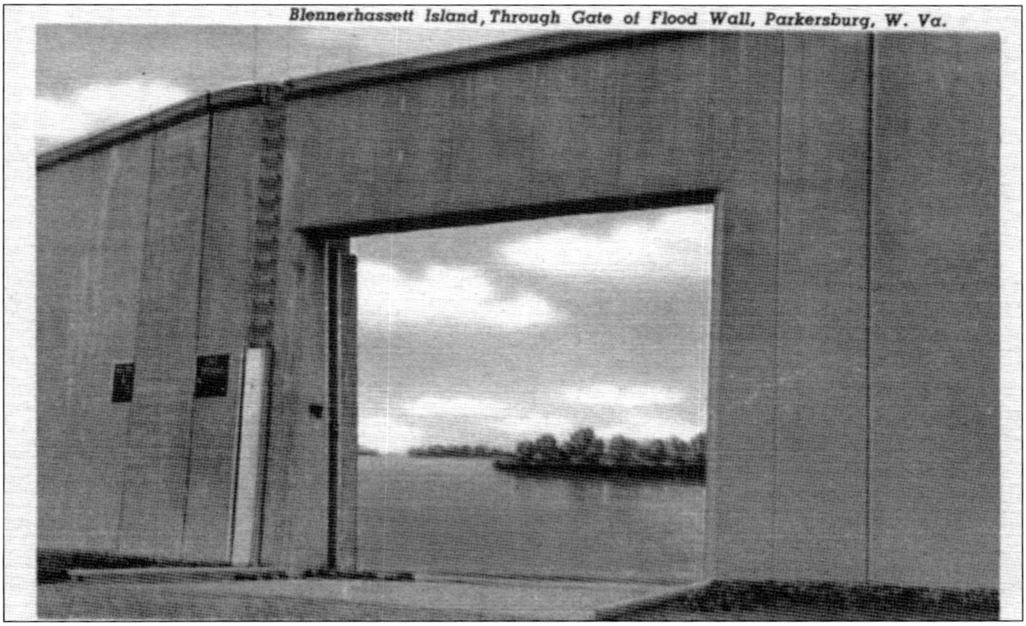

This souvenir postcard offers an unusual view of the Parkersburg, West Virginia, floodwall. Looking from the city toward the river, an open floodwall gate offers a glimpse of nearby Blennerhassett Island. Local support for erecting the Parkersburg floodwall was strong following the 1937 flood, but World War II delayed the start of construction until 1946. Completed in 1950, the wall is designed to protect Parkersburg against a flood equal to that of 1913, the city's worst ever.

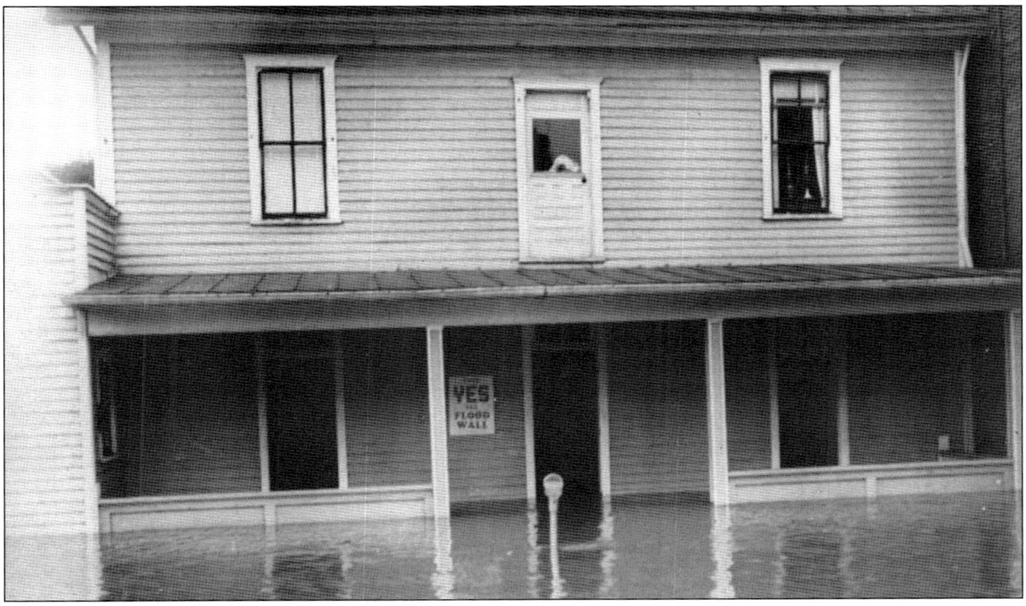

According to the U.S. Army Corps of Engineers, floods visited Catlettsburg, Kentucky, 36 times between 1884 and 1955. By 1955, frustrated residents and business people were no longer willing to see that keep happening. The voters backed a ballot measure providing the necessary local share of funding for a federally built floodwall. In this 1955 Catlettsburg photograph, a sign posted on a flooded house urges "Vote YES for the floodwall." The wall was completed in 1959. (Courtesy U.S. Army Corps of Engineers.)

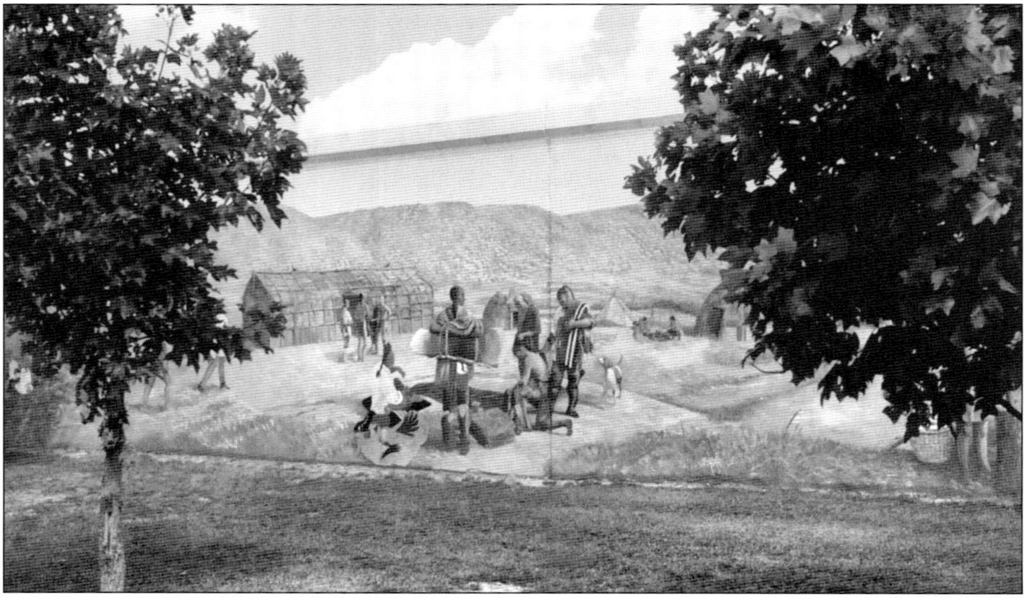

Point Pleasant, West Virginia, like a number of Ohio River communities, is decorating its floodwall with historical murals. Since 2006, renowned muralist Robert Dafford has been at work on a colorful series of murals, including this one depicting a Native American village. The murals on the river side of the wall are the first thing passengers see when they disembark from a visiting riverboat. Dafford also has painted floodwall murals in Portsmouth, Ohio, and Paducah, Kentucky. (Photograph by the author.)

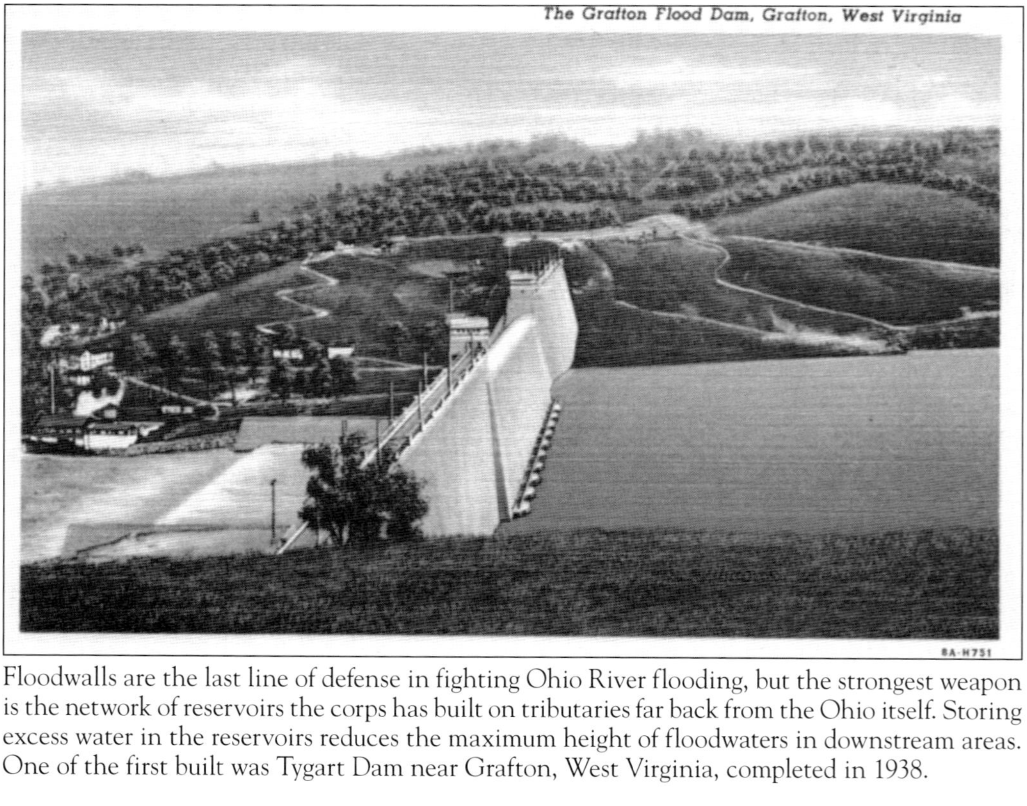

Floodwalls are the last line of defense in fighting Ohio River flooding, but the strongest weapon is the network of reservoirs the corps has built on tributaries far back from the Ohio itself. Storing excess water in the reservoirs reduces the maximum height of floodwaters in downstream areas. One of the first built was Tygart Dam near Grafton, West Virginia, completed in 1938.

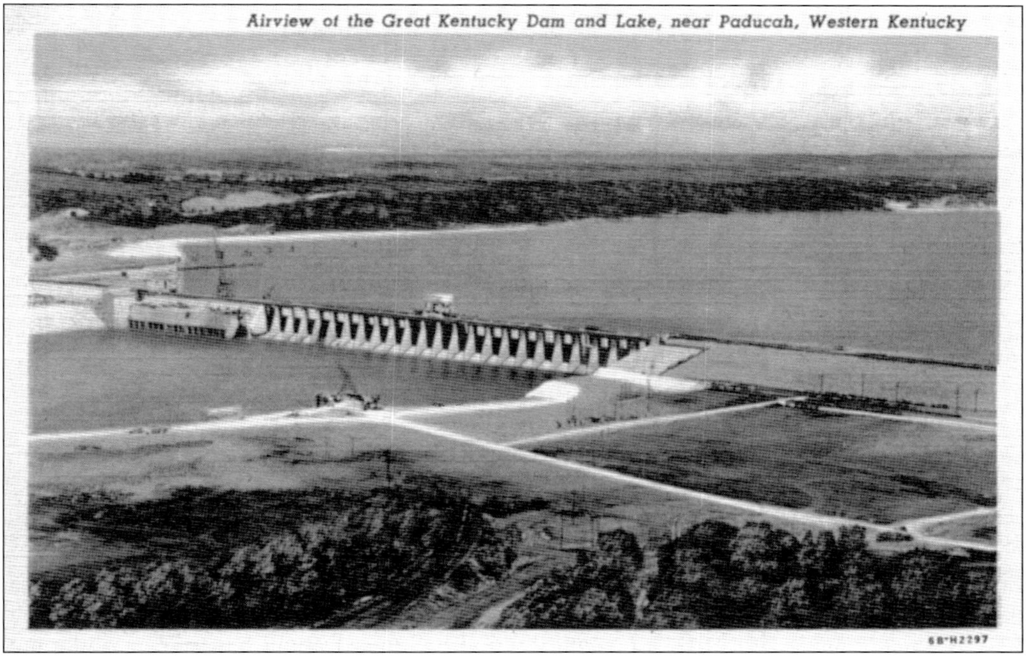

Flood control was one of the missions Congress assigned the Tennessee Valley Authority (TVA) when it created the TVA in 1933. In keeping with that mission, TVA built the Kentucky Dam on the Tennessee River about 22 miles upstream from Paducah, Kentucky. The dam, dedicated by U.S. president Harry Truman in 1945, created a reservoir 184 miles long with a shoreline of 2,200 miles, making it one of the largest man-made lakes in the world.

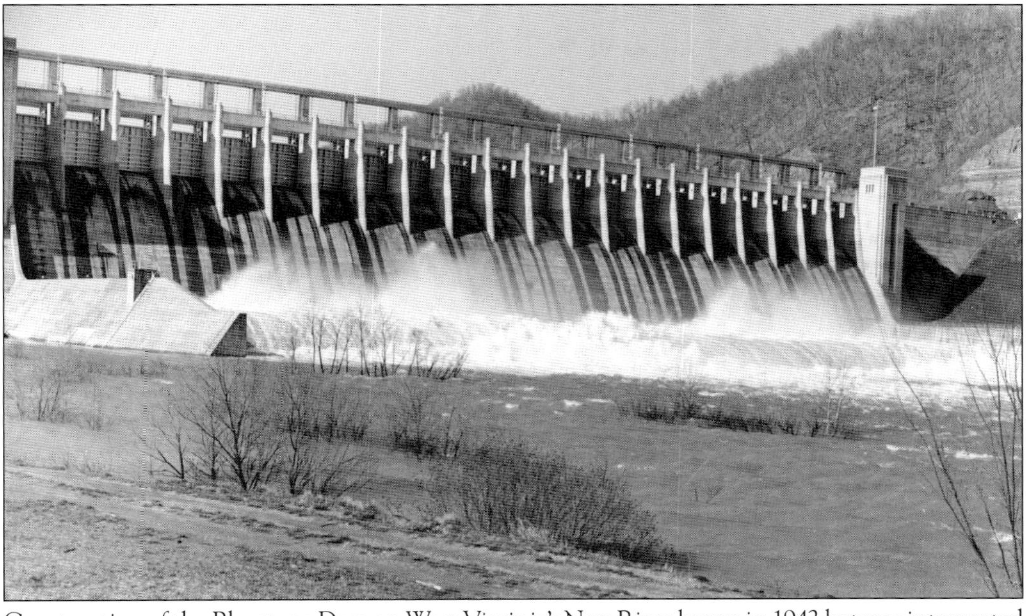

Construction of the Bluestone Dam on West Virginia's New River began in 1942 but was interrupted the following year because of World War II. Work resumed in 1946, and the dam became operational in 1949. The dam cost approximately $30 million to build. When it celebrated the dam's 50th anniversary in 1999, the U.S. Army Corps of Engineers estimated it had prevented more than $1.6 billion in flood damages. (Courtesy U.S. Army Corps of Engineers.)